RABBI YISROEL AND
RABBI OSHER ANSHEL JUNGREIS

COMPILED BY
REBBTZIN ESTHER JUNGREIS

TORAH FOR YOUR TABLE

© Copyright 2009 by Shaar Press

First edition – First impression / September 2009
                 Second impression / October 2009

ALL RIGHTS RESERVED
No part of this book may be reproduced in any form, *photocopy, electronic media, or otherwise without* written *permission from the copyright holder, except by a reviewer who wishes to quote brief passages in connection with a review written for inclusion in magazines or newspapers.*
THE RIGHTS OF THE COPYRIGHT HOLDER WILL BE STRICTLY ENFORCED.

Published by **SHAAR PRESS**
Distributed by MESORAH PUBLICATIONS, LTD.
4401 Second Avenue / Brooklyn, N.Y 11232 / (718) 921-9000

Distributed in Israel by SIFRIATI / A. GITLER
6 Hayarkon Street / Bnei Brak 51127

Distributed in Europe by LEHMANNS
Unit E, Viking Business Park, Rolling Mill Road / Jarrow, Tyne and Wear, NE32 3DP/ England

Distributed in Australia and New Zealand by GOLDS WORLD OF JUDAICA
3-13 William Street / Balaclava, Melbourne 3183 / Victoria Australia

Distributed in South Africa by KOLLEL BOOKSHOP
Ivy Common / 105 William Road / Norwood 2192, Johannesburg, South Africa

ISBN 10: 1-4226-0924-3 / ISBN 13: 978-1-4226-0924-8 Hard Cover

Printed in Canada
Custom bound by Sefercraft, Inc. / 4401 Second Avenue / Brooklyn N.Y. 11232

דיוקנו של אביו
"The image of the father never fades …"

We dedicate this book in memory of
our beloved father
**Harav Meshulem Halevi
Jungreis zt"l**
Whose image is forever with us.

TABLE OF CONTENTS

INTRODUCTION
Torah Thoughts for Your Table   17

THE BOOK OF GENESIS

PARASHAS BEREISHIS
The Power of Words   21

PARASHAS NOACH
Is He a Mentsch?   27
Do We See Ourselves As God Sees Us?   28

PARASHAS LECH LECHA
The Birth of the Jewish People   33
Finding Our Inner Strength   34
To Be Blessed or To Be a Blessing   35
God's Command or Our Desire   36
Bitter or Better   37
If We Will It   38

PARASHAS VAYEIRA
Jewish Character Traits   39
Character Traits That Distinguish a Jew   40

PARASHAS CHAYEI SARAH
Everything Is in God's Hands   47
Tips for Finding Your Life Partner   49
What One Should Look For   49
Prayer   50
Chesed   51
Don't Compromise Your Principles   51
Move On — Avoid Procrastination   52

Parashas Toldos

A Good Teacher Is Not Enough — You Also Need Good Peers ... 54
Thoughts To Ponder ... 55
Nature or Nurture — It's All in Our Hands ... 55
Our Roots — Our Treasures ... 57

Parashas Vayeitzei

Emes — Recognizing the Truth ... 59
Forever Engraved on Our Hearts ... 61
Maximizing Spiritual Growth ... 62
Never Be Afraid ... 63
Angels on the Ladder ... 63
Put Zest Into Life ... 64

Parashas Vayishlach

Less Is More ... 65
Formula for Survival ... 66
A Message for Today From Our Forefather Jacob ... 67
A Lesson for Survival — Recognizing The Trap ... 68
Character Traits To Aim For ... 69
Hakoras Hatov — Gratitude ... 70

Parashas Vayeishev

Sibling Rivalry ... 72
The Many Faces of Shalom ... 73
The Venom of Hatred and the Power in a Name ... 74
Withstanding Temptation ... 75

Parashas Mikeitz

Raising Jewish Children in a Hostile Environment ... 78
The Difference Between "But" and "Indeed" ... 79

Parashas Vayigash

Positive Criticism ... 82
Never Give Up ... 83
The Power of the *Shemah* ... 85

Parashas Vayechi

An Eternal Blessing From Our Forefather Jacob	87
Not When, But How Messiah Will Come	89
Messianic Times	89
Shabbos Chazak	90

THE BOOK OF EXODUS

Parashas Shemos

The Roots of Anti-Semitism — The Very First Holocaust	95
The Making of a Gadol — A Great Man	96
Torah Qualifications for a Leader	98
The Power of God in the Soul of Man	99
"Impossible" is Not in the Jewish Lexicon	100
Bitya's True Identity	102
The Eternity of the Jewish People	102

Parashas Va'eira

Admonishment Without Pain	105
The Professional Parent	107
Comfort and Consolation	108
Patience and Fortitude	109
Converting Suffering Into Blessing	110
The Power of Zeides and Bubbies	111
Hearing God's Voice in Good Times as Well as Bad	113

Parashas Bo

We Are Never Alone	114
Teach Others and Elevate Yourself	115
The Legacy of Parents and Grandparents	116
A Darkness That Transcends the Centuries	117
The Gift of Time	117
Do You Feel the Pain of Your Brethren?	119

Parashas Beshalach

Shabbos Shira: The Song of Faith	121
Converting Despair Into Hope	122
A Song That Springs From the Heart	123
Recreating Yourself	124

Parashas Yisro

The Art of Listening	126
Be Happy for Others: The Hallmark of Our People	128
The Ten Commandments: The Bedrock of Our Faith	129
Receiving the Torah in Every Generation	129

Parashas Mishpatim

Good Is Not Good Enough	131
Ethics and Trust in God	133
A Mother's Table	134

Parashas Terumah

Make Your Home a Sanctuary	136
Torah: The Heritage of Every Jew	138
A Study That Is Never Exhausted	139
Kosher (Honest) Money	139
A Solution to Every Problem	140

Parashas Tetzaveh

Moshe Rabbeinu: Putting Himself on the Line	142
The Menorah: More Than A Light	144
Garments That Are More Than Clothing	145
Bells and Pomegranates	146
Sacrifices: The Path to Commitment and Love	146

Parashas Ki Sisa

Measure Your Worth	149
Only When We Lose It Do We Appreciate It	151
Torah for Everyone	151

Parashas Vayakhel

We Need Only Will It and It Shall Be	154
Converting Liabilities Into Assets	156
Your Name and Your Faith	156

Parashas Pekudei

Reinventing Yourself	158
No Coincidences: Our Prayers Are Rooted in the Sanctuary	159

One Hundred Blessings	160
We Need Never Fear	161
Never Take Anything for Granted	161

THE BOOK OF LEVITICUS

Parashas Vayikra

The Meaning of Sacrifice	165
Make His Will Your Will	166
We Can All Make a Difference	167
In Humility We Find True Greatness	168
The Call of God is the Call of Love	169

Parashas Tzav

What You Wear Matters	170
The Power of Love	171
Download a Miracle	172
Would Hashem Approve?	173
Three Little Words	173
Dedicate Yourself	174
The Menial Is Also Sacred	175

Parashas Shemini

A Silence More Powerful Than Words	176
Whose Will?	177

Parashas Tazria–Metzora

The Power of Speech: Life and Death Are in the Tongue	179
Aaron's Legacy	180
Can *Lashon Hara* Ever Be Justified?	181
Guard That Which Enters and Leaves Your Mouth	182
The Healing Effects of the Torah	183
Remorse: Indication of True Sincerity	183

Parashas Acharei Mos–Kedoshim

Trust: The Basis of All Relationships	186
The Golden Rule	187
The Path to Holiness	188
Road Map to Sanctity	189

Parashas Emor

Reaching Beyond Yourself	191
Imparting a Life Lesson to the Young	192
An Ongoing Commitment	193

Parashas Behar

Total Trust in God	195
No Explanation Required	196
Take Care Not To Inflict Pain	197
Do Not Overburden Others	198

Parashas Bechukosai

Coincidence or the Hand of God?	199
Rediscovering Yourself	200
Three Pillars	201
The Way To Study Torah	202

THE BOOK OF NUMBERS

Parashas Bamidbar

We All Count	205
Discover Your Mission	206
You Are Special	207
Counting: An Expression of Love	207
Essential Tools for Torah Learning	209

Parashas Nasso

The Threefold Priestly Blessing: Blessings for All Eternity	210
The Meaning Behind the Blessing	211
Further Insights Into the Blessing	212
Know Yourself	213
We All Have a God-Given Mission	214
Custom-Made by God: It's Not What We Have, But Who We Are	215

Parashas Beha'aloscha

Elevate Your Life	217
A Jewish Litmus Test: When Do You Feel Deprived?	218

The Menorah and Its Many Dimensions	219
How Will You Be Remembered?	219
Maintaining Our Enthusiasm: A Key to Meaningful Living	220
A Second Chance	221
Life-Transforming Lessons From *Pesach Sheni*	222

Parashas Shelach

Not Affliction, but Correction	223
It All Depends on How We See It	225
The Power of Prayer and the Power of a Name	226
How Do You See Yourself?	227

Parashas Korach

The Root of All Evil: Jealousy, Lust, and the Thirst for Honor	229
Accusations, Libels, and a Formula for Peace	230
The Disastrous Consequences of Jealousy	232

Parashas Chukas

Voids Left by Those Who Die	234
Gratitude	235
Unwavering Faith	237
Unequivocal Faith	239

Parashas Balak

Wake-Up Calls: How Well Do We Listen?	240
Whose Fault Is It?	241
Never Give Up on Anyone	242
We Choose the Path	242
The Secret Power of the Jew	244

Parashas Pinchas

Love of God	246
Stand Up to the Plate	247
Converting Handicaps Into Assets	249
How Deep Is Our Love?	250

Parashas Mattos

Your Word Is Your Bond	251

Another Face of Gratitude	252
A True Leader	253
Life's Battles	254
How Much Do You Feel?	254
Jewish Priorities	255

Parashas Masei

Life's Journeys	257
The Land Is Our Destiny	258
Cities of Refuge: Spiritual Rejuvenation	259

THE BOOK OF DEUTERONOMY

Parashas Devarim

How To Criticize Without Offending	263
Three Steps	264
Less Is More	265
The Torah Speaks for All Eternity	265
It's Never Too Late To Start a New LiFe	266
Beware of Your Genetic Predisposition	267
You Can Redeem Your Ancestors	268

Parashas Va'eschanan

The Power of Prayer	269
Does God Answer All Our Prayers?	271
Perseverance in Prayer	272
Commitment to Mitzvos	272
Hands Off	273
The Covenant	273
The Ten Commandments	274
The *Shema*	274
Intermarriage	275

Parashas Eikev

A Mitzvah Litmus Test	276
God Does Not Punish	277
Formula for Maintaining Closeness With God	278
Prescriptions for Faith	279
The Torah: One Big Mitzvah	280

Grace	281
What Does God Require of Us?	282

Parashas Re'eh

Free Will: It's Up to Us!	284
You Need Only Open Your Eyes and See	285
How Well Do We Listen?	286
The Laws of *Tzedakah*	287
Tzedakah: Not an Option But an Obligation	288
Why Does God Allow the Poor To Be Poor?	289
If We Truly Seek Him, We Can Find Him	290

Parashas Shoftim

Road Map for Spiritual Growth	291
God Our King	292
Never Think You Are Smarter	293
Lessons To Be Learned	294
We Are All Stewards of God	295
We Are All Responsible	295

Parashas Ki Seitzei

Sensitizing Your Heart	297
Each of God's Creations Is Unique	299
Returning That Which Is Lost	299

Parashas Ki Savo

How To Give	302
Happiness — A Command, Not an Option	303
Gratitude: A Pillar of Judaism	304
Jealousy Leads to Hatred	305
You Need Not Be Blind To Have Faith, But You Have To Be Blind Not To Have Faith	306

Parashas Nitzavim

The Covenant of Mutual Responsibility	309
What If It's Beyond You?	311
The Eternity of the Jewish People	312
Steps Leading to Assimilation	313

Parashas Vayeilech

The Torah Is Engraved on Every Jewish Soul	315
When God's Face Is Hidden	316
Song of the Jewish People	317
God Is Always With Us	319

Parashas Haazinu

Eternal Witnesses	320
The Power of Listening	321
Formula for Jewish Living	321
Torah and Rain	321
Who Is To Blame?	323
Study Your Past To Understand Your Present	324
Red Flags To Watch For	324
Moses' Last Will and Testament	325

Parashas Vezos Haberachah

The Blessings Continue	326
The Uniqueness of the Jewish People	327
Torah Tziva Lanu Moshe, Morasha Kehilas Yaakov	328
Moses Died and Yet He Lives	329
The Last Letter	330

Glossary	331

INTRODUCTION

Torah Thoughts for Your Table

> If two sit together and there are no words of Torah exchanged between them, it is considered a session of scorners, but if two sit together and words of Torah are shared, then the Divine Presence rests upon them."
>
> Mishnah: *Ethics of the Fathers* 3:3

Man is not just a composite of flesh and bone, but, more significantly, he is a repository of the spirit of God. Within his being he carries a Spark of the Divine — his *neshamah*, his soul. In our materialistic, success-oriented, competitive world, we feed our bodies but neglect the spirit that God implanted within us. Torah study not only energizes our souls, but when shared with others, it creates an everlasting bond of friendship and invites the *Shechinah* — the Divine Presence — to rest upon us.

Having taught Torah for three decades for the Hineni organization founded by our esteemed mother, Rebbetzin Esther Jungreis, may God grant her long and blessed years, we discovered that ours is a generation that would be open to sharing Torah wisdom, but lacks the necessary tools with which to do so. In response to this need, for several years we have made available weekly Torah emails containing brief, concise, but life-transforming Torah insights that can be shared with family members and friends on formal and informal occasions and are especially meaningful around the Shabbos table. The response has been phenomenal. People from every part of the globe have written to express their appreciation. It is this interest that has inspired this collection of Torah thoughts.

The Torah is not just a compendium of Bible stories. Rather, it is a Book of Life authored by God Himself. Every word, every letter, every punctuation mark is laden with hidden meaning — all designed to ensure a meaningful and blessed journey on this planet. Therefore, we ask that God open our eyes, our minds, and our hearts to the Divine wisdom concealed in His sacred words. Every morning, when we recite our prayers, we pronounce a beautiful blessing and beseech the Almighty to make our study a *"sweet experience,"* not only for ourselves, but also for our children and children's children ... and for all Israel.

Our Sages divided the Torah into *parshiyos*, weekly portions that take a full year to complete, so that throughout the year, there is always a *parashah* to *sweeten* and elevate our daily lives.

It is our fervent hope and prayer that these teachings will spiritually enrich your lives and make the Torah a "sweet experience" that will inspire you and those with whom you share Torah thoughts, to explore further and to study on a regular basis. It is with this prayer and wish that we dedicate this book.

Rabbis Yisroel and Osher Anshel Jungreis

ספר בראשית

THE BOOK OF
Genesis

PARASHAS BEREISHIS

The Power of Words

Beginnings are always challenging. And so, as we commence the Book of *Genesis*, we express our appreciation to Hashem and ask that He help and guide us in the study of His Holy Torah.

In *Parashas Bereishis*, we learn many important lessons, but none more powerful and enduring than the significance and holiness of words and speech. The Torah teaches us that Hashem created the world through ten utterances: through Divine speech. With each holy command, our universe was formed. Hashem implanted this gift of speech within man. Of all earth's creatures, only humans are endowed with the ability to verbally communicate intelligently. We must be ever mindful that, even as God created through "words," on our own level, we too create through words.

Time and again, the Torah cautions us to be very careful with that which escapes our lips, for, as King Solomon tells us, "Death and life are in the tongue."[1] Before speaking, stop for a moment and consider how your words impact on others. What sort of environment and relationships do you create with your speech? Do you speak to your family and friends with love and respect? Do you think about what you're saying before you say it and the effect that it will have on those with whom you communicate? How careful are you with that which escapes from your lips?

There are more commandments in the Torah in regard to speech than to any other mitzvah: seventeen negative and fourteen positive mitzvos. It is through speech that we signaled our commitment to our Covenant at Sinai when we proclaimed, *"Na'aseh V'nishma* — We shall do it and we shall study it."[2] It is through speech — prayer — that we speak to God on a daily basis, bringing a positive spiritual influence into the mundane. Yet speech can have terribly negative effects as well: It was through speech that Hitler committed the most unspeakable evil ever to be perpetrated upon mankind. He himself never lifted a weapon; he used his lethal tongue to incite the world to hatred and slaughter. Indeed, "Death and life are in the tongue."

Think before you speak and ask yourself, "Will my words generate light or darkness, love or hatred, blessing or curse?" The choice is yours to make. Use your Divine gift of speech carefully and wisely, in the service of the Almighty.

☞ THE HOLY TONGUE — EVERY WORD IS DEFINITIVE

God invites Adam to identify each and every creature and give them *names* that reflect their essence.[3] Adam had incredible insight and was able to perceive the function of everything that God

---

1. See *Proverbs* 18:21: "Death and life are in the power of the tongue ...."
2. *Exodus* 24:7.
3. *Genesis* 2:19-20.

Kelev K'lev

brought before him. Thus, when he assigned names to the various animals, he revealed their true natures. For example, when he called the dog "*kelev*," the letters of which also spell "*k'lev*," which means "like a heart," he taught us that the dog can be a loyal friend.

Adam's own name indicates his mission, for if a man is to fulfill his mission, if he is to realize his potential, then first and foremost he must recognize his strengths and weaknesses. And so Adam called himself "Adam" — meaning that God fashioned him from "*adamah*," the earth. This designation is rather puzzling, for it is previously written that man was created in the image of God — that God breathed life into him,[4] and that the breath of God became the soul of man. So why didn't Hashem call him "*Neshamah* (soul)," rather than "*Adam* (earth)"?

Adam, with his amazing insight, understood from this that, no matter how spiritual a man may be, he is nevertheless grounded in the physical and material world, and precisely because of that he is vulnerable. Temptations surround him and, in a moment, he can forfeit his spirituality. The slightest wind can blow him away; therefore, he must be forever vigilant and protect the Divine spark with which God endowed him. Moreover, precisely because his soul is the breath of God, he must be careful not to sully it and be ever mindful that he is also "*Adam*" — made of earth and vulnerable. Also, the word *Adam* is constituted of the letters of the Hebrew word *m'od*, meaning *very* or *obsessive*, teaching us that if man is not vigilant, he can very easily become *obsessive* about his material needs and become addicted to them.

We see this teaching reinforced in our Yom Kippur services as well. Yom Kippur is our holiest day, on which we refrain from eating and drinking and from everything that is physical and material. Yet, at the afternoon service, *Minchah*, as the day draws to its close, the Torah reading deals with the laws of sexual morality. Once again we are reminded that our physical world is fraught with danger — there are so many allurements to which we may fall prey; therefore, we must be constantly alert and safeguard our *neshamos* (souls) by living moral Torah lives.

---

4. Ibid. 2:7.

Parashas Bereishis / 23

Unfortunately, in our world, very little attention is given to our spiritual well-being. Most of our activities revolve around the physical and the material. Our *neshamos* have become emaciated. The best way to revive and sustain our souls is to enhance our spirituality through prayer, Torah study, and the performance of mitzvos.

THE CREATION OF WOMAN

In contrast to Adam, of whom it is written, "*Vayetzer Hashem es h'adam afar min ha'adamah* ... — And God fashioned man from the dust of the earth ...,"[5] when it comes to the creation of the female, the word "*vayiven*,"[6] which literally means "to build," is used. The word "*vayiven*" shares the same root as the word "*binah* (understanding)." *Binah* goes beyond wisdom. Rather, it is an intuitive ability to see beyond — to construct, to build — teaching us that Hashem endowed the female with an added dimension of wisdom and charged her with the most sacred of all responsibilities — caring for children, building future generations. Our Sages were sensitive to this blessing of *binah* which God granted to the female, and they felt privileged to consult with their wives.

For example, Rabbi Elazar Ben Azariah consulted with his wife before he accepted the invitation to become head of the Sanhedrin, and Rabbi Akiva acted upon the recommendation of his wife, Rachel, who saw his potential to become a Rabbi in Israel and studied Torah with intensity for many long years. Thus, it is not by coincidence that, at the giving of the Torah, God instructed Moses, "*Ko somar l'beis Yaakov* — Thus shall you speak to the house of Jacob ...."[7] Our Sages explain that "*Beis Yaakov*" refers to the women. It is the women who were to be charged first, for it is they who possess the ability to inspire future generations and insure commitment. As it has been said, "Educate a woman and you educate a family — a nation .... Educate a man and you educate an individual."

---

5. Ibid. 2:7.
6. Ibid. 2:22.
7. *Exodus* 19:3.

ACCEPTING RESPONSIBILITY

It is common knowledge that the very first sin of which man was guilty was partaking of the forbidden fruit in the Garden of Eden. Upon closer scrutiny however, we discover that the history of mankind might have turned out differently had man had the courage *to accept responsibility for his transgression.* Having committed this first sin, Adam attempts to hide from God, whereupon the Almighty calls out, "*Ayekah* — Where are you?"[8]

But can man hide from God? Does man really believe that God is unaware of his whereabouts? With the question "*Ayekah* — Where are you?" God was challenging Adam to accept accountability for his sinful deed. "*Ayekah*" has a double meaning. It also means "*Eichah* — how," implying, "How did you do this? Examine your life. How did you depart so quickly from the path that I commanded you?" But instead of looking within himself, addressing the wrong, learning from his mistakes and accepting responsibility, Adam sought a scapegoat, and, showing a lack of *hakaras hatov* (gratitude; acknowledgment of the good), declared, "The woman that You gave me — *she* gave me of the tree and I ate."[9] Eve followed suit. She, too, looked for a scapegoat and claimed that the serpent had enticed her. Our Sages tell us that it was this unwillingness to accept accountability and thus redress the wrong they had done that sealed their fate and caused their banishment from the Garden of Eden.

Let us examine our own lives. Is it possible that when we rebel against God, we, too, try to hide from Him? Is it possible that we, too, scapegoat and hold others responsible for our shortcomings — blaming our homes, our friends, our schools, our workplace, our environment? If we wish to grow spiritually, we must demonstrate our integrity by saying, "I am accountable."

God is our loving Father Who is willing to forgive us, but in order for Him to do so, we must have the courage to say, "Forgive me, I was wrong." Indeed, that is the focal point of our Yom Kippur

---

8. *Genesis* 3:9.
9. Ibid. 3:12.

service, when we confess and "come clean" before God without "ifs," "ands," or "buts." When we pray, we must honestly mean the words we say, repent fully in our hearts, humble ourselves before God, and accept the responsibility for our actions. Only then can we be forgiven.

PARASHAS NOACH

Is He a Mentsch?

The *parashah* tells us: "These are the generations of Noah. Noah was a *man*, righteous and pure in his generation."[10] The Hebrew word for *man* is *"ish,"* for which the Yiddish equivalent is *"mentsch."* The Torah teaches us that first and foremost, each of us must try to be a *mentsch*. The word *mentsch* connotes integrity, respect, kindness — goals toward which we must all strive. The first questions that Jewish parents traditionally ask regarding a potential spouse for their daughter is, "Is he a *mentsch*? Does he have fine character traits?"

---

10. Ibid. 6:9.

Do We See Ourselves as God Sees Us?

A famous Midrash based on this week's *parashah* asks, "If there are so many ways through which God could have saved Noah, then why did He make him go through the difficult, arduous task of building an Ark that took 120 years to complete?"

The Midrash answers that Hashem, in His infinite mercy, did not want to bring the Flood upon the world. God desires to preserve life, not destroy it. Even as a father yearns for his estranged children, so too, God was hoping that His errant sons and daughters would heed His call, abandon their evil ways, and return to Him. Thus, if Noah were seen to be busily building his Ark day in and day out, people would ask him what he was doing. Then he would inform them about the impending Flood and tell them that they could cancel the evil decree through repentance. It was all in their hands.

But this Midrash begs yet another question: Why couldn't Noah speak to the people directly? Why did he need the Ark as a prop? Why couldn't he inspire the people to mend their ways? The answer to this question can be found in the beginning of the *parashah*: "Now the earth had become corrupt *before God*,"[11] teaching us that it was **only in the sight of God** that the earth was corrupt; man saw nothing wrong with his lifestyle. How does it happen that man can be so blind to his own faults and corruption?

The generation of the Flood was obsessed with hedonism and the pursuit of pleasure; in such a climate, the laws of God, which require discipline, are eclipsed. In a society without Torah guidelines, even the most depraved acts become acceptable. So Noah had no one with whom to talk; no one was willing to listen, for they all saw themselves as "righteous people," and it never occurred to any of them to ask **how God viewed them**.

Rabbi Yisroel Salanter, the founder of the Mussar movement, explains the process that brings about this moral blindness: The

---

11. Ibid. 6:11.

Easier to commit

first time a man commits a wrong, he feels guilty, but if he repeats that act often enough, his conscience will no longer bother him and eventually he will even see himself as a paragon of virtue. So it is that immorality, decadence, and degeneracy become the accepted way of life and are no longer considered sinful.

This lesson is of special significance to our generation, for ours is also a hedonistic society that does not recognize boundaries or discipline. We regard self-gratification as an end in itself and delude ourselves into believing that as long as we are *happy* with ourselves that is all that God requires of us. We never ask ourselves the all-important question, *"How does God see us?"*

How can we overcome this spiritual blindness?

Ongoing Torah study is the most effective remedy. When we study God's Word we hear His voice, and we come to realize how far we have departed from His path. We can then take steps to come closer to Him.

ARK REHAB

Still, you might ask why Noah had to enter the Ark. Why couldn't God have saved him in a different manner? The answer is that God wanted to make certain that when Noah and his family emerged from the Ark and undertook the task of rebuilding the world, they would be fortified with righteous deeds. In the Ark they had to care for all the animals that God had commanded them to gather; backbreaking labor consumed them day and night. Yet through that labor they learned the meaning of *chesed* — reaching out with *gemilus chassadim* (acts of loving-kindness) — one of the pillars on which God built His world.

It is in this light that we can understand the Midrash that relates that on one occasion, when Noah was slow to feed the lion, the lion injured him. Noah cried out in pain, and a Heavenly voice declared, "If only you had cried out in pain when the future of mankind was at stake!"

Parashas Noach

God's Infinite Patience — His Hand in Our Daily Lives

Noah was involved in the construction of the Ark for *120 years.* We ask ourselves why it took so very long for Noah to complete God's command. Surely, he could have completed his task in much less time, especially since Hashem gave him specific instructions on what materials to use and told him the exact dimensions of the Ark.

Once again, we behold God's compassion and infinite patience. Although He foresees the future, He nevertheless hopes for our repentance and gives us time — even 120 years — to mend our ways. Tragically, people mistook His *love* for His *absence,* but the lesson of the Ark continues to speak to us and demands that we see God's Hand in our daily lives, even if it is not always readily apparent. Another lesson that we can learn is patience. Even as the Almighty was patient with that generation, so should we try to be patient with the members of our family and our fellow man.

The Ark — The Holy Tabernacle — The Jewish Home

In the Torah we find that God commanded the construction of two edifices: Noah's Ark, and centuries later, after our forefathers left Egypt, the *Mishkan* (the Holy Tabernacle).

While these two structures were built light-years apart, for different reasons, and under different circumstances, they do share a common denominator: they serve as role models for the ideal Jewish home. The Ark represents security, protection, a safe place … which every home should embody, while the Tabernacle reflects a spiritual haven — a *Bayis Ne'eman,* a home that is a true bastion of faith … a place where husband, wife, and children live in peace and harmony; a place where the sacred light of Shabbos banishes all darkness; a place where loving-kindness and Torah wisdom prevail; a place where the *Shechinah* (the presence of God) dwells.

If ever there was a time when we needed such a home, with a fusion of the physical and the spiritual, i us strive for it.

☙ FEEL THE PAIN OF YOUR

God tells Noah to build an Ark in order to save his family and all the different animal species. Then God issues the somewhat puzzling command that Noah make a *tzohar* for the Ark.[12] There is a question as to what this light really meant. Our Sages explain that *tzohar* can mean "a window" or "a brilliant jewel that sheds light." But these definitions are problematic. What possible reason could God have for placing a window in the Ark? After all, how much light could enter as a fierce storm raged outside for forty days and forty nights? And what is the meaning of "a precious jewel"? Could a precious stone actually illuminate the entire Ark?

God wished to impress upon Noah his responsibility to humankind, for although Noah and his family were spared, he had an obligation to create *windows* through which he could see others and be sensitive to their pain and suffering. If he did, he would emerge from that painful tragedy kinder, wiser, and more caring. Thus, his windows would be converted into *jewels* that would illuminate his soul and enable him to better understand his obligation to his fellow man.

During the 120 years that Noah constructed the Ark, he didn't quite get that message. In contrast to the actions of Abraham, who pleaded with God to save the evil inhabitants of Sodom and Gomorrah, and Moses, who put himself on the line to save his people after the fashioning of the Golden Calf, Noah remained silent and was content to merely construct the Ark. As a result of this lack of compassion, Noah is not reckoned among our Patriarchs or Sages.

Today, this lesson speaks to us anew. We have a responsibility to gaze through our windows, empathize with our brethren, and do everything within our power to alleviate their suffering. Every challenge in life, every difficulty, becomes more bearable if you

---

12. Ibid. 6:16.

Parashas Noach / 31

that there is someone to share it with you and feel your pain.

So when we hear of hardships and when others around us are suffering, let's learn from the lessons of the *parashah*: let us make windows and create jewels.

PARASHAS LECH LECHA

THE BIRTH OF THE JEWISH PEOPLE

In this *parashah*, the history of the Jewish people commences. Until now, in the portions of Genesis and Noah, we studied about the creation of the world and the development of mankind, but now we meet the first Jewish couple: our grandparents, Abraham and Sarah.

The Torah goes into great detail regarding the fine nuances of their lives, for it is written, "*Ma'aseh Avos siman l'banim* — Whatever happened to our Forefathers is a portent for their children." Therefore, by studying the lives of our Patriarchs and Matriarchs, we can better appreciate the meaning of our own lives.

Our forefather Abraham was challenged with *ten tests*, all of which he passed with great distinction. All the trials and tribulations of future generations are traceable to those tests. If, through our long painful history we remained faithful to God and never lost sight of our calling, it is because Abraham created the character traits that enabled us to prevail.

The very first test with which he was confronted is to be found in the opening verse of the *parashah*: "*Lech lecha* — Go for yourself,"[13] meaning, "Divorce yourself from the immoral ways of the world, tap your inner resources, and discover your mission, your higher purpose in life. If necessary, be the lone voice standing up against the world, but stand steadfast in your commitment to Torah ... do not compromise!"

If we, the Jewish people, have had the courage to be that lone voice throughout the centuries and have lived by our own ideals proclaimed at Sinai, it is because our forefather, Abraham, paved the way for us; we need only follow in his footsteps.

Finding Our Inner Strength

Commentators teach that when Abraham was tested, he was not given Divine assistance, but had to seek strength from within himself. This appears rather paradoxical. Does not God help us fulfill every mitzvah? Isn't His guiding hand always there?

But if a test is to be truly a test that will accomplish its goal, then God has to restrain Himself from helping us, even as a parent or teacher has to refrain from providing the answers, and thereby encourage his children or students to research, study, and probe. Therefore, God denied Abraham assistance so that he might unearth the treasures buried within him and create those immortal character traits that would enable his descendants to survive for all time.

---

13. Ibid. 12:1.

Thus, because Abraham was able to pass that first test and depart from his country, from his birthplace, from his father's house, we too have been able to adapt to those new lands to which destiny has led us throughout the centuries. Because Abraham was able to retain his faith in the face of famine and the terrible ordeal of Sarah's abduction, we too have been able to retain our faith in days of total darkness, when all appeared lost. Because Abraham was able to respond to the call of God and offer his son Isaac on the altar, Jewish parents have been able to pass the tests of the Hitlers of every generation. Thus, every test that Abraham passed has become part of our spiritual genes. So when confronted by life's many trials and tribulations, we are not to despair. We have what it takes; our forefather Abraham prepared us well. We need only pray to God for His Divine Providence, summon our energies, our inner reserves and we will pass the test and triumph.

TO BE BLESSED OR TO BE A BLESSING

After blessing Abraham, God tells him, "*He'yei berachah* — "You shall be a source of *blessing*,"[14] words that imply a higher level of blessing than simply, "You shall be *blessed*." Most people seek blessings for themselves, and if given a choice, would opt to be *blessed* rather than be a *source of blessing* — receiving rather than giving, being served rather than serving, But the Torah teaches just the opposite: we will attain a greater level of fulfillment if we aspire to be a blessing to others. Our eminent *Zeide*, HaRav HaGaon Avraham HaLevi Jungreis, *z'tl*, would often say in Yiddish, "*Zolst eemer kenen* **geibon**, *un kein mol nisht darfen* **beiten**. — May God grant that you always be in a position to *give* and never need to *ask* [for financial assistance]." If we bear this is mind, we will not feel burdened when called upon to serve, and will become a blessing to our families, to our community, and to

---

14. Ibid. 12:2.

our people. If we can do that, we will make a difference in the world — and indeed, we will be truly blessed.

God's Command or Our Desire

Amazingly, the Torah introduces Abraham in a very modest manner, simply telling us that God commanded him to depart from his land.[15]

In contrast, in the previous *parashah*, Noah, the father of mankind, is presented as "righteous and perfect [wholehearted]." This is all the more puzzling when we consider the many wonderful, miraculous stories that we know of Abraham's early years, such as his emergence unscathed when King Nimrod cast him into a fiery furnace. Why doesn't the Torah relate them? The answer to this question defines the essence of our Jewishness.

Who is greater? He who performs a righteous deed because he is commanded by God, or he who does so because of the inclinations of his own heart? On first thought, you might think that the latter is superior, but our Sages teach that the person whose action is prompted by the command of God is on a higher level, for he sublimates his will for the sake of his Creator. Moreover, when one's action is based on one's own inclination, then one is subject to a change of heart, for while today he might find pleasure in doing something, tomorrow the very same deed may leave him cold. There is no permanence to his act.

But when a man is motivated by God's command, then no matter where life takes him, whether he is challenged by storms or calm, whether he is enveloped in darkness or showered with light, in illness or in health, his commitment will remain constant. That which occurred during Abraham's early years was the result of *his own feelings and thoughts and not God's command*, and therefore, in delineating his character, the Torah does not make reference to

---

15. Ibid. 12:1.

it. Our *parashah* introduces Abraham with the simple yet stirring words, "*Lech Lecha* ... — "Go for yourself." Thus, the first Jew is commanded to look within himself, *to dare to be different*, to defy the world and *live by the Word of God*.

Even as Abraham did, we perform our mitzvos because God spoke, and in every generation we are fortified by the knowledge that we have the ability to do so, for Abraham paved the way for us. But there remains a puzzling question. In the opening verses of the *parashah*, God promises Abraham, "I will make you a great nation and you will prosper."[16] The obvious question that arises is: If God promises that the Patriarch will benefit, then why is his obedience considered the fulfillment of God's Will?

We learn that even when God promised great blessings for the fulfillment of the commandments, Abraham acted solely for the sake of God and never thought of personal gain. As it is written, "So Abram went as God had spoken to him ...."[17] This is the key element in serving God: the ability to overcome our personal needs and desires and bow to His will. This trait of our forefather Abraham has been integrated into our psyches. No matter where life has taken us as a people, whether we bore the yoke of slavery and oppression or lived in freedom and had to battle assimilation, we cleaved to our Torah and mitzvos. It is that faith and that ability to sublimate our will for the sake of our Creator that enabled us to survive the centuries and remain Jews, no matter how great the odds were against us.

BITTER OR BETTER

You might ask why God imposed painful and difficult trials upon Abraham. Surely, God was aware of his lofty spiritual gifts. The answer can be found in the very word "test." In Hebrew, "test" is called *nisayon*, which literally means "to be lifted up," for in truth, every difficulty, every stumbling block that God

---
16. Ibid. 12:2.
17. Ibid. 12:4.

places in our paths is, in reality, a challenge through which we can become elevated.

Abraham understood that the hardships confronting him were orchestrated by God for his spiritual development. Therefore, Abraham accepted his trials with equanimity and serenity, and never complained. He transformed life's problems into windows of opportunity, and from each trial, he emerged stronger and greater, until he became the spiritual giant he was destined to be.

Our dearly beloved father, Rabbi Meshulem HaLevi Jungreis, z'tl, would often say that the difference between *bitter* and *better* is just one letter. So too, in life everything depends on attitude. One little letter can change everything. The way we react to onerous, trying challenges will either make us *better* or *bitter*. This message is especially significant to us today as we are beset by so many unknowns, so many fears. Let us convert our anxieties into challenges for growth. Let us become *better* and not *bitter*. This teaching should guide us in every aspect of our lives. Should the challenge be major or minor, big or small, the image of our forefather Abraham should remind us to seize the opportunity to make that which is *bitter*, *better*.

If We Will It

Hashem tells Abraham, "Go ... *from* your land, from your relatives, and your father's house to the land that I will show you."[18] Abraham leaves and *arrives* in the Land of Canaan, as it says, "Abram took his wife ... and they left to go to the land of Canaan, and they came to the land of Canaan."[19] From the two words "*left*" and "*came to*" we can glean a fount of wisdom that can help us throughout our lives. If we demonstrate the will to fulfill God's command, there is nothing that can stand in our way; we will surely achieve our goals.

---

18. Ibid. 12:1.
19. Ibid. 12:5.

PARASHAS VAYEIRA

JEWISH CHARACTER TRAITS

⁕ HUMILITY

"*Vayeira eilav Hashem ...* — And God appeared unto him"[20] are the opening words of *Parashas Vayeira*. Interestingly enough, although in context it is clear that God appeared to Abraham, the Torah does not explicitly name him. The last verse in *Parashas Lech Lecha* indicates that Abraham had just circumcised himself and the members of his household, so we know that Hashem came to visit him during his recuperation.

---

20. Ibid. 18:1.

~ Connecting With God

Some commentators wonder why the text omits the Patriarch's name. Why does he remain anonymous? Surely, his many merits rendered him worthy of the Divine visitation. There is a profound teaching behind this omission. The true greatness of Abraham (whose name means "father of all nations") could be found not only in his incredible *chesed* — loving-kindness, his all-encompassing faith in God, his ability to sacrifice … — but also in his genuine humility. "Behold, I am but dust and ashes,"[21] he proclaimed. He totally negated himself, divested himself of his ego, and became a complete spiritual being. It was this humility that enabled him to connect with God.

All of us who would strive to have a relationship with the Almighty should attempt to emulate Abraham's example. For our generation, this should not be too difficult, for if anyone should realize how fragile life is — how, in an instant, all our possessions can be wiped out and our very lives forfeit — it is we. On a universal as well as on a personal level, we live with uncertainty. It seems that no place is secure. Terrorism, economic instability, and fear of illness loom over us like sinister shadows. Certainly we can all echo the words of the Patriarch: "I am but dust and ashes …." Our only hope is to return to God and proclaim with the psalmist, "I raise my eyes upon the mountains, whence will come my help? My help is from Hashem …."[22]

Character Traits That Distinguish a Jew

~ Chesed — Loving-kindness

Our Sages teach that certain traits distinguish us and indicate that we are descendants of the Patriarch Abraham. One of those

---

21. Ibid. 18:27.
22. *Psalms* 121:1-2.

traits is *chesed*. In addition to *chesed*, yet another trait is associated with loving-kindness: *rachamim* (compassion). But there is no redundancy in Hebrew; thus, each of these terms has its own distinct component of loving-kindness, which we will discover in this *parashah*.

The *parashah* opens with Abraham, at the age of 99, recovering from his circumcision. For any adult to undergo such a procedure is no simple matter, but for a man of 99 it is a painful ordeal. This narrative takes place on the third day following the *bris*, which we know is the most difficult. Yet Abraham sat in the doorway of his tent, looking for guests so that he could perform the mitzvah of *hachnasas orchim* (hospitality). Therefore, Hashem compassionately caused the sun to shine in its full intensity to deter travelers so that Abraham should not be disturbed by wayfarers.

But Abraham's heart was bursting with *chesed*. He had a need to give, and he suffered more at the thought of not being able to welcome guests than from the physical pain of his circumcision. He anxiously sat at the threshold of his tent, searching for passersby to invite into his home. When the Almighty saw Abraham's yearning to reach out, to be of service to others, He sent him three angels in the guise of nomads. Although ailing, Abraham was so overjoyed to see them that he actually *ran* to greet them, offered them hospitality, and prepared a lavish meal for them.

Herein is to be found the difference between the traits of *chesed* and *rachamim*. The word *rachamim* is derived from the word *rechem*, which means "womb." Even as a mother has compassion on the child growing within her, so, too, the individual with *rachmanus* has his/her compassion aroused by a certain need. But *chesed* operates *independent of need*. It throbs in the heart and demands expression. The *baal chesed* — he who personifies *chesed* — desires to give because that is his *raison d'etre*. Doing so lends meaning to his life; that is the spiritual gene that our forefather Abraham transmitted to us: the desire to *give, to make the world a better place* by extending a helping hand.

From whom did our forefather Abraham learn this? From the Almighty Himself. It was on pillars of *chesed* that God built this world.[23] Prior to the Creation, there was no life in need of God's compassion, but it is God's "desire," so to speak, to do *chesed*. Therefore He created the world in order to dispense His loving-kindness. We have a mandate to emulate the Almighty God: to live our lives in such a way that we become *gomlei chasadim*, men and women who impart loving-kindness to others.

Our bobbe, Rebbetzin Miriam Jungreis, *a'h*, was a true embodiment of this trait of *chesed*. Her life was one of constant giving, and even in her last days, as illness racked her frail body, she continued to organize *chesed* programs for needy Russian immigrants, explaining that if she could not offer help to others, her life had no meaning.

⁓ Bikur Cholim — Visiting the Sick

Our Sages impart yet another reason why Abraham's name is omitted as God makes His compassionate visit in the opening verse of this *parashah*. Had the Torah identified the Patriarch by name, we might have concluded that God visits only the righteous. To the Almighty, however, every human being is holy and the *Shechinah* hovers over every sickbed. Therefore, the lesson that we should glean from this is that we, too, must visit the sick and express concern, not only for friends, family, and prominent individuals, but to all those in need.

Acting upon this teaching, *Bikur Cholim* organizations (for visiting the sick) have been important to Jewish life throughout the centuries. Timeless lessons are to be found in the very words "*Bikur Cholim*," as well. The Hebrew word *bikur* (to visit) is related to *bikores* (investigation), to teach that when we visit someone who is ill, we should investigate and determine how we may best help the patient and family members. The word *bikur* is also related to *boker* (morning), reminding us to bring cheer and sunshine with our very presence and not to depart from the sickroom without pronouncing a prayer for good health. The importance of visiting the sick is just one of the concepts of *chesed* that we can learn from this *parashah*.

---

23. *Psalms* 89:3.

⁌ Hachnasas Orchim: Lessons for Life

Although the Torah had not as yet been given, Abraham felt God's word in every fiber of his being. The Torah describes in great detail the mitzvah of *hachnasas orchim* — welcoming guests.

When we open our home to guests, we transform it from a residence into a spiritual abode in which we share God's blessings. Our home is not simply a residence in which we eat, drink, sleep, and relax, it is also a place in which we welcome guests, impart joy to others, and help all those in need.

We can learn many lessons for life from *Parashas Vayeira* and can readily apply them to our own situations. Among these lessons are:

1. **The *Chuppah*: Abraham's Model for the Jewish Home:** Abraham's tent was open on all sides so that it might be accessible from every direction. To this very day, in remembrance of the Tent of Abraham, the *chuppah* (marriage canopy) is open on all sides, in the hope that the home of the young couple will replicate Abraham's tent, in which guests were lovingly provided with hospitality. This teaching applies to *all* guests, for even though Abraham thought that his guests were simple desert nomads, he welcomed them with great honor.

2. **Enthusiasm:** Abraham *ran* to greet his guests and he ran to serve them, teaching us that when we perform a mitzvah, it should be done with alacrity and joyous enthusiasm. It is not only *our performance* of mitzvos that is critical, but *the manner* in which we do so: grudgingly or happily, angrily or kindly, warmly or coldly.

3. **Attend to the needs of guests:** Abraham had many servants, but he and his wife Sarah *personally* attended to the needs of their guests. Thus we learn that it is proper to honor visitors by serving them.

4. **Say little, but do much:** Abraham invited his guests to partake of "a little water" and "a morsel of bread,"[24] but then proceeded to prepare a lavish banquet, teaching us that a host should say little — so as not to make his guests feel beholden — but deliver much.

5. **Thank God:** Abraham did not allow his guests to express thanks to him, but instructed them to thank God. He impressed upon them that all that he possessed and shared was from Hashem. From this we learn that when we entertain guests, we must also consider their spiritual needs and make them aware of God's presence and bounty.

6. **Escort Guests:** It is written that when the angels took their leave from the tent of Abraham, he "walked with them to escort them"[25] – reminding us that not only is it a mitzvah to invite guests to our homes, but when they depart, we should accompany them (for example, if we live in an apartment building, we should escort them to the elevator; if we have a private home, we should walk them to the door). To this very day, we can recall our grandparents, Rabbi and Rebbetzin Abraham Jungreis, of blessed memory, walking us to our car and waving until we turned the corner. This same tradition was continued by our beloved father, Rabbi Meshulem Jungreis, *z"tl*, and lives on today in our mother, Rebbetzin Esther Jungreis. *tichyeh*.

7. *Lifum Tzara Agra* — The reward is commensurate with the pain: Although Abraham was suffering intensely due to his circumcision, he transcended that pain so that he might perform the mitzvah of *hachnasas orchim*, and experienced great joy in doing so. We learn that the greater the effort and *mesiras nefesh* (self-sacrifice) that the mitzvah entails, the greater the satisfaction in doing it. Today, we go to synagogue despite distance and inclement weather; we study Torah despite our fatigue; we give *tzedakah*, despite the fact

---

24. *Genesis* 18:4-5.
25. Ibid. 18:16.

that we are on a tight budget, and we grow spiritually as we perform each mitzvah.

8. **Hospitality:** *Hachnasas orchim* may be proffered on many different levels. People are lonely. They yearn for warmth and family. People are perplexed; they need guidance. They are spiritually deprived and are yearning for something to hold on to, something to believe in. The hospitality that Abraham extended encompassed all this. By following in his footsteps, we can bring people closer to God. A most auspicious time to extend such hospitality is Shabbos, for the spiritual power of the day is all encompassing and will leave a life-transforming impression on our guests.

9. **Responsibilities of guests:** "They [the angels] asked Abraham, 'Where is Sarah, your wife?'"[26] Rashi explains that the angels knew where Sarah was. Nevertheless, they inquired about her whereabouts to praise her to Abraham. Their question called his attention to her fine character traits and modesty, thus making her even more beloved to her husband.

    The Torah teaches that we should always try to enhance the *shalom bayis* (peace and harmony) of those whom we visit by praising one spouse to the other. Similarly, the most meaningful gift that we can give parents and grandparents is to notice something praiseworthy about their children. Such expressions of kindness are the most meaningful gift that visitors can impart.

10. *Makom kavua* — Designating a set place for prayer: We should have a special place for prayer. For the Torah tells us that Abraham spoke with Hashem regarding the destruction of Sodom[27] and then returned the next day "to the place where he had stood before Hashem."[28]

11. *Hamispallel B'ad Chaveiro*: "He who prays on behalf of another when he himself needs that very same thing is

---

26. Ibid. 18:9.
27. Ibid. 18:23-32.
28. Ibid. 19:27.

answered first." God granted Sarah a son after Abraham prayed for Abimelech to be blessed with children.[29]

Find someone who has the same problems as you and pray for that person, and God will hearken to your prayers. Admittedly, this is not an easy challenge, for we tend to be consumed by our own needs. We see only our own requirements, but if we can transcend ourselves, if we identify with the pain of our neighbors and sincerely beseech God on their behalf, that is our best reason to hope that God will answer us.

---

29. Ibid. 20:17, *Rashi* to ibid. 21:1.

PARASHAS CHAYEI SARAH

Everything Is In God's Hands

Our Torah is a Book of Commandments, yet *Sefer Bereishis* (Book of *Genesis*), the longest of the Five Books, deals mostly with the history of our Matriarchs and Patriarchs. It is through their lives that we learn proper conduct, morals, and values. It is they who impart to us the road map for our lives. It is they who teach us how to deal with our many challenges and respond with strength to the ups and downs of life.

In this *parashah* we encounter the very first funeral mentioned in the Torah, with the death of Sarah Imeinu (our mother). The Sages tell us that Sarah died of grief upon hearing that Abraham had actually sacrificed their only son, Isaac. After sacrificing a ram at the site of the *Akeidah* (Binding of Isaac), Abraham and Isaac returned only to discover that their beloved Sarah was no longer alive. Sarah's death was extremely painful to Abraham. In all such situations, so many thoughts could plague a mourner. Perhaps the death could have been prevented ... perhaps something more could have been done ... perhaps .... Nevertheless, we find that Abraham never resorted to this type of self-destructive speculation or grief. While he wept for his beloved wife, he did so with limitations. The Torah text testifies to this as the word *"V'LIVkoSAH* — to bewail her"[30] is written with a small letter *kaf,* teaching us that Abraham did not succumb to depression, but restrained his grief, mourned with dignity, and thus brought honor to the memory of his beloved wife.

Significantly, as soon as the time of mourning passed, Abraham resumed his responsibilities as a father and began the search for a bride for his son, Isaac. The lesson to be drawn from this is obvious: no matter how trying and how sorrowful our lot may be, we must nevertheless pick ourselves up and continue to fulfill our life mission.

Ultimately, we have to understand that *everything that occurs is in God's Hands,* so to speak. It is He Who determines the number of the days of our lives. Even if there had been no *Akeidah, Sarah would have died on that very same day.* To reinforce this teaching, the passage opens with "the lifetime of Sarah," and concludes with "[these are] the years of Sarah's life," emphasizing that our years are designated by God. We should never berate ourselves by second-guessing:"If I had called a different doctor...." "If we had gone to a different hospital...." "If I had been more alert...:" "If... if... if...." Know that there is a God above you. Do what is in your power, trust the One Above, and respond to the challenges of life with strength.

Two passages in the Book of Genesis announce death, but, paradoxically, both convey death using the word "life." We are informed of Sarah's demise with the words "*Chayei* Sarah — the

---

30. Ibid. 23:2.

life of Sarah,"[31] while the death of Jacob is prefaced by the words, "*Vayechi Yaakov* — And Jacob lived,"[32] to teach us that if people are truly righteous, even when they pass on, their legacy continues and they remain alive.

TIPS FOR FINDING YOUR LIFE PARTNER

This *parashah* is sometimes referred to as "the *Shidduch parashah*" and we will share just a few points on the ins and outs of finding a life partner.

WHAT ONE SHOULD LOOK FOR

Abraham Avinu asks his trusted servant Eliezer to swear that he would not take a wife for Isaac from among the Canaanites in whose midst he dwells, but would return to Abraham's birthplace and seek a wife for Isaac there.[33]

We wonder why Abraham is so adamant that Isaac not marry a Canaanite girl. It couldn't simply be because the Canaanites were idolaters, for the people of Charan (Abraham's birthplace) were also idol worshipers. In fact, at that time, the entire world was mired in paganism. Abraham's decision can be understood when we realize that idol worship is an intellectual error; it is a belief in a fallacious theology, and that can be overcome. However, the Canaanites were *morally degenerate*; they were innately dishonorable. While people can become enlightened and renounce their erroneous beliefs, corrupt character traits cannot easily be overcome. It was that which concerned our forefather Abraham. He

---

31. Ibid. 23:1.
32. Ibid. 47:28.
33. Ibid. 24:3-4.

knew that the future Matriarch of the nation destined to stand at Sinai could not be found in such a population.

The test of a truly good family is evidenced by the *middos* (character traits) of its members. These character traits are passed down from generation to generation through the example set by the parents. In our world today, where the trappings of financial success are often the criteria for a "good match," we would do well to remember this teaching. Exterior trimmings, such as wealth, have no substance; they can disappear overnight, leaving darkness and pain in their wake. So, when seeking a life partner, first and foremost, look for exemplary character traits: kindness, refinement, patience, humility, generosity, and *simchas hachaim* (a positive attitude toward life). Moreover, beware of those who gossip, are quick tempered, arrogant, cynical, unforgiving, miserly, jealous, and selfish. Don't be blinded by good looks and glamour. If positive character traits are lacking, then even the most beautiful face can turn ugly overnight.

PRAYER

Eliezer *prayed* to God that He do *chesed* for his master Abraham and grant that he find a wife for Isaac. It is difficult to understand why one would have to pray for a match for Isaac, a man who had it all. He was the scion of a great family, fabulously wealthy, magnificent in appearance, and brilliant; in short, a great catch. Who would *not* want to marry him? But from this we learn that when it comes to finding our life partners, we all need God's help. It's easy enough to get married, but to marry the *right one* — for that we need Divine assistance, for that, we have to *pray*. An especially auspicious time for prayer is during *Minchah*, the afternoon service, for that was the prayer that Isaac was reciting when he first beheld Rebecca.

Chesed

The litmus test that Eliezer used to recognize Isaac's *basherte* (Divinely destined life-partner) was *chesed*. "Let it be that the maiden to whom I shall say, 'Please tip over your jug so I may drink,' and who replies, 'Drink, and I will even water your camels,' her will you have designated for Your servant, for Isaac ...."[34]

To appreciate the awesomeness of this test, let us remember that drawing water from a well is no easy task, and satiating the thirst of ten camels can be backbreaking labor. It would have been reasonable for Rebecca to have told the stranger to draw his own water; however, not only did she refrain from responding in such a manner, but her offer of help exceeded Eliezer's expectations, as she watered the camels until they were satiated and then, when Eliezer asked for lodging for the night, offered him food and stabling for his animals as well.

Don't Compromise Your Principles

Although Abraham made Eliezer take an oath that he would not seek a wife for Isaac from the daughters of Canaan, he also told him that if the girl refused to return with him, he would be absolved from the oath. Nevertheless, under no circumstances should Eliezer consider taking Isaac out of the land of Israel.

From this we learn that, as critical as it is to make a *shidduch*, it should never be made at the price of moving to a community that might stunt one's spiritual growth. Indeed, we must always make the effort to reside in a place where we can continually grow spiritually as Jews.

---

34. Ibid. 24:14.

But if Eliezer were freed of his oath, whom would Isaac marry? Since he could not marry a woman from the land of Canaan, as Abraham had previously stipulated, and if no woman were willing to accompany Eliezer to Eretz Yisrael, what would happen to God's promise that the children of Abraham would be as numerous as the stars in the heavens?

Abraham had perfect faith in Hashem and knew that His promise would be fulfilled. If there were no suitable matriarch of the Jewish People in Haran, one would be found elsewhere, *somewhere*. We learn that even if it appears that we are undertaking an impossible task, if that task is assigned by Hashem, we nevertheless follow God's commandments and trust that He will do the rest, as He did for our forefathers. Today, assimilation is rampant, intermarriage is rife, and people very often try to justify marrying out by claiming that there is no one else available. But God is the ultimate *shadchan* (matchmaker). We must trust Him to *send us our destined life partner* and He will surely do so.

MOVE ON — AVOID PROCRASTINATION

Eliezer very clearly challenged Rebecca's family. "And now, if you intend to do kindness and truth with my master, tell me," he demanded, "and if not, tell me, and I will turn to the right or to the left."[35] Eliezer wanted a clear *yes* or *no*, without delay, so he could continue to fulfill Abraham's command.

Once again, this is a teaching that we would do well to remember. Ours is a society in which procrastination is in vogue. People have a tendency to date endlessly, only to see their efforts end in futility. Often, critical months and even years are wasted and leave much heartbreak in their wake. Our Torah teaches that if a *shidduch* isn't working out, move on!

This teaching is also applicable in situations that end in painful breakups because one of the parties has a change of heart. Very

---
35. Ibid. 24:49.

often, the rejected party feels that his/her life has been put on hold and fears that the *basherte shidduch* has been lost. The teaching of *our parashah* comes to fortify such people. Eliezer could certainly have lost hope had they said no. After all, there were so many miraculous signs that indicated that Rebecca was Isaac's *basherte* and she was even a descendent of Abraham's own family. Yet Eliezer said "Tell me yes or no, so that I may know whether I should turn right or left and continue my quest for a wife for Isaac."

PARASHAS TOLDOS

A GOOD TEACHER IS NOT ENOUGH — YOU ALSO NEED GOOD PEERS

The Torah tells us that Rebecca was pregnant with twins and the children struggled within her womb, *"Vayissrotz'tzu habanim b'kirbah."*[36]

Rashi explains that whenever Rebecca passed a house of idolatry, Esau fought to emerge, and when she passed a house of Torah study, Jacob struggled to be born. We can understand why Esau was anxious to be born, but why would Yaakov wish to leave his mother's womb early? Do we not have a tradition that an angel

---

36. Ibid. 25:22.

teaches the entire Torah to the fetus while in the womb? Could Jacob have found a better Torah teacher than God's angel?

From this we learn that a negative environment or a bad friend can overcome even the best teacher. Jacob had to escape from Esau so that his negative influences would not taint Jacob's character or his soul. If this holds true for Jacob, how much more must we be vigilant regarding our friends and environment.

THOUGHTS TO PONDER

Who is strong? He who subdues his personal inclination.
(Ethics of the Fathers 4:1)

"He who masters his speech will not be overcome."
(Rabbi Nachman of Breslov)

NATURE OR NURTURE — IT'S ALL IN OUR HANDS

In *Parashas Toldos*, we find that when Esau was born, he emerged from the womb red in appearance.[37] It was only later, however, when he was full grown and demanded of his brother Jacob, "Pour into me, now, some of that very red stuff,"[38] that he was called *"Edom"* (red). Edom is a metaphor for cruelty and blood lust. At birth, Esau already had the potential to be a killer, but he also had the potential to channel his inclinations in a positive way. It was only when he used his talents negatively that he received the name Edom. We learn that all tendencies and character traits can be directed either for the good or for the bad. The choice is ours, and it is by the choices we make that we are

---

37. Ibid. 25:25.
38. Ibid. 25:30.

measured. Once Esau expressed himself in such a crude and cruel manner, "Pour into me, now, some of that very red stuff," he was called *Edom* because he had chosen to be a crude and cruel person.

From this we learn that our words not only impact on others, but perhaps even more significantly, they influence and shape our own personalities. Thus, if you speak in a cold, uncaring manner, you will eventually become cold and uncaring; if you speak in loving, caring language, the possibility that you will become loving and caring can become a reality. The Torah is alerting us to the far-reaching effects of our deeds and words as they shape and mold our character. Therefore, we must be ever on guard to use refined language and gentle, compassionate words, not only so that we might interact with others with warmth and love, but also so that we ourselves might become better, kinder people.

One might argue that Esau can hardly be held responsible for his barbaric ways. After all, he was *born red*, and his propensity for evil was inborn. Moreover, isn't it true that everything is pre-determined, that the script of our lives is written before we are born? To a certain extent, this is true; nevertheless, we have been given free choice in the most crucial of all decisions: that is, shaping our character. The Talmud states, "Everything is foretold except our *yiras Shamayim* [reverence for God]." Thus, for example, before birth, it is determined how high our I.Q. will be, but it is our decision (based on our reverence for God) whether we will use that high I.Q. to bring blessing to others, or God forbid, to inflict harm and pain upon them. Just consider how different the world would have been had Hitler used his ability to sway public opinion for good rather than for evil. The same holds true in every area of life.

David, king of Israel, is a perfect example. He demonstrates how one can harness one's inborn characteristics and channel them for the benefit of mankind. It is written that he, too, was born *red*, but his *yiras Shamayim* was the guiding light of his life. Thus, with his words he created psalms and with his courage, he defeated the evil Goliath and forever changed the course of mankind. These thoughts from the *parashah* should inspire us to scrutinize our own personalities, measure our own words, and evaluate our own deeds so that we may convert our weaknesses into strengths, our failures into wisdom and our apathy into caring. Let us each do our share to create a better world.

Our Roots — Our Treasures

We are all familiar with the story of Jacob and Esau, which is the focus of this *parashah*. There are, however, also passages of which we may be less aware and which at first glance appear to have less personal meaning or significance. Upon closer examination, however, they reveal to us the history of our people and our eternal resilience.

Even as in the days of Abraham, when famine forced the Patriarch to leave his home, so, too, Isaac was confronted by hunger and, as commanded by Hashem, went to dwell in the land of Gerar, where King Abimelech reigned. There, Isaac became very prosperous and re-dug the wells that the servants of his father, Abraham, had dug, wells that produced "living" water. Those wells had been stopped up by the people of Gerar because of hatred and jealousy. Isaac not only opened the wells, but he called them by the very same names as his father had.[39]

The message of these wells is profound and has direct bearing on us today. Wells that produce living waters are symbolic of Torah. Those who hate us cannot bear for us to dig deeply into our wells and bring forth the spiritual treasures buried in our souls. In every generation they find different ways to persecute us and close our wells. But even as Isaac re-opened the wells of his father, so too must we open our ancient wells, keep digging, and plumb the Torah to its depths so that its living waters may pour forth and refresh our souls. We learn that we are never to be disheartened, never to give up. Torah study is not just an avocation: it is our very life, the essence of our being, and no force on earth can separate us from it.

---

39. Ibid. 26:15-18.

Furthermore, when Isaac called the wells by the very same names designated by his father, he taught us that, when it comes to spirituality, we must go back to the very roots and foundation that our parents set forth for us. We dare not even change names; how much more so must we retain the way of life that our ancestors paved for us. Our prayers, our mitzvos, our *chesed,* are all symbolized by those wells, and therein lies our resilience. Isaac renewed Abraham's wells, and those three wells are reminders of our Holy Temples: the first two that were destroyed and the third that is yet to be built and will stand eternally.

Our generation has encountered those who would shut down our wells. The Nazis, the Communists — they tried, and failed. The Torah that was once studied in the mighty yeshivos of Europe was not consumed in the flames of the Holocaust; that Torah found new life on these shores, in Israel, and the world over — wherever the descendants of Isaac live. Fortunately for us, in this blessed country our wells have not been shut down. We do not have to endanger our lives in order to study Torah. We just have to dig deeply into our hearts and renew our commitment to our covenant with God, and we will discover a wellspring of treasures.

PARASHAS VAYEITZEI

Emes — Recognizing the Truth

In this week's *parashah* we discover how we might best develop our spiritual potential and find more meaning in our lives. The Torah tells us that upon the advice of his parents, Jacob departs from the land of Israel and travels toward the city of Haran in search of his life partner. And then the passage continues, "*Vayifga bamakom* — He encountered 'The Place.'"[40] This very unusual usage of the word *makom* (place) teaches us that on his way to Haran, Jacob realized that he had neglected to stop at the Temple Mount where his father and grandfather had prayed, and

---

40. Ibid. 28:11.

to rectify his mistake; he immediately turned around to return to the site of the future *Beis HaMikdash*.

To appreciate the awesomeness of this, just try to imagine how you would react upon returning from Israel, drained and exhausted, having survived a terrorist attack (just as Jacob had narrowly escaped Esau's son's murderous intent). While waiting for your luggage at J.F.K. you suddenly realize that you had neglected to pray at the Western Wall. Would you make an immediate about-face and go back, especially in view of the fact that Hamas and company were lying in wait for you, just as Esau and his clan were in Jacob's case?

Jacob's attribute was *emes* (truth), and above all, he was committed to the pursuit of that truth, even if it meant undertaking an arduous and hazardous journey, and even if it meant admitting his mistakes. We can appreciate the awesome strength of Jacob's character when we contrast his reaction to that of his brother Esau. In last week's *parashah*, Esau sold his birthright for a pot of beans, but his arrogance would not allow him to admit that he had acted foolishly and impetuously; therefore, instead of doing *teshuvah* (repentance), he became further embedded in lies and spurned his birthright by expressing contempt for it.[41]

The ability to recognize one's mistakes and shortcomings is what elevates a person. It's not so much the mistakes that we make that condemn us, but how we react to them that counts, and that is the meaning of *teshuvah*. When God sees that we are determined to embark upon His path, then He meets us more than halfway, comes to our aid, and performs miracles on our behalf. Thus, as soon as Jacob admitted to his mistake and expressed his desire to return, God shortened his journey and the Temple Mount actually appeared before him: he encountered *The Place*. It is this ability to admit the *emes*, recognize one's mistakes, and do *teshuvah* that distinguishes the great among our people.

The kings of Israel descended from Judah because he had the strength of character to openly admit that he erred. In this same vein, his descendant, David, conceded to Nathan the Prophet, "I

---

41. Ibid. 25:34.

have sinned to Hashem."[42] Those words of David have inspired people throughout the centuries. In these difficult times, when we are challenged to examine our lives, we would do well to follow the example of Jacob, Judah, and David and summon the courage to say, "I was wrong — I will learn from my mistakes! I will do *teshuvah* and do my share to make the world a better place." And if we do, we can hope that God will make miracles for us, miracles to ease our paths even as He did for Jacob "and we too will encounter *The Place*."

Forever Engraved on Our Hearts

There is yet another way of understanding this very same incident: "*Ma'aseh Avos siman l'banim*." Jacob was the Patriarch who had to struggle with exile. Therefore his life experiences speak to us with great relevance. When Jacob arrived in Haran, he yearned for the Temple Mount and Jerusalem. His yearning was so intense that Hashem actually brought the Temple Mount to him. Thousands of years have passed since Jacob dreamed at Mount Moriah, but we, his descendants, have never forgotten. Even as he, we too yearn for the Temple Mount — for Jerusalem. We may have been dispersed to the four corners of the earth, but no matter where destiny has taken us, in all our prayers we turn toward Jerusalem. At every wedding, in the midst of our joy, we break a glass — *Zeicher l'Churban* — in memory of the destruction of the Holy Temple in Jerusalem. And when we extend comfort to mourners, we do so with a prayer that they "find consolation among the mourners of Zion and Jerusalem."

Our holy city has never left us. May we behold the rebuilding of our Temple speedily in our own day.

---

42. *II Samuel* 12:13.

Maximizing Spiritual Growth

Our forefather Jacob had a dream in which he beheld a ladder anchored to the ground and reaching heavenward, with angels ascending and descending. This dream raises many questions. Why do angels need a ladder? And should they not descend before they ascend? Why is a ladder, rather than a bridge, the connecting link between heaven and earth? What is the lesson of this ladder?

The Torah teaches us that if we are to realize our spiritual capabilities, we must keep *shteiging* (growing). Even as we climb a ladder rung by rung, so too must we be constantly climbing, striving to reach ever-greater spiritual heights. On a ladder, we can never stand still, we can never just coast; either we go up or we go down. Similarly, we cannot be content with our status quo, for if we do not progress, we regress. *To be a Jew is to be in a constant state of development.* We never graduate from the university of life. As long as we are alive, our Torah learning and observance of mitzvos must continue to develop.

The ladder in Jacob's dream is firmly planted on the ground, but the top reaches the heavens. Similarly, we, too, must be firmly planted in our convictions, but always looking heavenward, always striving to enhance our spirituality and our connection to God.

The metaphor of the ladder is an allusion to Mount Sinai, since the word "*sulam*" (ladder) and *Sinai* have the same *gematria* (numerical value) of 130. The word *sulam* in the verse is spelled without a *vav* (סלם), which gives it the same numerical value as Sinai (סיני, 130). *Sulam* can also be spelled with a *vav*, (סולם) which would give it the numerical value of 136, like *Kol* (קול), *Tzom* (צום), and *Mamon* (ממון). These words can help us further expound on the meaning of the ladder. *Kol* (voice, prayer), *tzom* (fasting/repentance), and *mamon* (money/charity) are all vehicles through which we build our ladder. It is this concept that we proclaim in our High Holy Days liturgy: "Repentance, Prayer, and Charity cancel the evil decree."

Yet another lesson can be gleaned from the money and ladder comparison: We may use our resources for *tzedakah* — as a means to climb the ladder — but if that money is used for self-indulgence and temporal pleasure, then that very same wealth may cause us to fall from the ladder.

Never Be Afraid

In his dream, Jacob saw God Himself at the top of the ladder, teaching us that God is in charge of the world. Things don't happen at random; rather, everything is orchestrated by the Almighty. That very knowledge is fortifying, for when we are overwhelmed by the seemingly senseless chaos that surrounds us, it is strengthening to know that there is a God above who will make it all come right. Therefore, we must never be afraid. We need only turn to our Heavenly Father and He will help us climb the ladder, attain spiritual fulfillment, and realize our destiny as Jews.

The ladder also teaches us not to feel intimidated as we embark upon a life of Torah and mitzvos. We must not delude ourselves into thinking that we can achieve perfection immediately, or that if we have setbacks, there is no hope to improve. Rather, we must climb the ladder rung by rung, going "from one mitzvah to another mitzvah." As it is written, "*mitzvah gorreres mitzvah* — One mitzvah gives birth to another mitzvah." The point is that we must always aim for the next level.

Angels on the Ladder

As to why angels ascend prior to descending, it is because we create those angels through our deeds, through our Torah, mitzvos, and *chesed*. The righteous angels testify on our behalf in the heavens above, but alas, the reverse is also true: when we lack faith and abandon our sacred heritage, those angels cannot remain on high. When we fall, we drag down our angels, and they become our prosecutors, reporting on our sins and failures.

We can also learn a prophetic teaching from these angels: The nations that have oppressed us throughout history are represented in the heavens above by their own angels. Jacob saw them ascend. But fear not; their ascendancy was only momentary, for ultimately, they all must descend. Indeed, we have seen many empires, many great nations, attain glory and might, but we also have seen them disappear in the sands of time.

Therefore, we must never be afraid. We need only turn to our Heavenly Father.

Put Zest Into Life

When Hashem reassures Jacob that he will return whole and safe to the Land of Israel, the Torah states, "So Jacob *lifted his feet* and went toward the land of the easterners."[43] Rashi explains that this great news removed a heavy burden from Jacob's heart and energized him. When we feel that God is with us, when we know that we are fulfilling His will, no task is too difficult, no mountain is too high to climb. But when that assurance is missing, even the smallest step becomes an arduous task that taxes our resources. It is all in our own hands: if we remain loyal to Hashem's teachings, we will confront life's challenges with confidence, but if we betray His Word, we will invite our own undoing.

To apply this to our own families, let us try to emulate God's teachings and inspire our dear ones; let us impart our blessings and love to them, so that, even as Jacob, they too may lift their feet with joy as they embark upon life's journey.

---

43. *Genesis* 29:1.

PARASHAS VAYISHLACH

For many people, the events that we read about in the Torah are just charming Bible stories, but that is the furthest thing from the truth.

LESS IS MORE

From Jacob we learn that the material gifts that we possess should not be flaunted. Although at this juncture he is a wealthy man, he describes his assets by saying, "I have *an* ox, *a* donkey, *a* lamb, *a* servant ...."[44] Jacob's words remind us to be humble and modest. Once again we find a lesson that is so important for our generation, in which people feel compelled to ostenta-

---

44. Ibid. 32:6.

tiously display their wealth, or, worse still, inflate it. Who among us does not know individuals with the constant need to brag about their latest acquisitions, be they real or imaginary; people who believe that their worth is judged only through their possessions. Such people are spiritually and morally bankrupt. They lack self-esteem and inner peace. Their entire lives revolve around trying to keep up with the latest, and topping it. But there is always someone whom they cannot top. Moreover, there is no security in their possessions, no matter how solid they consider their assets to be.

In Aramaic, one of the terms for money is *"zuzim,"* which, literally translated, means "moving," teaching us that money is always on the move. Today, it is here and tomorrow it's gone, and if anyone should know this, it is our generation. Who cannot cite sad examples of people who, to all intents and purposes, were "riding high" but whose possessions evaporated overnight, leaving them with nothing to fall back on? Thousands of years ago, our forefather Jacob taught us that life is not about *having* more, but about *being* more.

Formula for Survival

Jacob's strategy for his reunion with his brother Esau was to divide his family: "If Esau comes to the one camp and strikes it down, then the remaining camp shall survive."[45] Jacob's foresight was meant to save at least part of his family in case Esau attacked.

Thus, Jacob laid the foundation for one of the principles that would ensure Jewish survival during our turbulent, painful years of exile. We see the pattern of sunset and sunrise throughout our history; following are just two examples for us to ponder:

As the First Temple in Jerusalem was destroyed, the great Jewish community of Babylon (where the Talmud was arranged) was born. Many centuries later, as the sun set upon European Jewry, it

---

45. Ibid. 32:9.

rose in America and Israel. Our forefather Jacob laid the foundation well, for no matter what our enemies sought to do, their plans came to naught. *Am Yisrael Chai!* — The Jewish nation lives! *"Al tira ...* — Do not fear sudden terror or the holocaust of the wicked when it comes."[46] "Plan a conspiracy and it will be annulled; speak your piece and it shall not stand, for God is with us."[47]

A Message for Today from Our Forefather Jacob

Every occurrence, every word in the Torah is a message to us today. It is written, *"Maaseh Avos siman l'banim."* Indeed, the Torah is the blueprint of the future, so if we wish to understand our contemporary world and know how we may best respond to the many challenges that confront us, we need only delve into the *parashah*.

Jacob is the Patriarch who foreshadows the exile. The pain and the extraordinary suffering that we have endured throughout the millennia in all the lands of our dispersion were all experienced by him. Jacob taught us how to respond to the terror of the night when we are overwhelmed by feelings of loneliness and fear. It was not by coincidence that Jacob is the composer of *Maariv* (the evening prayer service). He showed us how to illuminate the darkness with words that emanate from our hearts. He taught us that even in the most difficult moments, when all appears to be lost, we are never to give up, but we must turn to God in heartfelt prayer.

The Patriarch Jacob prayed not only for himself, but also for us, who followed him many generations later. When Jacob looked up and saw Esau coming, he also saw the Inquisitions, the pogroms, the Holocaust, and he begged for mercy. God heard his prayers, and promised that we, the Jewish people, would forever survive.

---

46. *Proverbs* 3:25.
47. *Isaiah* 8:10.

As King David wrote, "May Hashem answer you on the day of distress; may *the Name of the God of Jacob* make you impregnable."[48]

A Lesson for Survival — Recognizing the Trap

Upon confronting Esau, Jacob cried out, "Rescue me, please, *from the hand* of my brother, from the *hand of Esau* ...."[49] Our Rabbis discuss the meaning of these two hands, and the meaning of "my brother ... Esau." After all, Jacob had no other brother, and we know that nothing is redundant in the Torah, so why did Jacob use these apparently repetitive phrases? Our Sages explain that the Patriarch is teaching us a lesson for survival. Esau will confront us in two different guises: There are times when he will extend to us the hand of a brother in friendship, and in so doing, will attempt to destroy us through assimilation; there are times when he will attack us with Esau's hand, the ruthless hand of oppression.

Esau greets Jacob with a kiss, but the word "kiss" is dotted; the Sages teach us that the kiss was really a bite.[50] What seemed to be an act of friendship on Esau's part disguised a threat to Jacob's life. The Midrash tells us that Hashem, in His infinite mercy, changed Jacob's neck into a pillar of marble, thereby preventing Esau from injuring his brother. While we must be vigilant in regard to both hands of Esau, Jacob feared the hand of friendship more, pleading first for rescue from the hand of his brother. The danger from the hand of Esau is clear; it attempts to destroy our very lives, but the brother's hand, the hand of friendship, is the more dangerous, for when that hand is outstretched, we may be taken unawares, and can, God forbid, lose our identity, our heritage, our very Jewishness. The hand of friendship can make it very easy to forget

---

48. *Psalms* 20:2.
49. *Genesis* 32:12.
50. Ibid. 33:4.

that we stood at Sinai and are bound to Hashem by an eternal covenant. So let us treasure the awesomeness of our survival and protect our identity, our Torah, our Judaism with vigilance and love.

Character Traits To Aim For

After many years of separation, Jacob once again meets his brother, Esau. From the subtlety of Jacob's language, we discover the character traits to which we, as Jews, should aspire. The reverse is also true: From Esau we learn those characteristics that we must shun.

In an attempt to appease Esau, Jacob presents him with gifts. Initially, Esau demurs, saying *"Yesh li rav* — I have plenty." Nevertheless, Jacob presses the gifts upon him saying, "... inasmuch as God has been gracious to me and ... *Yesh li kol* — I have everything."[51] In this exchange we discover two world views: the philosophy of the Torah Jew and the outlook of those who live lives devoid of God.

When Esau says, "I have plenty," he is also telegraphing the message, "I want more." His statement reveals his greed and arrogance. Our Sages teach, "One who has one hundred desires two." More than enjoying the hundred that he *does* possess, he covets the hundred that he *does not* as yet own.

Such a person is never at peace; there is always something more for which he lusts. He remains forever dissatisfied, for, as far as he is concerned, his possessions are not gifts from God, but the fruits of his own labor, reflections of his own achievements. Therefore, he does not understand the concept of gratitude or the implications of *tzedakah*, which is based upon giving back.

On the other hand, from our forefather Jacob we learn that if a man recognizes that his possessions are gifts from God, he can indeed proclaim, "I have everything," for a genuinely spiritual person perceives that God gives everyone that which he requires

---

51. Ibid. 33:9, 11.

to fulfill his potential. Therefore, if he lacks something, he does not feel deprived, but is sustained by the knowledge that if God does not deem it important for him to have, he does not need it.

"Who is rich?" our Sages ask. "He who is content with his lot"[52]; that contentment can only be attained by recognizing God's presence in our lives. Jacob was totally connected to God, and even in his most difficult moments, he was tranquil in the knowledge that God was above him and would provide. Since Jacob viewed his possessions as gifts from the Almighty, he was committed to sharing them with others. But for Esau, his possessions reflected his own achievements; therefore the only compulsion that he felt was to acquire even more. In our materially obsessed society, in which we work ourselves into a frenzy to obtain ever more, we would do well to remember the teaching of Jacob and proclaim with him, "God has been gracious unto me ... I have everything."

HAKARAS HATOV — GRATITUDE

Hakaras hatov is yet another teaching that is imparted to us by Jacob, and it is one of the basic tenets of our faith. The words of our forefather Jacob, "I have everything," reminds us to be constantly aware of God's many bounties. As descendants of Jacob, we take nothing for granted; no sooner do we open our eyes in the morning than we say the *Modeh Ani* prayer: "I gratefully thank You, O living and eternal King, for You have returned my soul within me with compassion — abundant is Your faithfulness!." From a glass of water to an elaborate meal, to our bodily functions, to our possessions, we are forever blessing God, as did Jacob, who proclaimed, "I have everything!"

Conversely, he who does not see God's Hand in his daily life cannot understand the meaning of *hakaras hatov*. As far as he's concerned, he is *entitled* — never *indebted*; he has "much" but always wants more and never knows the sweetness of contentment. This is

---

52. *Ethics of the Fathers* 4:1.

a most meaningful lesson for our lives. We must recognize that all that we possess is from God, given to us in trust to share with others. Thus, those who understand the meaning of *hakaras hatov* will also understand that life is not about *acquiring*, but about *giving*. Just as God gives to us, we are meant to share His bounty with others, to show that we truly appreciate His generosity and are aware that it is a *chesed* He does for us that we are required to emulate. This pertains not only to our material possessions, but to all the gifts with which God endowed us: our talent, our energy, our time. If we bear that in mind, we, too, will be able to echo the words of our forefather Jacob: "I have everything."

PARASHAS VAYEISHEV

SIBLING RIVALRY

In this week's *parashah*, we read the story of Joseph's betrayal by his brothers. This is one of those vexing, painful incidents that are difficult to comprehend. How can brothers be so callous? How can they be so cruel? By closely examining this passage from the Torah, we can gain some insight.

The Torah states, "They saw him [Joseph]) from afar, and when he had not yet approached them they conspired against him to kill him."[53] The words "from afar" and "he had not yet approached" seem to be redundant. It would apparently have sufficed to say, "… they conspired against him." Why stress that he had not yet approached? Hatred can only prevail in hearts where there is no

---

53. *Genesis* 37:18.

communication. The brothers saw him from a distance because *they did not allow him to approach them*: it's easier to condemn, resent, and hate from afar. This distancing was the tragedy that led to the betrayal of Joseph by his brethren.

To prevent such deterioration in relationships, the Torah commands us, "You shall not hate your brother in your heart,"[54] calling upon us to resolve our differences and not allow animosity and hatred to fester within us. Let's try to apply this teaching to our personal lives; let us communicate in an amicable and civilized manner with those against whom we harbor resentment. We must do this, not only for the sake of others, but more — for our own sake. When jealousy and hatred are permitted to overtake us, they can literally consume us and render us bitter, angry people who not only destroy others, but more significantly, destroy ourselves.

If we wish to eliminate the rivalries and controversies (as subtle as they may be) in our own families, we have to learn to communicate with respect, "judge each person favorably"[55] and give them the benefit of the doubt. After all, isn't that what we wish others to do for us? Focus on their redeeming qualities rather than on their character flaws, and you will find that life will be more pleasant and relationships more rewarding.

THE MANY FACES OF SHALOM

In this week's *parashah*, the word *shalom* is mentioned several times, and, we detect different dimensions of the word. *Shalom* means *greeting*, shalom means *peace*, shalom means *welfare* or *wellbeing*, and its Hebrew letters also connote *complete*, as in the word *shalem*, whole.

In this *parashah*,[56] we find that the brothers of Joseph hated him and could not speak to him "*l'shalom*," peaceably, which literally translates, "to peace." Moreover, in this passage, we note the eli-

---

54. *Leviticus* 19:17.
55. *Ethics of the Fathers* 1:6.
56. *Genesis* 37:4.

sion of the word *shalom*, which is spelled here without the letter *vav*. There are many lessons that we can derive from this. If we want to attain peace in our relationships, we have to take steps toward peace, hence "*to peace*," and each little step becomes part of the mosaic until *completion* — *shalem* — *total peace* is attained. Because the brothers hated Joseph, they could not even take the first small step: they could not even greet him.

Without the *vav*, the *gematria* of the word *l'shalom* — to peace — is 400, which is equal to the value of *ayin ra* — an evil eye. The brothers looked upon Joseph with an evil eye, unable to see the good in him or to interpret his actions favorably. On the other hand, when the Patriarch Jacob/Israel said that he intended to send Joseph to his brothers in Shechem, Joseph responded, "*Hineni* — here I am*.*" Jacob charges Joseph with looking into the welfare of his brethren; once again the word *shalom* is used, but this time, the word is spelled fully,[57] teaching us that Jacob instructed Joseph to seek completeness in his brethren and disregard their flaws — and Joseph was ready to do his bidding. It's all in our hands: Will we look at one another with an "evil eye" or will we see "wholeness"? Obviously, it's much easier to see another's faults, but the challenge is to search for the goodness, for the positive attributes in each person. How we judge others speaks volumes about our own character. Let us kindle the lights of love and compassion in our hearts.

The Venom of Hatred and the Power in a Name

Through this *parashah* we can understand the terrible consequences of jealousy and animosity, which, if allowed to go unchecked, can lead to such intense hatred that even simple communication becomes impossible. *Chazal* tell us that when Joseph greeted his brothers, saying "Shalom," they mocked his greeting, but when he remained silent, they jeered, saying, "He

---

57. Ibid. 37:13-14.

does not even say 'Shalom.'" This teaches us that, in face of jealousy and hatred, nothing that one does is right. On the other hand, when love is present, there is always a willingness to look away and forgive.

A further manifestation of jealousy and hatred is evidenced when the elderly Jacob is told, "Identify, if you please: Is it *your son's* tunic or not?"[58] The brothers' hatred was so intense that they couldn't bear to pronounce Joseph's name. To prevent such destructive deterioration in our relationships, let us be careful to refer to others by their names and see them as real people rather than as impersonal objects: "he" or "she."

Our mother, Rebbetzin Esther Jungreis, has often related that very often, in troubled families who come to her for consultation, hostile children simply cannot pronounce the words, "my mother" and "my father," but insist on referring to their parents as "she" or "he." There is a world of difference between the two. When you say, "my mother" or "my father," you are acknowledging that no matter what, whether you see eye to eye or not, you are connected … you know that they care for you and are concerned for your welfare. But when parents become *she's* or *he's*, they are transformed into objects that have no bearing upon your life. Monitor yourself: How do you refer to the members of *your* family? Enhance your relationships through the simple exercise of referring to them by name. It is not by coincidence that when Hashem expresses his love for the Patriarch Abraham and for Moses our teacher, He repeats their names.

WITHSTANDING TEMPTATION

So many enticements continually assail us. Sometimes it appears as though we are in a constant state of struggle. How do we withstand these allurements, these temptations?

---

58. Ibid. 37:32.

Joseph is our perfect role model. At the very sensitive age of 17, he finds himself alone, the only Jew in Egypt. In the ancient world, Egypt was known for its wealth, decadence, and perversion. Not only is Joseph the lone Jew in Egypt, not only is he at an impressionable age, but he is also vulnerable because he was betrayed by his own brothers, who sold him into slavery.

By all rules of logic, he should have been a ready candidate for submission to the tentacles of temptation that wound throughout Egypt ... and he had to undergo the most difficult of all trials. The beautiful wife of his Egyptian master cast her eyes upon him. Day after day, she tried to seduce him. She used all her feminine wiles, and when they did not work, she threatened him with physical punishment, humiliation, and imprisonment. But Joseph remained true to his beliefs and adamantly refused her advances.[59] Then, one day, it appeared that his resolve finally weakened. Regarding the passage, "... he entered the house to do his work,"[60] the Gemara expounds that his resistance was about to crumble, but he miraculously mustered inner strength and escaped from the clutches of Potiphar's wife with his morals and values intact. It was not for naught that he became known as *Yosef HaTzaddik* — Joseph the Righteous One!

What was Joseph's secret? How was he able to resist this cunning seductress? The Torah teaches that the *"d'yukno shel aviv,"* the image of his father Jacob, appeared before him. That image imbued him with faith and vision. That image gave him inspiration and courage. That image made him probe his soul and ask himself, "How can I betray the teachings of my father, my rebbi who taught me Torah? How can I forfeit his legacy?"

This is a most critical and significant lesson for us to absorb. Life is one big struggle, during which we are constantly assailed by myriad temptations. How can we prevent ourselves from compromising? How can we protect our children when they set forth on the road of life?

If we follow the example of Joseph and always keep in our hearts

---

59. Ibid. 39:7-10.
60. Ibid. 39:11.

and minds the image of our Torah teacher, be he our father or our rebbi, we will be secure, for that image will keep us anchored in even the most critical moments.

In our generation, not all fathers are capable of being Torah teachers, so we are taught "*Asei lecha rav* — Accept a teacher upon yourself ...."[61] Each of us must have someone to whom we can look for Torah guidance and wisdom; someone we can trust and respect; someone who can advise us and insure our spiritual survival, for that is the task of a true Torah teacher. Such a teacher takes on the role of a father.

Someone once asked, "Why can't I acquire my wisdom simply from books?"

"From books," he was told, "you can gather wisdom, but from a Torah teacher, you will learn how to **live wisely**."

---

61. *Ethics of the Fathers* 1:6.

PARASHAS MIKEITZ

Raising Jewish Children in a Hostile Environment

In this *parashah*, we find Joseph confronting the difficult challenge of bringing up his two sons in a hostile environment in which no other Jews were to be found. To insure their Jewish survival, Joseph made certain to give them only Jewish names and, perhaps even more significantly, was a perfect role model, for he lived what he preached. Although Pharaoh gave him an Egyptian name — Zaphenath-paneah — Joseph never used it. The Torah states that it was *Joseph* (not Zaphenath-paneah) who "emerged in charge of the land of Egypt." [62]

---

62. *Genesis* 41:45.

Joseph's example was emulated by all our forefathers. Our Sages teach that one reason our ancestors were deemed worthy of redemption was that they never altered their Jewish names. To this very day, whenever we bless our sons, we do so by beseeching God to make our sons like Ephraim and Manasseh — the sons of Joseph who carried their Jewish names with great pride, total commitment, and unflinching loyalty.

We would do well to emulate the example of Joseph and call our children by their Jewish names, not only on special ceremonial occasions, but at all times. These names not only remind us of our bubbies and zeides, but they also invest us with a sense of history. They charge us with our legacy, with our responsibilities as Jews. "*Shem Yisrael Kodesh* — a Jewish name is holy." Let us not lose sight of the awesome gift that our names represent.

THE DIFFERENCE BETWEEN "BUT" AND "INDEED"

In this week's *parashah* we read the dramatic story of Joseph, now viceroy of Egypt, meeting his brethren after 22 years of separation. The brothers do not recognize Joseph, and when he accuses them of espionage they are overcome with trepidation. They immediately attribute their troubles to the heinous sin that they committed so long ago, when they sold Joseph into slavery.

In voices full of torment, they cry out, "*Aval* — *Indeed* — we are guilty concerning our brother inasmuch as we saw his heartfelt anguish when he pleaded with us and we paid no heed; that is why this anguish has come upon us."[63] The brothers could, of course, have ascribed Joseph's accusation to the whim of a mad Egyptian despot, but herein lies their greatness. Instead of shifting blame, they searched their souls and looked within themselves for the cause of their misfortune.

We can appreciate the depth of their self-scrutiny through an

---

63. Ibid. 42:21.

examination of the Hebrew word *aval* (indeed) which has a double meaning. It can also be translated *but*. At first glance, these disparate words appear contradictory. The Torah, however, is teaching us a profound lesson. Most people, when explaining themselves, prefer to use the word *aval* as "but" in order to justify their negative behavior. They readily concede that their conduct was incorrect, but then go on to say, "*But*, there were mitigating circumstances beyond my control ...," "I know that I was wrong, *but* I was provoked ...," "I probably shouldn't have said that, *but* she/he pushed my buttons ...," etc., etc. Thus, with that little *but*, they give themselves license to continue to follow the same ill-advised path.

The brothers, the Tribal Patriarchs of the Jewish people, teach us how to repent, to do *teshuvah*. They teach us how to shed our bad habits, improve our character traits, and rediscover our true essence. They use the word *aval* — not as "*but*" (a loophole) — but rather as *indeed*, acknowledging, "Yes, *indeed*, we have sinned, we are accountable." Thus they display the path of *teshuvah* for all generations.

On Yom Kippur, when we recite *Vidui* (Confession), we repeat these very words: "***Aval** anachnu va'avoseinu chatanu ... Indeed*, we and our fathers/ancestors have sinned" — no ifs, ands or buts! On the other hand, when people say, "I know I did such and such, **but** —," qualifying their confessions with that little insidious *but* attempts to justify continuing to follow the same corrupt path and cancels out their *teshuvah*.

That which *we choose* to forget, God will remember, but that which *we choose* to *remember* and do *teshuvah* on, God will not only forget, but He will cancel the evil decree — the painful consequences of our sin — and convert the transgression into merit. "If your sins are like scarlet, they will become white as snow ...."[64]

Most of us are good and decent people. It is the excuses that we make with *but* that allow us to stray from the path. We have a choice: We can emulate the Tribal Patriarchs by saying "Indeed," and grow, change, and realize our potential, or we can indulge ourselves with "but" and sink into our weaknesses. *It all depends on us.*

---

64. *Isaiah* 1:18.

There is yet another lesson that we can learn from the brothers' confession. To all intents and purposes, the sin of which this apparent Egyptian despot is accusing them has no connection to the family squabble that took place 22 years previously in Canaan. And yet the brothers see a direct link between the tragedy that is now befalling them and the events that occurred so long ago. Nothing happens in a vacuum, and there is no forgetfulness before God. If we choose to ignore the transgressions of our past, if we fail to do *teshuvah* and ask forgiveness for them, then Hashem will find ways to remind us. God's time is different from ours, Eventually all our transgression will catch up with us in the most unexpected way. Time and again we see the law of *middah k'neged middah* (measure for measure), which, in our contemporary world, is often referred to as "what goes around comes around."

PARASHAS VAYIGASH

Positive Criticism

This *parashah* is perhaps the most emotional *parashah* in the Torah. After 22 years of separation, Joseph reveals himself to his brothers and declares, "I am Joseph — is my father still alive?"[65] These words were the most devastating admonishment that Joseph could have given to his brothers. Instead of berating them for having sold him into bondage, he simply said, "I am Joseph," implying, "My dreams, which you attributed to delusions of grandeur, were fulfilled; God did make me king, and He did send you to bow down before me." But note that nowhere does Joseph actually utter those words.

The declaration, "I am Joseph," was sufficient. He allows his

---

65. *Genesis* 45:3.

brothers to infer the rest and his question, "Is my father [rather than *our* father] still alive?" cuts to the core of the issue, for it suggests that they had not conducted themselves as sons should, else they could not have sold their brother and led their elderly father to believe him dead. But again, Joseph does not introduce himself with these words. Rather, with his terse "Is my father still alive?" he invites his brothers to judge themselves.

From this we learn that admonishment is most effective when used as a mirror and that it can never be accomplished through painful jokes, shouting, cynical remarks, or name-calling. Such tactics can only result in secondary problems that lead to further resentment and alienation.

When Joseph embraces his brother Benjamin, he falls on his neck and weeps profusely, and Benjamin, in turn, does the same.[66] The Gemara explains that Joseph was crying over the Holy Temples that would be destroyed in the land allotted to Benjamin, and Benjamin was crying over the Tabernacle that would be destroyed in the portion allotted to Joseph. The question remains, however, why they chose this particular moment to weep over the Temples and the Tabernacle. The message that the Torah imparts is that, tragically, they foresaw that the very same acrimony that led to the splintering of the House of Jacob would continue to divide our people and lead to the destruction of the Temples. Joseph and Benjamin cried for each other's pain, teaching us that the only remedy to this plague of hatred is for us to learn to empathize with one another, to feel each other's pain, and reach out with *chesed* — exemplifying kindness and love.

NEVER GIVE UP

In this *parashah* we discover some of the ways through which the name "Jew" defines us as a people. When the sons of Jacob are confronted by the irrational accusations of the viceroy of Egypt (Joseph), and realize that the life of their younger brother

---

66. Ibid. 45:14.

Benjamin is at risk, then Judah (whose name connotes "Jew," for a Jew is called a *Yehudi*) rises like a lion and does battle for his brother. As desperate and as hopeless as the situation appears to be, Judah — a man of *complete* faith — does not *give up*. Similarly, we, his descendants, have never given up.

The obstacles that Judah confronts are many. The Egyptian viceroy (Joseph) pretends that he doesn't speak or understand Hebrew. An interpreter acts as an intermediary, and the evidence weighs heavily against Benjamin. Nevertheless, speaking Hebrew from his heart, Judah cites Jewish sensitivity. One may ask what Judah could possibly have hoped to accomplish by speaking in Hebrew and referring to Jewish values to this supposed Egyptian, Joseph.

A wonderful story about the great Sage, the Chofetz Chaim, explains it all. The Polish government had passed an edict that would have the effect of prohibiting independent Jewish education, thus jeopardizing the continuation of Torah life. The Chofetz Chaim requested a meeting with the Polish president. Even as Judah spoke in Hebrew, the Chofetz Chaim spoke in Yiddish and a Jewish senator stood by to translate. Although the president did not understand Yiddish, the Chofetz Chaim's heartrending plea touched him so deeply that tears filled his eyes. When the interpreter began to translate, the president quickly interrupted him and said, "Although I do not speak Yiddish, I understand the words of this holy man. He spoke from the heart, and one heart understands another heart. The edict is rescinded." This is the legacy of Judah: If we speak in the name of God, if we uphold our Torah, and are prepared to put our lives on the line for the sake of our brethren, there will be no barrier that we cannot overcome.

We, the Jewish people, have survived the centuries with the Torah as our guide. Our *emunah* (faith) has sustained us. We have never lost hope. So, if we feel overwhelmed by life's struggles, we must remember that we are Jews — descended from the family of Judah. Let us connect with our Torah, with our faith, and God will surely come to our aid. Let us remember that the name Judah also means "to give thanks and praise to God."[67] Ultimately, that is

---

67. Ibid. 29:35.

probably the most compelling definition of us as a Jewish people: In times of joy as well as in times of adversity, we give thanks to our Creator; we never give up, knowing that He will always protect us.

THE POWER OF THE *SHEMA*

In this *parashah*, we are witness to an amazing, miraculous reunion. After 22 long years, during which time our Patriarch Jacob was led to believe that his beloved son, Joseph, had been killed, the two reunite. Joseph, now viceroy of Egypt, harnesses his chariot and goes forth to greet his beloved father, The Torah tells us, "He (Joseph) appeared before him [his father], fell on his neck, and he wept upon his neck excessively."[68]

Rashi, the great commentator, points out that while Joseph cried, Jacob recited the *Shema* (see below). Why would Jacob have chosen this moment for the recitation of the *Shema*, which precluded him from speaking or giving his son a kiss or a hug? Surely, he could have greeted his long-lost son before uttering this prayer.

The Maharal explains that when a righteous person experiences the goodness of God, he seeks to connect with Him, not only to express gratitude, but also so that that goodness might impact on future generations and become an eternal blessing. Thus, when our forefather Jacob beheld his son in all his grandeur, his first thought was to connect that moment to the glory of God — the establishment of *Malchus HaShamayim*, the Kingdom of God here on earth, which is symbolized by the recitation of the *Shema*.

Joseph wept on the neck of his father because the neck is a metaphor for the Holy Temple, since it is the neck that joins the head (the spiritual) to the body (the physical). Joseph foresaw the terrible suffering that would befall the Jewish people with the destruction of the Holy Temples, so he wept on Jacob's neck. But Jacob recited the *Shema*, for he knew that through the *Shema* the Jewish people would persevere and triumph.

---

68. Ibid. 46:29.

Indeed, the *Shema* is our most powerful prayer. It is the essence of our faith; we commence and end each day with it, it is encased in our mezuzahs on our doorposts; it is in the tefillin that our men don every morning as they stand before God in prayer, and it is the prayer that has accompanied us throughout the long years of our exile and imbued us with courage in even our most darkest moments. So let us proclaim the *Shema* with fervor and commitment. In all situations, let the *Shema* guide us, and let us learn from Jacob, the Patriarch: When good fortune befalls us, let us not be content with celebrating with a mere party or a dinner, but rather, let us transfer our feelings of joy to God and express our gratitude to Him. And when we are tested by life's trials, let us once again remember the teachings of our Patriarchs and cling tenaciously to the *Shema*.

PARASHAS VAYECHI

An Eternal Blessing From Our Forefather Jacob

In this *parashah*, the final segment of the Book of *Genesis*, our forefather Jacob dies and we bid farewell to the Patriarchs and Matriarchs. The Book of *Exodus* begins the story of the Jewish people.

Jacob, on his deathbed, blesses all his children, assigns them their unique missions, and also chastises them for their failings. He singles out, however, two of his grandsons, Ephraim and Manasseh, the sons of Joseph, and adopts them as his own: "And now, your two sons who were born to you in the land of Egypt before my coming to you in Egypt shall be mine; Ephraim and Manasseh shall be like Reuben and Simeon."[69]

---

69. Ibid. 48:5.

Additionally, Jacob gives the two lads a special blessing and proclaims "By you shall Israel bless, saying 'May God make you like Ephraim and like Manasseh.' "[70]

At first glance, this elevation of Ephraim and Manasseh is somewhat puzzling, but there is a deep teaching therein. These two boys grew up in Egypt, in a land that was renowned for its immorality, corruption, and decadence. Moreover, they grew up in the opulence and luxury of the palace and, more significantly, they were the only Jewish children in the land of Egypt. And yet, despite it all, their commitment and faith in God remained unwavering and they were as dedicated to Judaism as the sons of Jacob were.

This, in and of itself, is a phenomenal feat, for usually, with the passage of each generation, there is a spiritual downturn, as each generation becomes one step further removed from its source. But Ephraim and Manasseh reversed that process. They linked themselves to the previous generation as though they had been born to be Tribal Patriarchs. Thus they defied the odds and reached beyond the spiritual level into which they had been born.

Now we can more readily understand the blessing which Jacob proclaimed, "By you shall Israel bless, saying, "May God make you like Ephraim and like Manasseh," for even as Ephraim and Manasseh withstood the ultimate test and were able to maintain their high standard of faith in a hostile environment, so too, to this very day, all Jewish parents pray that no matter where destiny may take their children, they will remain staunch, loyal Jews, upholding Torah and mitzvos. Therefore, on the eve of the Sabbath and on the eve of Yom Kippur, parents pronounce the ancient words of Jacob and bless their children with these immortal words: "May God make you like Ephraim and like Manasseh."

There is yet another reason why Ephraim and Manasseh were chosen to be the ultimate role models for our children. They were free of jealousy and arrogance and rejoiced in each other's attributes and success, as we see that Manasseh did not complain that Ephraim, the younger brother, was mentioned first and received the blessing of the right hand.

---

70. Ibid. 48:20.

Not When, But How Messiah Will Come

As our forefather Jacob was about to expire, he called upon his children to unite, teaching us that in our unity, we will find blessing and strength. At that time, Jacob wanted to reveal the date of our final redemption, but God prevented him from doing so. For a moment Jacob became agitated. Could it be, he wondered, that God was denying him this privilege because his children were unworthy? The Tribes, sensing their father's distress, called out in unison, "*Shema Yisrael, Hashem Elokeinu, Hashem Echad!*" — Hear, O Israel, Hashem is our God, Hashem is the One and Only."[71] They proved their dedication to God, showing their father that they were indeed worthy to be redeemed, when God would will it to occur. And to this very day, we, the descendants of Jacob, greet and conclude every day with the *Shema*. It is our most ancient prayer, first recited by our forefather Jacob, then by his sons, the twelve Tribes of Israel, and is engraved in our Torah for all eternity. Let us make a special effort to recite the *Shema* with commitment and fervor; our commitment to God will surely bring the redemption more quickly.

Messianic Times

Nowadays there is much fascination with the end of days. Messianic fervor has taken hold of our generation; people have myriad questions: What will life be like when the Messiah comes? When will he come? When will the Temple be rebuilt? At what point will resurrection take place? In this week's *parashah*, the Patriarch Jacob on his deathbed tries to answer all these questions. "Then Jacob called for his sons and said, 'Assemble yourselves and I will tell you what will befall you in the

---

71. *Deuteronomy* 6:4.

End of Days.'"[72] However, God removed his *Ruach Hakodesh* (gift of prophecy) precluding him from making that revelation.

Since belief in the coming of Messiah is a test of faith, we can readily appreciate why God would not want Jacob to disclose this information. However, the question remains: Why was it necessary to remove *Ruach Hakodesh* from the Patriarch? The Rebbe of Radomsk once wrestled with this question and concluded that when Jacob prophetically foresaw the terrible tribulation that would be visited upon his descendants in pre-messianic times, he became terribly saddened, and when a man falls into a state of sadness, his *Ruach Hakodesh* automatically departs from him.

We are the generation that is experiencing all those tribulations, but, while there is much darkness in our world, there is also a great light in the awareness that Jacob foresaw it all and the knowledge that that which befalls us is not a random occurrence: God is guiding our destiny. Moreover, while the Patriarch may not have been able to tell us when the Messiah would come, he did inform us how we might bring him. The answer is in *Genesis* 49:1: "Assemble yourselves." That unity is the key to our redemption. Tragically, we are a nation that is fragmented, and unity continues to elude us. While we may not be able to control the acrimony that divides us as a nation, we can certainly neutralize the bickering that plagues our families and our communities.

Let us, then, make a concerted effort to hearken to the words of the Patriarch. Let us start by reaching out to the members of our family, friends, and community, and unify. In that merit, we shall behold the coming of Messiah very soon in our own day.

Shabbos Chazak

The Shabbos on which we conclude the reading of the portions of *Sefer Bereishis*, the first of the Five Books of the Torah, is referred to as *Shabbos Chazak* — the Sabbath

---

72. *Genesis* 49:1.

of Strength. This is because, as we conclude the Book of Genesis, the entire congregation rises and proclaims, "*Chazak, Chazak, V'Nis'chazeik* — Be Strong! Be Strong! And may we be strengthened!" We ask the Almighty to give us the strength to continue with and succeed in our Torah studies. At first glance it may appear strange that we extend wishes for strength at this time; one might think that it should really be at the commencement of our undertaking that we do so. However, beginnings are always marked by enthusiasm and zeal. The trick is to retain that same level of enthusiasm at the end. Therefore, upon concluding the Book of Genesis, we make a commitment to continue our Torah studies with strength and devotion and pray that this conclusion be a steppingstone for further growth and development.

Additionally, we learn that that which is first is always definitive; since this is the first time that we recite "*Chazak*," it behooves us to ask what special lesson or teaching we can derive from it. This is the *parashah* in which the death of the Patriarch Jacob is announced, but, strangely enough, instead of saying that Jacob died, the Torah states, "*Vayechi Yaakov*," which, literally translated, means, "And Jacob lives." But how can that be? Isn't this a contradiction? Our Sages teach us that as long as the children, the descendants of Jacob, keep his teachings alive, as long as we live by them, "Jacob did not die — rather, Jacob lives!" *And that is the true meaning of "Chazak — Be strong."* We must find strength in the knowledge that our Patriarchs and Matriarchs — our *zeides* and *bubbies* — live on in us. We need only follow in their footsteps.

ספר שמות

THE BOOK OF Exodus

PARASHAS SHEMOS

The Roots of Anti-Semitism — The Very First Holocaust

> ... Joseph died, and all his brothers and that entire *generation*. The Children of Israel were fruitful, teemed, increased, and became strong ... and the land became filled with them. A new king arose over Egypt, who did not know Joseph."
>
> Exodus 1:6-8

These verses reveal the seeds of anti-Semitism. The Tribal Patriarchs, the *zeides* — the entire *generation* who kept the nation anchored to their faith — died. At the same time, the Jewish people increased, multiplied in great numbers, *spread out all over Egypt,* and became part of the Egyptian culture. And with that acculturation, we encounter the beginnings of anti-Semitism.

There is a new Pharaoh, "who did not know Joseph." But how can that be? Would the president of the United States claim that he does not know who preceded him in the White House? Our Sages explain that Pharaoh *did not want* to know Joseph. He did not want to acknowledge that Joseph literally saved Egypt from doom. Nor did he wish to recognize the contributions of the Jewish people. We see this very same pattern of anti-Semitism throughout our history. Our mother, Rebbetzin Esther Jungreis, who lived through the horrors of the Holocaust, has often related that many assimilated Jews in Europe had proudly averred that they were Germans, Hungarians, etc., and Jews *not at all*. These Jews were totally shattered emotionally and spiritually when they discovered that, despite their loyalty, contributions, and sacrifices for their respective countries, they were overnight labeled "Jews, enemies of mankind," and were marked for extermination. Yes, there was a new king in Europe who did not know Joseph. Millennia have passed and nothing has changed; we, the Jewish people, have yet to comprehend that anti-Semitism is rooted in assimilation and that there is only one place where we can find shelter: It is within our God-given Torah way of life.

THE MAKING OF A GADOL — A GREAT MAN

In *Parashas Shemos*, we meet for the very first time the greatest prophet who ever walked on Planet Earth, the man who actually spoke to God face to face — *Moshe Rabbeinu* — Moses, our Rabbi, our Teacher. Moses was brilliant, strong, handsome, and powerful, yet it was not for any of these reasons that he was chosen to be a leader.

What rendered Moses great? What are the qualities that enable a man to transcend himself and become a spiritual giant?

It is written, "... *vayigdal Moshe* ... — ... Moses grew up and went out to his [enslaved] brethren and observed their burdens ...."[1] Moses not only *saw* his people's pain, but he *felt* it, and he not only felt it, but he strove to *do* something about it, as we see further in the verses.

Raised in the palace of Pharaoh, Moses was a royal prince in the mightiest empire in the world. He could have shut his eyes and remained indifferent to the anguished cries of his brethren, but he chose to give up the opulence of the palace, the power of his royal position, to commiserate with his oppressed brethren in the slave camps. He took on their torment; he wept for them, he prayed for them, he fought for them, and as a child he had even convinced Pharaoh to allow them to rest one day in seven. Thus, Moses enabled the Jewish people in Egypt to observe Shabbos, and to this very day, every Shabbos, we recall his gift in the *Amidah* (the *Shemoneh Esrei*) of *Shacharis* (the morning prayer service) when we declare, "*Yismach Moshe* ... Moses rejoiced in the gift of his portion." And keep in mind that at this point in his life, he had not been charged with a mission. No Divine voice had yet summoned him. He did what he did out of the goodness, the purity of his own soul, and herein is to be found his greatness.

The pain and the love that Moses felt for his fellow Jews remained forever etched on his heart. When he was forced to flee from Egypt and his first son was born in Midian, Moses called him "Gershom," which reminded him that he too was sojourning in a strange land, just as his brethren were. And at the burning bush, God spoke about the suffering of his brethren, who were engulfed in the fires of Egypt, but who, despite their torment, were not consumed and remained Jews.

The Midrash relates that, prior to commissioning Moses with his mission, God gave him yet one more test. While Moses was shepherding the flock of Jethro, his father-in-law, in the desert, a little lamb ran away. Concerned for his charge, Moses went in search of it. After a while, he found the animal drinking at a brook. "My poor little lamb," Moses said, reaching out for it. "I didn't know

---

1. *Exodus* 2:11.

you were thirsty; forgive me. You must be weary." And with that, he picked up the lamb, placed it on his shoulders, and carried it back to the flock.

Then a Heavenly voice was heard: "This is the man who is worthy of shepherding My people." And so, Moses became the *"Ro'eh Ne'eman* — the loyal shepherd of Israel."

One need not be a rabbi or rebbetzin; one need not major in psychology, nor need one take a special course in leadership to be a *loyal shepherd*. One need only *feel love* toward those whom one guides, be concerned for their welfare, and dedicate oneself to them. With understanding and empathy, and guided always by God's laws, one will be able to lead one's family in the path of righteousness.

TORAH QUALIFICATIONS FOR A LEADER

The Torah testifies that no other person even came close to the greatness of Moses in his perception of God's prophecy. While we cannot possibly fully comprehend his majesty, we will try to note some of the great abilities that made him unique. Perhaps one way to do so is to contrast his life to that of Noah.

Initially, the Torah describes Moses in very modest terms. The daughters of Jethro even refer to him as "an Egyptian man."[2] On the other hand, Noah is described in glowing terms as a *tzaddik*, "a perfectly righteous man."[3] At the end of their lives, however, their roles are reversed. Moses is called "the servant of God,"[4] and Noah is called "the man of the earth."[5] What was it that led to the spiritual ascent of Moses and the spiritual descent of Noah?

Yes, Noah built the Ark as God had commanded, but he never

---

2. Ibid. 2:19.
3. *Genesis* 6:9.
4. *Deuteronomy* 34:5.
5. *Genesis* 9:20.

put his life on the line to save others. He did not plead with God to save his generation. In contrast, when the survival of the Jewish people was in jeopardy following the sin of the Golden Calf, Moses pleaded with God to forgive the people or "erase my name from Your Book." The Torah teaches that we measure our success not by what we *achieve for ourselves*, but rather, by *how we impact on our fellow man and the extent through which we become a blessing to others*. This does not mean that we should neglect ourselves or our own needs, but rather, that we should expand ourselves to include others and make their concerns our own.

The average person may better relate to this concept through the oneness he feels with his immediate family, but if he can extend this oneness, this love, to encompass a larger circle, his own soul will expand and he will emerge stronger and better for the experience. Moses came by this love naturally; it was in his genes. His mother, Jochebed, and his sister, Miriam, were the midwives of the Jewish community who courageously defied Pharaoh's decree and saved the babies. And more: they lovingly cared for every infant as if it were their own.

To Moses, every soul was dear and precious. He cared for and worried about each and every person in his flock. Awed by the greatness of Moses, we can endeavor to emulate him in some measure and bond with our brothers, feel their pain, rejoice in their joy, and extend *chesed* to them.

THE POWER OF GOD IN THE SOUL OF MAN

> And the king of Egypt said to the Hebrew midwives [Shifrah and Puah] ..., "When you deliver the Hebrew women, and you see them on the birthstool; if it is a son, you are to kill him, and if it is a daughter, she shall live." But the midwives *feared God*, and they did not do as the king of Egypt spoke to them, and they caused the boys to live.
>
> *Exodus* 1:16-18

These awesome words testify to the superhuman courage of the two midwives. One might well ask from where they obtained their strength. How did they have the fortitude to take a stand against Pharaoh?

Yes, two simple Jewish women dared to stand against the most powerful man of the day, as well as against the Egyptian taskmasters who constantly monitored them. Not only did they refuse to follow the king's orders, but, more significantly, they ensured that the Jewish baby boys *lived*.

The first midwife was Jochebed, and she earned the name *Shifrah* for she was committed *l'shaper* — to strengthen and beautify the babies. The second midwife was Miriam, known as *Puah*. She was given this name because of the loving, cooing sounds she produced to soothe the babies. The sacrifice and valor of these two women transcend the centuries and cry out from the pages of the Torah, condemning the powerful Nazi officers and all other tyrants who, when brought to trial for their unspeakably evil deeds, try to exonerate themselves from responsibility by proclaiming, "We were just following orders."

Those who truly fear and believe in God stay the course. No force can intimidate them; no power on earth can make them compromise the truth, for God's presence is ever before them. Two simple Jewish women testify to the indomitable spirit of mere mortals, who through their reverence for God soar higher than the angels.

"Impossible" Is Not in the Jewish Lexicon

> Pharaoh's daughter went down to bathe by the River ....
> She saw the basket among the reeds ....
> *Exodus* 2:5, 6

The basket that Pharaoh's daughter spotted contained the infant Moses, and the Torah teaches us that she instructed *amosah* (her maidservant) to fetch it. But the Hebrew word "*amosah*" can also be translated, "her *arm*." From this we learn that she stretched out her arm to retrieve the basket although the basket was a great distance from her and there was no logical way in which she could have pulled it to shore. So why did she make the attempt?

Our Sages explain that her determination to do a mitzvah — to save a life — was so all consuming that she *reached beyond herself* and, because of that, God enabled her to transcend her physical limitations and He miraculously extended her arm. We learn from the daughter of Pharaoh that when it comes to doing a mitzvah and thereby fulfilling our spiritual goals, the word *"impossible"* doesn't exist. If we do our *hishtadlus* and put forth our best efforts, then God will do the rest.

Chazal teach us that the daughter of Pharaoh came to the river, not merely to bathe, but to immerse herself for the purpose of conversion to Judaism, and the river was her *mikveh*. Spurning her pampered royal lifestyle, she yearned to join the Jewish people, and that, in and of itself, was proof of her sterling character and high spiritual level. In recognition of her greatness, God named her *Bitya*, which means "the daughter of God." Bitya, in turn, named the infant *"Moshe,"* for she said, *"Ki min hamayim m'shee'seehu* — For I drew him from the water,"[6] and thus, her charitable act engraved upon her adopted son's heart his mission to save others, even as he had been saved.

Moses had many names, given to him by many people — including his own biological parents — but it is *Moshe*, the name bestowed upon him by the daughter of Pharaoh, that God recorded in the Torah. Bitya was honored and revered by Moses and the Jewish people, and when the redemption came, she went forth with the nation. She stood at Sinai, she entered the Promised Land, and like Elijah, she did not die in the normal manner, but ascended alive to the heavens. The legacy that she imparted is a lesson to all of us. When it comes to mitzvos, we are never to give up. *If we are sincere and determined, nothing is beyond our reach; the word "impossible" simply does not exist.* We need only stretch forth our hands to discover that **with God, everything is possible.**

---

6. *Exodus* 2:10.

Bitya's True Identity

Were we to be told that, during the Holocaust, Hitler's daughter decided to convert to Judaism, we would dismiss the idea out of hand. It simply wouldn't be credible. So how can we explain the phenomenon of Bitya's desire to convert? After all, her father was the "Hitler" of his generation, attempting to destroy the Jewish nation even before it became a reality.

The Kabbalah teaches that Bitya was a *gilgul* (reincarnation) of Eve, the first woman. In the Garden of Eden, Eve *stretched out her hand* to take the forbidden fruit,[7] thereby extinguishing the light of the world — the law of God. Centuries later, she is reborn to perform a *tikun* (rectification) of her misdeed, so she *stretches out her hand* again, this time to rescue the basket that contains the light of the world: Moses, who would ascend Sinai, give us the Torah, and restore God's light.

We have no way of knowing whether we lived in an earlier life or what failings we may have been guilty of perpetrating. But one thing we *can* know with certainty: Whatever tests or challenges come our way, we must rise to the occasion and reach beyond ourselves to pass them. It is God Who is Master of the world, and He places tests and challenges in our paths so that we may fulfill our true purpose and mission in life. So, when confronted by challenges, let us never feel overwhelmed or paralyzed. Hashem would never test us with a mission which we are not capable of fulfilling.

The Eternity of the Jewish People

> An angel of Hashem appeared to him in a blaze of fire from amid the bush. ... and behold! the bush was burning in the fire but the bush was not consumed.
>
> *Exodus* 3:2

---

7. See *Genesis* 3:6.

The bush represents the saga of the Jewish people. Our enemies have tried to destroy and annihilate us, but even as the bush was not consumed by fire, we too have survived the deadly flames of the centuries. Our survival has been nothing short of miraculous. Even non-Jews have been awed by it. Listen to the words of Mark Twain:

➣ THE IMMORTAL JEWS

If the statistics are right, the Jews constitute but 1 percent of the human race. It suggests a nebulous dim puff of star dust lost in the blaze of the Milky Way. Properly the Jew ought hardly be heard of, but he is heard of, has always been heard of.

He is as prominent on the planet as any other people, and his commercial importance is extravagantly out of proportion to the smallness of his bulk. His contributions to the world's list of great names in literature, science, art, music, finance, medicine, and abstruse learning are also away out of proportion to the weakness of his numbers. He has made a marvelous fight in this world, in all the ages; and has done it with his hands tied behind him. He could be vain of himself and excused for it. The Egyptian, the Babylonian, and the Persian rose and filled the planet with sound and splendor, then faded to dream stuff and passed away, the Greek and the Roman followed, and made a vast noise, and they are gone; other peoples have sprung up and held their torch high for a time, but it burned out, and they sit in twilight now or have vanished. The Jew saw them all, beat them all, and is now what he always was, exhibiting no decadence, no infirmities of age, no weakening of his parts, no slowing of his energies, no dulling of his alert and aggressive mind. All things are mortal but the Jew; all other forces pass, but he remains. What is the secret of his immortality?

Mark Twain

Parashas Shemos

Mark Twain's question is well placed. In his heart, every Jew knows the answer. Let us never lose sight of it …. We are a nation whose might and very life comes solely from God.

PARASHAS VA'EIRA

Admonishment Without Pain

When we study Torah, we not only learn of our past, of our heritage, and of our mitzvos, but we also discover how to conduct ourselves in our daily lives. From the Patriarchs and Matriarchs and all the spiritual giants whom we meet in the Torah, we learn how to react to life's challenges, and also how, at times, *not* to react. We have a unique opportunity to learn this lesson from the Almighty Himself: "God spoke (*vayidabeir*) to Moses and said (*vayomer*) to him, 'I am Hashem ....'"[8] In English, there is not much difference between the words "spoke" and "said," but in *lashon haKodesh* (the holy tongue) there is a

---

8. *Exodus* 6:2.

world of difference. The word *"vayidabeir"* (spoke) connotes harsh language, while the word *"vayomer"* (said) implies gentle speech.

The Almighty was displeased with Moses because, in the previous *parashah*, he questioned God, asking, "My Lord, why have You done evil to this people?"[9] While Moses was prepared to accept his own trials and tribulations, he could not bear to see the suffering of his people. What he found most agonizing was that from the moment he called for their redemption, their plight worsened. Pharaoh, in his madness, intensified their workload and their lives became even more unbearable. It was because of this that Moses called out unto God.

But the darkness is most intense before the dawn, and this pain was a necessary prelude to redemption. Even as medicine cannot be described as evil, so this suffering could not be termed "evil." *Bitter, yes; painful, yes; but not evil*. To bring this point home, God used strong, harsh language (*vayidabeir*) when He began to speak to Moses, but once that point was made, He immediately reverted to the gentle, soft, *"vayomer."*

This lesson in admonishment has left a profound imprint upon the souls of our people. In our relationships, in our teaching methods, in all our communications, we have to be cautious not to impart an impression of rejection. Thus, our Sages in the Talmud teach, "With the left hand you push away [the left, as the weaker hand, is used to rebuke], and with the right [the stronger hand] you immediately draw the person near." It is crucial that this "drawing near" follow immediately upon the rebuke, so that no time elapses during which the rebuked person might feel that he has been rejected. The lesson is obvious: *Admonishment and criticism* should always be followed by *comforting words* so that the person may realize that our intention is only to *help* and not, heaven forbid, to *hurt* or to *censure pointlessly*.

---

9. Ibid. 5:22.

The Professional Parent

> And I appeared to Abraham, to Isaac, and to Jacob as *Keil Shakai*, but with My Name *Hashem* I did not make Myself known to them.
>
> *Exodus 6:3*

This enigmatic passage becomes even more puzzling when we study the interpretation of the commentator par excellence, Rashi, who, in a simple but cryptic passage, indentifies Abraham, Isaac, and Jacob as "the Patriarchs."

Surely, one need not study Rashi to know that. Any young yeshivah child can identify Abraham, Isaac, and Jacob as the Fathers of our people. So what lesson is Rashi imparting to us?

Our *Zeide*, HaRav HaGaon Avraham HaLevi Jungreis, *z"tl*, explained that Rashi wants to impress upon us that *the Patriarchs were quintessential fathers*. A professional parent understands that, as painful as it may be, there are times when he has to say "no," when he has to choose the difficult rather than the easy path. For example, when a mother takes her baby to the pediatrician for a vaccination, the infant does not comprehend why Mommy is so mean. In vain would she try to explain that it's all for his benefit; the shot will protect him from devastating disease. The baby can relate only to the *here and now*. Nevertheless, he trusts his parents and instinctively knows that Mommy and Daddy are his protectors, and that without them, he is lost. When the injection is over, he turns his face into Mommy's shoulder to comfort him, regardless of the fact that it was she who brought him to the doctor.

As the years pass, the stakes get higher. "No, you can't go to the party"; "No, you can't take the car"; "No, you can't use that credit card"; etc., etc. The role of the professional parent is never quite over.

Similarly, there was a reason why we had to endure bondage in Egypt, and why, to this very day, we are challenged by the many tests and trials of life. Throughout, we must place our trust in the Father of all Fathers Who does everything for our welfare, even if the reason eludes us. The Patriarchs understood that. They experienced suffering and disappointment, but they never questioned, they never doubted — their faith remained constant.

God has many different names, each of which reflects His attributes. The name *Keil Shakai*, which is related to the word *"dai"* (sufficient), is the name upon which our Patriarchs staked their lives. Whatever fate overtook them, whatever the tests or challenges, they never complained — it was always *Keil Shakai* — everything that comes from God is good and sufficient. They never demanded that God relate to them with the name *"Hashem,"* which implies the attribute of mercy.

To be sure, *Moshe Rabbeinu* also underwent arduous, painful ordeals and he accepted all his trials with love and equanimity, but when he witnessed the torment of his enslaved people, he could not bear to see their terrible suffering — and it was that which he protested.

It's not easy to be a professional parent. It is always easier to give in. But if we truly love our children, we must be strong for them and teach them how to walk with honor on the bumpy road of life.

COMFORT AND CONSOLATION

> Hashem spoke to Moses and Aaron and commanded them regarding the children of Israel ....
>
> *Exodus 6:13*

It often happens that we find ourselves in situations in which we are called upon to extend comfort and encouragement to people who are in distress and feel they can no longer go on.

Finding the proper words on such occasions is never easy, but that was the challenge faced by *Moshe Rabbeinu* as he addressed his brethren who were suffering in Egyptian bondage. At the beginning of the *parashah*, God charged Moses with the mission of announcing to the Jewish people that the time of their liberation was at hand. Hashem used four different expressions in describing their redemption:

> ... I shall take you out from under the burdens of Egypt; I shall rescue you from their service; I shall redeem you with an outstretched arm and with great judgments. I shall take you to Me for a people, and I shall be a God to you; and you shall know that I am Hashem your God, Who takes you out from under the burdens of Egypt. I shall bring you to the land about which I raised My hand to give it to Abraham, Isaac, and Jacob; and I shall give it to you as a heritage — I am Hashem.
>
> *Exodus 6:6-8*

Despite this awesome promise, however, the Jewish people remained dispirited and incapable of absorbing the good news. The explanation for this reveals the nature of suffering and how one may best comfort those who are hurt. When someone is in pain, he does not have the patience or the ability to comprehend *that which will occur in the future*. His agony is so overwhelming that he is aware only of his present state. Therefore, the Almighty God instructs Moses and Aaron once again and commands them to bring the Children of Israel forth from Egypt,[10] teaching us that when someone is in distress, we have to extend *immediate help*. Thus, when encouraging those who have lost hope, let us not content ourselves with visions of the future. Rather, let us immediately do something concrete to relieve their pain and infuse them with faith and strength.

Patience and Fortitude

In this same passage, God also instructs Moses to be gentle and patient with the people — a basic ingredient that is required of all leaders. The Midrash teaches that Hashem told Moses and Aaron: "My children are often stubborn and recalcitrant. They are quick to anger and are troublesome. It is under

---

10. Ibid. 6:13.

these conditions that you should undertake to accept leadership over them ...." This teaching has relevance, not only for leaders, but for each and every one of us. In every family, there are situations in which one's patience is sorely tried. At such times, we must exercise patience and forbearance, remain calm and respond with strength and dignity.

CONVERTING SUFFERING INTO BLESSING

The passage above has yet a third interpretation. It is written in the Talmud that it was at this moment of crisis for the Jewish people that God told Moses to command the nation regarding the emancipation of slaves that would take place once they entered the Promised Land. At first glance, this appears farfetched. The nation is in bondage, so what possible relevance can such instructions have? But the Torah is teaching us that it is precisely when you are in the throes of suffering that you must make a commitment to *banish* suffering — to convert that pain into a healing experience ... into a blessing. It is in this spirit that the Torah calls upon us to remember our bondage and the Exodus from Egypt. Again and again, our Torah connects our mitzvos to *Yetzias Mitzraim* — our experiences during the Exodus from Egypt.

One example of this connection is the verse, "And you shall love the proselyte, for you were strangers in the land of Egypt."[11] Our suffering in Egypt enables us to empathize with the pain of others, to come to Sinai, and to become "a nation of *rachmanim* and *bnei rachmanim* — compassionate ones and descendants of compassionate ones."

One who has never suffered, who has never experienced pain, cannot relate to someone who cries out in anguish. One who has never experienced the pangs of hunger cannot identify with those who are starving. Yet we all have options regarding how we

---

11. *Deuteronomy* 10:19.

respond to adversity. Suffering can render us cruel, bitter, and cynical — or it can make us sensitive, compassionate, and loving. By accepting the Torah at Sinai, we opted for the latter.

THE POWER OF ZEIDES AND BUBBIES

> And these are the names of the sons of Levi in order of their birth: Gershon, Kehath, and Merari; the years of Levi's life were a hundred and thirty-seven years.
>
> *Exodus 6:16*

Lèvi's impact on his descendants had far-reaching effects, as is evidenced by the fact that when the Torah cites his descendants, the verse states, "These are the *names* ... " of Levi's sons, but the word *"names"* is omitted in the case of Reuben and Simeon, as is their age at their demise.

The *Sforno* explains that Levi was blessed with longevity; this attribute enabled him to impart to his descendants the greatness of his father Jacob, and thus Levi became a living link to the Patriarch.

From this we learn how critical it is for us to connect our children to our past ... to our grandparents and great-grandparents — to relate stories of our families and to teach our children to emulate the *chesed*, goodness, and devotion of our ancestors. If children are to thrive, they need spiritual role models to sustain and invigorate them. But Levi was not content to relate only to the past. He gave expression and life to his teaching. Although Levi was not enslaved, he knew of the decree that would come to pass, and he felt his people's future bondage with such intensity that he gave his three children names that reflected the pain he would feel for his suffering brethren: *Gershon*, which means, "We are strangers in the land"; *Kehath*, which reflects the agony that was so great that it set the people's teeth on edge[12]; and *Merari*, derived from *mar* (bitter),

---

12. In the Haggadah, the response to the wicked, sarcastic son is introduced with the words, *"Hak'heh es shinav* — Set his teeth on edge."

Parashas Va'eira / 111

describes the bitterness of their fate. Now we can understand why, when enumerating the heads of the tribes of Reuben and Simeon, the Torah introduces them by simply declaring that they are sons,[13] but when the progeny of Levi are listed, the Torah states, "These are the *names* of the sons," because Levi chose their names to imply his distress about the future suffering.

It was not by coincidence that the three spiritual giants, Miriam, Aaron, and Moses, are descendants of this noble tribe. According to the Midrash, Moses, raised in the palace of Pharaoh, was consumed by the suffering of his people and visited them in the slave camps. Aaron was known for his great and boundless love of his fellow Jews; Miriam, the prophetess, was renowned for her indomitable faith. The love and empathy that Levi felt for his fellow Jews encompassed the entire nation and was one of the reasons why the Jewish people merited redemption. As Hashem proclaimed: "*Moreover*, I have heard the groan of the Children of Israel ...."[14] Our Sages explain that when Hashem *heard* how, despite his own pain, every Jew was willing to *listen*, feel, and reach out to his brother, He proclaimed, "I, too, have heard — and the time for redemption has now come!"

We live in a world in which people have a tendency to focus only on their own needs, and have little patience for the concerns of others. The example of our ancestors in Egypt speaks to us and reminds us that precisely because we have tasted the bitter sting of pain, we should feel empathy for the anguish of our fellow man.

We learn from the Torah how vital it is to identify with the pain and struggles of others. There is so much suffering in the world today, and we have a responsibility to try to help alleviate some of that pain: to pray for and help our beleaguered brethren. Yes, we *are* our brothers' keepers!

---

13. *Exodus* 6:14-15.
14. Ibid. 6:5.

Hearing God's Voice in Good Times as Well as Bad

> Pharaoh saw that there had been a relief [from the plague of the frogs], and kept making his heart stubborn.
>
> *Exodus* 8:11

The Torah teaches us a lesson regarding human nature. Under stress we feel impelled to call out to God and beseech His help. But no sooner does the crisis pass than we revert to "business as usual." Indeed, this obtuseness is the "Pharaoh syndrome"; with each plague, the affliction intensified, but Pharaoh refused to "get it," and fell back into his old habits.

Would it not be wonderful if we could maintain the promises that we make in times of distress: to be more charitable, to be more understanding, to be more compassionate, to be more committed to the observance of mitzvos, the study of Torah, and the attainment of genuine prayer. It is a well-known adage that there are no atheists in foxholes, but the measure of a man can be recognized by his ability to call out to God in times of plenty, when fortune smiles, and to recognize that all his blessings are gifts from God. Our goal is *to pray from inspiration rather than from desperation.*

PARASHAS BO

WE ARE NEVER ALONE

> *Bo el Paroh* ... Come to Pharaoh ....
> *Exodus* 10:1

Our Sages expound upon this declaration: Surely, it would have been more appropriate to say, "*Lech* — Go," to Pharaoh rather than, "*Bo* — Come," to Pharaoh. What, then, is the deeper meaning of this passage, and what can we learn from it?

The word *bo* always connotes going with or coming to someone: "Come with me" or "Come to me." *Bo* is an expression that reminds us that we are never alone.

On the other hand, *lech* implies that we are on our own. So when Hashem told *Moshe Rabbeinu*, "*Bo* — Come to Pharaoh," He assured Moses that he would not be going alone — He, Hashem, would accompany him. This holds true not only for *Moshe Rabbeinu*, but for all of us, for all our generations, for all time. If we will it, through our mitzvos, through our Torah study, and through our prayers, Hashem will always be at our side. The *Shechinah* will always be above us, as will the angels who are the creations of our own mitzvah observance. And still more, Hashem invites all our *zeides* and *bubbies* to walk with us on the road of life, so we should never fear ... because we are not alone.

Teach Others and Elevate Yourself

At the beginning of the *parashah*, we are told that one of Hashem's goals for the Exodus from Egypt was to insure that we tell that story to our progeny: "... and so that you may relate in the ears of your son and your son's son that I made a mockery of Egypt, and My signs that I placed among them — that you may know that I am Hashem."[15]

After reading this passage, an obvious question comes to mind: If we are commanded to teach our children, then it is *they* who will know, but the text reads "that *you*," the teller of the story, may know. Furthermore, the order appears to be reversed: Should not one have knowledge before teaching? The Torah is revealing a profound truth regarding human nature.

The best way to acquire understanding is by accepting responsibility and instructing others, for that experience compels us to study and seek insights. Thus, it is not unusual for men or women who never gave too much thought to their Judaism to undergo a total transformation once they become parents. They realize that if they are to convey something of lasting value, and if they are to tell "the story" to their children, they must first and foremost possess that knowledge. This logic holds true, not only vis-à-vis

---

15. Ibid. 10:2.

raising children; every time we are challenged to explain ourselves as Jews, we are prompted to explore our roots.

THE LEGACY OF PARENTS AND GRANDPARENTS

The text also shows us how we might best impart this lesson: "Relate in the *ears* of your son" — the teaching must be personalized and intimate. The study of Torah cannot be simply a cerebral experience, but it must be an emotional and spiritual one as well. It must be transmitted from heart to heart with love and passion. It is this that enabled Joseph to retain his faith as a lone Jew in Egypt. Despite his suffering, he never faltered, for engraved upon his heart and mind was the image of his father's teaching.

From this passage our Sages also conclude that if three generations (fathers, sons, and sons' sons) in one family are committed to the study of Torah, we may be assured that the Torah and the mitzvos will never depart from that family. The litmus test of Jewish continuity is whether Judaism continues into the third generation. In our contemporary society, in which demographics demonstrate that so many of our people are assimilating and intermarrying, this question weighs heavily upon us. Every Jew must ask himself, *Am I doing enough to insure that my grandchildren will remain Jews?*

Tragically, ours is a generation that has become spiritually orphaned, and most of us do not have *zeides* who can tell the story. Therefore, we must seek out our rabbis and Torah teachers and ask them to "relate the story in [our] ears." We have survived the centuries because this commandment to tell the story to our children and our children's children is at the heart of our faith. No matter where destiny may have taken us, we continued to relate that tale and shall continue to do so until the end of time.

A Darkness That Transcends the Centuries

> Hashem said to Moses, 'Stretch forth your hand toward the heavens, and there shall be darkness upon the land of Egypt, and the darkness shall be tangible."
>
> *Exodus* 10:21

Thus, the ninth plague is introduced. All the plagues that were visited upon Egypt were "measure for measure," so that the Egyptians might know that the afflictions were not random occurrences, but represented the Hand of God. Thus, even as the Egyptians were blind to our suffering, so they were punished with a darkness that was akin to blindness.

However, everything that we study in the Torah contains a message for future generations, and herein is a *remez* (hint), regarding the Holocaust. The verse teaches us that the darkness was so terrible, so dense, that it was actually tangible. The Hebrew word for tangible is *"v'yameish,"* spelled *vav, yud, mem, shin*. If we skip back to the letter preceding each one, we will see that the letter before *vav* is *hei*, the letter before *yud* is *tes*, the letter before *mem* is *lamed*, and the letter before *shin* is *reish*. The word we have just spelled is "Hitler."

The darkness that Hitler would create would be so dense that it would eventually become tangible, but we must remember that after that terrible darkness came the tenth plague that spelled our *geulah* (redemption), the redemption we hope to see again, speedily in our day.

The Gift of Time

"This month shall be for you the beginning of months ...."[16] With this proclamation, Hashem endowed us with the greatest of all gifts: *time*.

---

16. Ibid. 12:2.

During our bondage in Egypt, our time did not belong to us. Our days meshed one into the other. Every day was painfully and monotonously the same. In the life of a slave there is no hope, there is no creativity, there is no future. But free men have choices to make, and the most important choice is to *use time wisely* and not fritter it away.

This teaching is especially pertinent to us in the 21st century. While technology and modern scientific inventions have freed us from much drudgery and hard labor, and we have more time at our disposal than our forefathers ever dreamt possible, we have also, unfortunately, come to abuse that time and squander it on pointless, meaningless pursuits.

Our technology has actually created inane programs that serve only to kill time. However, when God spoke to us and entrusted us with that great gift of time, He demanded more from us than just using time expeditiously. He charged us with the command of *sanctifying* time and making it holy. The court would do this through sanctifying the New Moon.

In contrast to the solar calendar used by much of the Western world, ours is a lunar calendar; in that, too, there is a profound teaching to be found. Unlike the sun, the moon does not generate its own light, but reflects the sun's rays. Similarly, we, the Jewish people, do not put forth our own light, but reflect the light of God; it is not our own will or desire that is the focus of our lives, but rather, the fulfillment of the will of God. Even as the moon illuminates the night, our task is to illuminate the darkness of the world with the Word of God: the Torah.

Another reason why we have a lunar calendar is that the moon waxes and wanes every month; even as the moon renews and regenerates itself, so, too, we have a mandate to rejuvenate and revitalize ourselves through *teshuvah*. This mitzvah of establishing the calendar and thus sanctifying the new month was chosen by God to be among the first of our 613 commandments. Freedom from Egyptian bondage did not mean that we became free from responsibility. It did not mean that we could do what we chose with our time. On the contrary, when God charged us with the mitzvah of sanctifying time, He entrusted us with the greatest of all responsibilities: to utilize every moment of our lives for His Holy Name's sake.

As Jews, we must be ever cognizant that our lives here are temporary and that we must make the most of every moment, for the time will come when God will ask us to give an accounting for every day of our existence. So let us sanctify our time here on earth through our holidays, through our Sabbaths, through our Torah studies, through our prayers, and through our mitzvos, and let us be ever mindful that there is only one thing that, if lost, can never be retrieved: not money nor precious gems, but the time that God has granted us on this earth.

Do You Feel the Pain of Your Brethren?

> And Pharaoh rose up at midnight ....
> *Exodus* 12:30

Regarding this passage, Rashi, whose commentaries are always concise and pithy, and whose work is a key component to understanding the Torah, explains: "Pharaoh got up from his bed." It is difficult to understand what Rashi intends to teach with this comment. It seems so obvious; from where, if not from his bed, would Pharaoh have risen? Our beloved father, Rabbi Meshulem HaLevi Jungreis, z"tl, told us a story that clarifies Rashi's remark.

During World War II, Hungary was one of the last countries in Europe to be occupied by the Nazis, but prior to the German takeover, young Jewish men were conscripted for slave labor. Our father's older brother, Yosef Dov, a brilliant young Talmudist, was forced onto a truck one night by the Hungarian military police and taken to a slave-labor camp. From that day, his mother, our grandmother, the Rebbetzin Chaya Sora, o.b.m., refused to go to bed. Instead, she sat in her chair the entire night, weeping and praying for Yosef Dov. The youngest son, our father, was the only one remaining at home. He felt a responsibility to care for his mother, and ever so gently, he would plead with his mother to lie down and rest.

"How can I rest? How can I lie down in my bed when my Yosef Dov is not here?" she wept. And so, she sat in her chair, night after night, until the day that the Nazis came and deported her and the entire family to Auschwitz, where most of them were murdered in the gas chambers.

Egypt was on fire. In every home there was devastation, but the heartless Pharaoh slept in his bed.

PARASHAS BESHALACH

SHABBOS SHIRAH: THE SONG OF FAITH

The Shabbos that *Parashas Beshalach* is read is known as *"Shabbos Shirah* — the "Sabbath of Song" — because it is in this *parashah* that Moses leads the Jewish men, and Miriam the prophetess, leads the Jewish women in singing *the Song of Praise and Exultation to the Almighty God* following the crossing of the Sea of Reeds. The special song that Moses composed is *"Az Yashir* — Then Moses *will* sing." The use of the future tense teaches us that Moses not only sang at the Sea of Reeds, but he will lead us in song once again when we behold our final redemption: the coming of Messiah. In the interim, we, the Jewish people, recite the song of Moses every morning in our prayers as we express gratitude to God.

How does one sing unto God? Is it possible for mere humans to praise Him?

Moses opened his song with the awesome words, *"Ashirah la'Hashem* ... I shall sing to Hashem for He is exalted above the arrogant ...."[17]

But how high is God? Can we compare Him to anything that we human beings have experienced? Moses, the greatest man ever to walk on planet Earth, was keenly aware of this human inadequacy, so he contented himself with the phrase, *"ga'oh ga'ah,"* which is literally translated "high, high" (exalted above), followed by a blank space in the text. In fact, every stanza of Moses' song is followed by a blank space, so that we might realize that no mortal can even hope to comprehend the infinite, the Divine.

In our culture of hedonism and instant gratification, it is vital to absorb this message, for ours is a generation that may lose faith at the slightest disappointment. "How could God have allowed this to happen to me?" we protest indignantly. So, when events do not turn out as anticipated, let us remember the message of Moses: leave a blank space and remain silent, anchored to our faith.

Converting Despair Into Hope

Miriam the prophetess not only led the women in song, but she did so with tambourines and drums. From where did she obtain those instruments? The desert was hardly a place to purchase them. A profound lesson is to be found in those instruments. While enveloped in brutal bondage in the "Auschwitz" of Egypt, Miriam the prophetess prepared drums and tambourines, in the faith that one day redemption would come and give the nation cause to sing and celebrate. It is this pure faith that Jewish women instilled in our people, it is this faith that

---

17. Ibid. 15:1.

enabled us to survive the centuries, and it is this faith that we must summon whenever we find ourselves in predicaments that appear to be hopeless.

When counseling people embroiled in trying and untenable situations, our esteemed mother, Rebbetzin Esther Jungreis, often advises them to take their cue from Miriam: The name *Miriam* means "bitter" (as in *maror* of the Seder table); but through her faith, Miriam converted bitterness into hope and renewed life. So, instead of giving in to despair, get a tambourine and trust God. Our mother, a survivor of the infamous Bergen-Belsen concentration camp, is living testimony to that trust.

A Song That Springs From the Heart

Shirah is more than a song: It is an expression of jubilation and exultation that springs from the inner recesses of the soul.

At the Splitting of the Reed Sea, the Jewish people, in its entirety, witnessed events of a magnitude that even the illustrious prophets did not behold. The heavens opened as the Children of Israel beheld angels, the Patriarchs, and the Matriarchs; they saw the very Hand of God. A simple handmaiden was able to point and cry out in joy, "This is my God ...."

But there is yet another dimension to this song of Moses that makes it so special, and this uniqueness is to be found in the Hebrew word, "*az*" with which Moses commenced the song. It was with this very same word, "*az*," that Moses previously questioned God and complained, "*Mei'az* ... — From the time I came to Pharaoh to speak in Your Name, he [Pharaoh] did evil to this people, but You did not rescue Your people."[18] And now, with this very same word, "*Az*," Moses proclaims God's praise.

Sometimes we sing songs of praise to thank God for having

---
18. Ibid. 5:23.

saved us from danger and suffering, and we also sing to acknowledge the miracles He performed on our behalf. But that gratitude takes on a totally different dimension when we become aware that even the danger and suffering that we experienced were for our own benefit, and realize that through that affliction, we came to realize our potential and achieved greatness. Our bondage in Egypt enabled us to come to Sinai and accept God's Covenant, for only a nation that endured suffering could appreciate the true meaning of Hashem's *chesed*. Only such a nation could be worthy of accepting God's covenant and all the responsibilities entailed therein — to become a "light unto the nations," witnesses to God's Presence.

Now we can better understand why, when the Torah speaks about Moses singing the song at the Splitting of the Sea, the word used is *Yashir* — *will sing*, for when the Messiah comes, Moses will once again lead us in song with the word "*Az*" and we will understand the meaning of our long exile and our pain.

In the interim, we must always keep that vision in mind. We must always be aware that even when problems overwhelm us, even when we find ourselves enveloped in darkness, God's Presence is always there and our suffering is not random or for naught. As Isaiah states, "I thank You, Hashem, for You were angry with me and now ... You have comforted me."[19]

RECREATING YOURSELF

It is written that when our Forefathers departed from Egypt, God took them via a circuitous route rather than on the way that would lead them directly to the Land of Israel. At first glance, this is difficult to understand. Why would God have us traverse an inhospitable desert where there was no provision for food or water when we could have passed through the land of the Philistines and be assured of sustenance? There is an important teaching to be

---

19. *Isaiah* 12:1.

learned here. The Almighty was concerned that we would not be able to withstand the temptations and the pressures of Philistine society; contact with them might prompt us to return to Egypt, not only in a physical sense, but in our outlook as well. It is not only from the land of Egypt that we had to depart. More significantly, we had to remove the immorality and corruption of Egypt from *ourselves*. We had to experience the desert so that we might be re-created, re-shaped, and thus become the Priestly Kingdom, the holy nation that God willed us to be.

We must derive a lesson for life from this. That which appears to be short and comfortable sometimes turns out to be arduous and hazardous. Physical risks can be overcome, but once we lose our values and our morals, we lose the very essence of our lives. Accordingly, we must be vigilant and guard our souls; we must carefully choose the neighborhood in which we live; the environment in which we work, and the place where we vacation. We are never to underestimate the deleterious effects of living in a corrupt environment. Sometimes, it is more prudent to take a longer, circuitous path and, if necessary, change direction, in order to avoid a situation that would prove destructive to our spiritual well-being.

PARASHAS YISRO

The Art of Listening

Revelation at Sinai, the greatest moment in the annals of mankind, is recorded in this *parashah*. Incredibly however, the portion is entitled *"Yisro,"* in honor of Moses' father-in-law, Jethro, who, prior to his conversion, had been a pagan priest. Logically, one would have expected that the portion be called "Moses" or "Sinai," but surely not *"Yisro."* How are we to understand this?

The *parashah* opens with the simple but piercing words, *"Vayishma Yisro* — Jethro *heard."* The voice of God was audible throughout the universe, but it was only Jethro who *heard*, it was only Jethro who reacted and chose to abandon his prestigious position as a priest of Midian to join the Israelites at Sinai. Our Sages teach that when the kings of the nations heard those awesome sounds, they thought that a cataclysmic event was about to occur and there would be yet another Flood. For a very brief moment, they stopped to listen, but then Bilaam, their prophet, assured them that it was *"only"* God giving His commandments, so they returned to their old ways.

At first glance, one must feel appalled at such obtuseness: *"Only God giving His commandments"* — How could they have justified such a stance? But let us examine our own lives. How different are *we* from those pagans? Are we not guilty of the same dense callousness? Do we pay heed to the Word of God, or is it only when catastrophe strikes that we hear His voice? Yet, God's call never ceases. Every day, a *Bas Kol* (a Divine Voice) issues us a summons to our unique destiny, but in our pursuit of "the good life," the glitter, and the gold, we no longer hear God's voice. Like the pagans of old, it is only when the sinister shadow of disaster looms over our heads that we stop to listen. But how many of us truly stop to hear the Word of God?

In every generation, those who rise to their calling and fulfill their life missions are those who have mastered the art of listening, of hearing and noticing the messages implicit in the universe. The Talmud relates that Rabbi Akiva, one of the greatest Sages of our people, at the age of 40 was an impoverished, illiterate shepherd, who had an awakening when he saw that water continually dripping upon a stone had eroded the rock. *If water can erode a stone, then surely Torah can alter a mind or a heart,* he reasoned. He therefore embarked upon a life of Torah study. To be sure, many others had also witnessed the same phenomenon, but only Akiva truly observed and "heard" this message. The challenge of *listening*, of becoming aware, set forth in the examples of Jethro and Rabbi Akiva, speak to us anew today. Unfortunately however, most of us hear only that which we want to hear and see only that which we wish to see. Our challenge is to listen to the messages — and respond properly to them.

Be Happy for Others: The Hallmark of Our People

The greatness of Jethro was further evidenced when, upon arrival at the desert encampment, he was told of the wondrous events that had rescued the Jewish people. The Torah relates: "*Vayichad Yisro* — Jethro rejoiced." Our Sages explain that the word *vayichad* is an expression of joy tempered by reservation, for even as Jethro heard the amazing events, he also felt a pang of sadness for his former friends, the Egyptians.[20] Nevertheless, Jethro proclaimed the two majestic words that have become the hallmark of our people throughout the centuries: "*Baruch Hashem* — Blessed is Hashem!" "*Baruch Hashem*" has been our response to all the challenges of life — to the joys as well as to the trials.

At first glance, it may be difficult to comprehend why this phrase, *Baruch Hashem*, should be attributed to Jethro. Surely there were others who blessed God before him. After all, didn't Moses praise God at the crossing of the Reed Sea, when he composed his glorious song? There is one fine difference, however. Moses praised God for the miracles He performs for His own people, but Jethro thanked God for the blessings that He bestows on others.

The concept of being happy for someone else is a goal toward which we must strive. When we realize that we can find our own joy in the happiness that is visited upon others, we become elevated spiritual beings. To be sure, this is a difficult concept to accept in a culture that has conditioned us to measure our happiness by that which we acquire rather than by that which we give. To maintain our Torah values, we would do well to bear in mind that God did not command us to become rich and successful, but He *did* command us to become giving, generous people, to personify lovingkindness, and to full-heartedly proclaim, "*Baruch Hashem*," when we behold the happiness of others.

---

20. *Exodus* 18:9.

The Ten Commandments: The Bedrock of Our Faith

Like every word in the Torah, every aspect of the Ten Commandments[21] is laden with profound meaning; even the structure speaks. For example, the first commandment, "I am Hashem, your God," is parallel to the sixth — "You shall not kill," teaching us that, because every person was created in the image of God, when someone is killed, not only the person dies, but the spark of God, which was within him, is removed from the world. In this same way, the placement of each of the commandments on the tablets is significant.

The Ten Commandments are the bedrock of our faith, for they represent the entirety of the Torah and its 613 mitzvos, and therefore it is a tradition for the entire congregation to rise in awe as they are read in the synagogue.

Receiving the Torah in Every Generation

It is written that the Jewish people entered Midbar Sinai to receive the Torah *"bayom hazeh* — on *this* day"[22] rather than "on *that* day."

This is not a grammatical error; rather, it is a profound teaching for all of us. The giving and the receiving of the Torah is an *every day* occurrence. Every day we must see ourselves as if we were standing at Mt. Sinai, and every day we must re-commit ourselves to the covenant and attempt to muster the same fervor and enthusiasm as on the day when we first heard the voice of God at Sinai.

Even the setting, the place where the Torah was given, is instructive. God chose the desert, for the desert is empty. Similarly, if we

---

21. Ibid. 20:2-14.
22. Ibid. 19:1.

wish to absorb this Divine Wisdom, we must become like a desert, free ourselves of all preconceived notions, and allow the Torah to shape and mold us. The Torah was given on Mt. Sinai — a lowly hill — to teach us that it is only in a humble heart that the Word of God can find a home. Once again, vital lessons for us to learn, for ours is a generation that is replete with many voices. So many voices, so many sounds pull at us, demanding our attention. Ours is also a generation in which arrogance abounds; everyone is an "expert," convinced that he *can* "make it" — and *is* making it — on his own, without God's help. And so, the Torah was given to us on a lowly hill, Sinai, to remind us that a precondition to receiving God's Word is a humble heart.

> The Kotzker Rebbe once asked a child, "Tell me, where is God?"
> "Everywhere," the little boy responded.
> "No, my son," the Rebbe said. "He can only be found in the hearts of those who allow Him to enter. In an arrogant heart, there is no room for His presence."

Finally, let us be mindful that at Sinai God designated us as His "beloved treasure" — "a kingdom of ministers and a holy nation."[23] Let us attempt to conduct ourselves accordingly.

---

23. Ibid. 19:5-6.

PARASHAS MISHPATIM

Good Is Not Good Enough

> And these are the ordinances that you shall place before them:
>
> *Exodus* 21:1

This *parashah* opens with the words *"V'eileh hamishpatim ... —* And these are the ordinances ...." At first glance, it seems grammatically inappropriate to commence a chapter with the conjunction "and," but nothing in the Torah is to be taken for granted. Every letter, every syllable, every punctuation mark comes to teach us a lesson. The conjunction "and" reminds us that this *parashah* is connected to the preceding one, in which Revelation — the giving of the Torah — takes place, teaching us that even as the laws in the previous *parashah* were given at Sinai, the commandments pertaining to civil laws that are the focus of *Parashas Mishpatim* were also proclaimed at Sinai. But would we not understand this on our own? Do we really require the conjunction "and" to remind us that *all* of the Torah emanates from Sinai? Sadly enough, yes!

Most of us have a tendency to rationalize regulations that deal with our interpersonal relationships. It is *"our life,"* we argue, and therefore we have the right to determine what is appropriate or inappropriate. The Torah, however, reminds us that it is only the One Who created us Who can make such a determination. Only He can decide what is honest or dishonest, kind or cruel, moral or immoral, and precisely because of that, the Torah reminds us that those laws that legislate our personal relationships also emanate from Sinai, just as do the rituals and ceremonies enumerated in *Parashas Yisro*, which govern our relationship with God.

This message speaks to our generation, for we tend to interpret laws to accommodate our own needs and predilections. Morality, honoring parents, gossip, inflicting pain and injury, theft, can all be manipulated to justify our own desires. No matter how selfish our behavior may be, we can find a rationale for our actions or inactions. We pride ourselves on being *good people* who deal fairly, and forget that the Torah does not specifically command that we be "good." The word "good" is too ambiguous: every culture, every society, even the most base, has its own interpretation of goodness. Moreover, the definition of "good" is ever changing. That which yesterday was termed good may no longer be considered so today, and the converse is also true. That which in the past was regarded as evil and immoral can, regrettably, today be viewed as good and moral. But the goodness by which we live, which was legislated at Sinai, is *rooted in eternity*. It comes from God Himself, Who created us. Thus, our Torah defines "good" and tells us how we must interact in our relationships on a personal, intimate level as well as in our general interaction. Nothing is left to chance. Life is too precious; we can't afford to live it in error. Therefore, everything emanates from Sinai, showing us how to live a good life.

ETHICS AND TRUST IN GOD

There is yet another dimension to this connection between Sinai and our civil laws. As noted above, the Ten Commandments open with the words, "I am Hashem, Your God." By placing the laws of business ethics after the Ten Commandments, the Torah teaches us that he who is not ethical in business does not really trust God, for if he believed in Divine Providence, he would understand that, ultimately, it is God Who provides, it is He Who determines our income and therefore, it is futile to cheat, steal, or surrender to greed, for in the end, it will all catch up with us. We cannot outsmart God.

This connection once again reminds us that we must adhere to our moral and ethical laws, not necessarily because they appeal to our intellect, but because they were legislated by God and guide our behavior in the workplace as well as in the synagogue. This is a lesson that we dare not forget: **"The beginning of wisdom is fear of Hashem."**[24] If we lack that awe and awareness, all our wisdom, all of our morals and ethics can be twisted, corrupted, and rationalized to justify the most horrific evil. Just consider the evil that has and continues to plague us in our "civilized" and "enlightened" 20th and 21st centuries.

The Torah gives us a mandate to strive to emulate God and live by His commandments. Even as He is compassionate, we must strive to be compassionate. Even as He is forgiving, we must be forgiving. Our ethics and morals are all from Hashem, and are therefore immutable and non-negotiable. How blessed are we to have laws that guarantee the integrity of our human interaction … and what a pity it would be to be unaware of this gift.

This teaching is reinforced throughout the Torah. So it is that the Ten Commandments are engraved on two tablets: one for those establishing a relationship between man and God, and one for those establishing a relationship between man and his fellow man. The two tablets remind us that both relationships are equally holy. It was also for this reason that during Revelation, God pro-

---

24. *Psalms* 111:10; *Proverbs* 9:10.

nounced all Ten Commandments simultaneously, so that it would be clear that no one commandment takes precedence over another. Moreover, a special section in the Mishnah is entitled *Ethics of Our Fathers*. It deals with human relations, but significantly, it commences with the monumental words, "Moses received the Torah from Sinai,"[25] once again impressing upon us that *all our ethical and moral commandments are of Divine origin.* In a world in which values, ethics, and morals seem to have lost their meaning, how powerful it is to know that our Torah has anchored us to timeless truths.

Even on a most elementary level, 21st-century man has yet to accept "You shall not kill." From Hitler to Arafat to Bin Laden to Ahmadinejad, it is obvious how desperately man needs God to regulate his behavior.

A Mother's Table

The *parashah* opens with a most unusual expression, *"V'eileh hamishpatim asher tasim lifneihem* — And these are the commandments that you shall place before them."[26]

Normally, the Torah instructs Moses with the words "speak," "command," or "teach" — so why is Moses here commanded to "place"?

Rashi, whose commentaries are a key to understanding Torah, gives a brief but cryptic explanation: "Placed in front of them like a *set table.*" But this leaves us even more puzzled. Our revered grandfather, HaRav HaGaon Avraham HaLevi Jungreis, explains that a good mother prepares a beautiful table for her children, bearing in mind the needs and tastes of each of them (one may like meat, the other prefers chicken, sweet or spicy, etc.). And once her children are seated at the table, the mother urges them to taste the many other delicacies that are available there. Similarly, when imparting the commandments, the Torah teacher must bear in mind the needs of each of his charges. He must offer something that will draw the

---

25. *Ethics of the Fathers* 1:1.
26. *Exodus* 21:1.

student to the table. He must invite the student to experience the many other mitzvos and thus imbibe the wisdom of the Torah.

This commandment speaks to us with great relevance, for ours is a generation that has seen many young people fall through the cracks and lose their way. We must find a way to bring them to the Torah table and reach their hearts, and this teaching reminds us how we may do so. We need only set a beautiful table for them, taking into account their special needs, and, with the help of God, the transformation will surely take place.

PARASHAS TERUMAH

Make Your Home a Sanctuary

> "They shall make a Sanctuary for Me — so that I may dwell among them …."
>
> *Exodus* 25:8

Our Sages ask, "Is it possible for man to build a home for God? Isn't it true that even the heavens cannot contain His holy Presence?" How then can we mere mortals build a Sanctuary for Him?

The response to this challenge speaks personally to each and every one of us. God, in His infinite mercy, does not expect us to achieve the impossible; we need only develop ourselves to our fullest potential and dedicate ourselves to Him with love and devotion.

If we do so, God promises to enter our hearts, our sanctuaries, and even our homes. Our homes can become replicas of the Tabernacle. Our tables can become altars at which guests are welcomed and the word of God is spoken; where blessings and grace over meals are pronounced and the laws of kashruth are observed. Our sacred books — the Chumash, the Mishnah, the Talmud, the Prophets, the Psalms, the Siddur — remind us of the Holy Ark. In the Jewish home, books are not mere ornaments or means of entertainment. Rather, they are road maps that give direction to our lives.

The Shabbos candles and menorahs serve to remind us of God's eternal light. Thus, although the Tabernacle and the Holy Temple no longer stand, we can transform our homes into *sanctuaries in miniature*, until such time as God in His infinite mercy rebuilds our Holy Temple in Jerusalem.

Following are practical suggestions on how we can convert our homes into sanctuaries. In every home, a room or a place should be set aside for *davening* (prayer) and Torah study. Every home should have a Jewish library. Today, Torah-based *sefarim* are available with fine English translation and commentary. There is a vast body of rich Jewish literature for young and old, and there is no longer an excuse for ignorance of Torah.

Moreover, if our homes are to be converted into sanctuaries, we must be meticulous in our preparations for welcoming the Sabbath Queen. Even as the Levites in the Holy Temple sang beautiful hymns to God, you, too, can sing *zemiros* — songs of praise and thanksgiving. Even as the Kohanim and the Levites prepared to serve God, you, too, can prepare lessons of Torah to share with your family and friends. The awareness that your home is a sanctuary should place you on your guard, remembering to lace your words with kindness and gentleness and to avoid *lashon hara* and hurtful words. Expand your home by making it a gathering place for Torah study, so that your family and friends may share in its wisdom. To initiate such a program, enlist the help of a local rabbi. You will quickly discover that the sweet sound of Torah will transform and elevate your home and, yes, convert it into a sanctuary. Finally, while we no longer have sacrificial offerings as we did in the days of the Holy Temple, if you wish your home to be a sanctuary, make sacrifices for *shalom bayis*. Learn to control your temper; give others the benefit of the doubt and you will be performing a holy service. These are all goals that are within our human capability, and, if we so desire, we can attain them.

"Make a Sanctuary for Me — so that I may dwell among [you]"; it's all up to us. If we will it, our homes can be God's Sanctuary.

Torah: The Heritage of Every Jew

The method of construction of the Tabernacle is also instructive. The measurements of its vessels and furnishings and how they were fashioned were not left to our discretion, but were ordained by God. Consequently, they are laden with hidden meaning. For example, when it comes to the construction of the Holy Ark, the verse states in the plural, "*V'asu* ... — And they shall make ..."[27] — rather than the singular, "*V'asisa* ... — and *you* shall make...,"[28] the expression used in regard to the Menorah and the *Mizbei'ach* (Altar) which were generally the domain of the Kohanim, the priests. From this we learn that we all have a share in the Torah, which is in the Ark, that *Torah is the heritage of every Jew*. We can *all* plumb its depths and become Torah scholars. Our Sages teach us that there are three crowns: the crown of Torah, the crown of priesthood, and the crown of kingdom. The crown of kingdom belongs strictly to Judah — the House of David. The crown of priesthood is limited to the descendants of Aaron — the Kohanim, but the crown of Torah is the possession of each member of the entire nation. And if we attain it, we can acquire the fourth crown: the crown of a good name, and that, our Sages teach, excels them all.

---

27. Ibid. 25:8.
28. Ibid. 25:31, 27:1.

A Study That Is Never Exhausted

The measurements of the Ark were given in fractions[29] to teach us that as much as we study Torah, we can comprehend only a fraction of it. The Torah was written by God Himself and its true intent is beyond our human understanding. This awareness is very humbling, and yet elevating, for it reminds us that this is a study that can never be exhausted, and which, if pursued, can take us to celestial heights.

The half-measurements have yet another message: We cannot do it alone. If we are to succeed in our Torah study, we must interact with a Torah teacher. The interdependence of student and teacher is the path to the acquisition of Torah wisdom.

The positioning and the method of carrying the Ark are also instructive. Even when the Ark rested, the poles that lifted it were not permitted to be removed, impressing upon us that those who support Torah study have an equal share in it.

Throughout our long and turbulent history, as we were forced to wander from country to country, these lessons remained imbedded in our souls. Even under the most trying circumstances, we gathered for Torah study, and in every generation, there were those who volunteered to give of their means to support those who devoted their lives to Torah study, for it is the very essence of our lives. It is that which renders us Jews, and it is that which enables us to survive. Wherever destiny takes us, the Torah must accompany us at all times and under all circumstances, for it is only Torah that can illuminate our paths as we journey on the rocky road of life.

Kosher (Honest) Money

Parashas Terumah, which focuses on the building of the Sanctuary, follows the portion of *Mishpatim*, which, in great measure, deals with the laws of honesty and ethics.

---

29. Ibid. 25:10.

The obvious question is, "What is the connection between these two portions?"

The Torah is teaching us an important lesson. The money that we contribute must be "honest money." We are never to rationalize or delude ourselves into believing that it's acceptable to be dishonest or unethical in business as long as we contribute to good and just charitable causes. This lesson is further reinforced by the Hebrew word *terumah*, which means "an uplifted portion." If the letters of the word are rearranged, they spell, *"hamutar,"* meaning "the permissible." Only money that is "kosher" — "honest money" — may be donated to *tzedakah*. Even as our goals must be honorable and noble, so, too, the means by which we achieve them must be permissible — untainted and free of corruption.

A Solution to Every Problem

Our Sages teach us that at Mount Sinai we attained such majestic heights that, if not for the sin of the Golden Calf, we would never have needed to build a Sanctuary. That being the case, it is rather puzzling that in this *parashah* we are commanded regarding the Sanctuary, although the sin of the Golden Calf had yet to occur. So why are we instructed to build the Sanctuary at this point?

Nothing in the Torah is random. The construction of the Tabernacle — which served to keep God close to His people — was commanded before the sin of the Golden Calf — which distanced Israel from God — is mentioned in the Torah. God teaches us a lesson to fortify us through all life's tests: Before a tragedy occurs, God provides the solution.

Our mother, Rebbetzin Esther Jungreis, often explains this teaching through a popular parable. At one time or another, through our own foolishness, or for some inexplicable reason, we find ourselves in "hot water" and feel we cannot continue. Under such circumstances, what's to be done? We have three choices, which can be compared to a carrot, an egg, or coffee.

If a carrot is placed into boiling water, after a while it disintegrates and becomes mush. If an egg is placed into boiling water, it becomes hard and tough, but when coffee is placed into boiling water, the boiling water becomes a delicious drink. These are the choices that we all have when we suddenly find ourselves in boiling water. We can disintegrate like carrots, fall apart, and become depressed; we can become as hard as a boiled egg, tough, cynical, angry, and bitter; or we can become like coffee, converting that water into a delicious drink.

Similarly, we can transform our difficulties, our tragedies into something positive and find our way back to our Creator. God showed us the way: The Tabernacle that would bring atonement for the sin of the Golden Calf was commanded to be built before the sin of the Golden Calf occurred. Moses ascended Mount Sinai again, and beseeched God to forgive His people. Then he ascended once again to receive the Ten Commandments anew. The day the forgiveness was complete and Moses was given the Second Tablets became a Day of Atonement for all eternity — Yom Kippur.

These then, are our choices: In the face of onerous difficulty do we become "carrots," depressed? Do we become "hard-boiled eggs," tough and angry? Or do we convert that boiling water into something positive and create something desirable from our adversity? Learn from that experience! Move on, become wiser and more sensitive, and fulfill the purpose for which you were created by continuing to serve our Creator.

PARASHAS TETZAVEH

Moshe Rabbeinu: Putting Himself on the Line

> Now you shall command the Children of Israel that they shall take for you pure olive oil, pressed, for illumination, to kindle a lamp continually.
>
> *Exodus* 27:20

Parashas Tetzaveh opens with the words, "*V'atah tetzaveh* ... — Now you shall command ...." The words "now you" are puzzling. Who is meant by "you"? Why is "you" not identified?

"You," is, of course, a reference to *Moshe Rabbeinu*, and, for the very first time since his birth, his name does not appear in the *para-*

shah. Rather, Hashem refers to him using the anonymous pronoun, "you." But in this anonymity, Moses speaks with even-greater force and gives us a glimpse of his majesty.

Following the sin of the Golden Calf, fearing that God would destroy the Jewish people, Moses pleaded, "And now if You would but forgive their sin! — but if not, erase me now from Your Book that You have written."[30] With those words, Moses put himself on the line and was prepared to sacrifice his own life for his beloved people.

But what sort of defense is this plea? How did Moses hope that by asking that his name be erased from God's Book his nation would be saved?

One's calling, one's mission, is to be found in one's *name*. Therefore Moses reasoned, "If they committed such evil, it must be *my* fault — I must have failed as their rabbi and teacher. Hence, erase my name." Just as a parent pleads on behalf of his wayward child, "He's really a very good boy. It's all *my* fault. I wasn't the parent I should have been," so, too, Moses, with his unflagging love, accepted responsibility for the sin of the nation. God forgave Moses' people, but Moses' name was omitted from the *parashah*.

This omission is difficult to understand. After all, why should Moses have been penalized for his self-sacrifice? In reality, he was not. The omission of his name reveals the greatness of his person more powerfully than ever before, for we are reminded that he was prepared to lay down his life for his people. And more, this *parashah* is usually read during the week that we commemorate *Moshe Rabbeinu's yahrzeit*, which falls on *zayin Adar*, the seventh day of Adar. It is on this day that he was born and it is on this day that he died. Thus, forever and ever, when we come to this *parashah* and realize that Moses' name is missing, we are also reminded that it is the *yahrzeit* of our beloved *Rebbi, Moshe Rabbeinu*, the holy teacher of all Israel.

---

30. Ibid. 32:32.

The Menorah: More Than a Light

Everything in the Tabernacle has a deeper meaning. For example, the Menorah represents the sacred light of the Torah and therefore, everything about it is significant: the material to be used to create the flame, the method of its kindling, and the placement of the Menorah in the Tabernacle.

- **The material:** The oil used for the lighting of the Menorah must be *pure olive oil*, free of sediment, teaching us that our Torah study must be pure and not compromised by alien concepts and influences.
- **The method:** When lighting the Menorah, we must be certain that the flame burns brightly, teaching us that when we teach Torah, we must impart the lesson in such a way that the student fully understands. The Torah teacher is charged with the responsibility of tenaciously staying with his students until the lesson is fully absorbed.
- **The placement:** The Torah instructs us to place the Menorah "outside the Partition that is near the Testimonial-tablets,"[31] teaching us that the light of the Menorah, which reminds us of the eternal light of the Torah, must guide us not only when we are in the confines of the Sanctuary immersed in study and prayer, but even when we are "outside the Partition." That light of the Torah must direct our lives, in our homes, in our workplace, and wherever life may take us.

We live in such menacing times; we have so much stress to contend with. Every day the world becomes more frightening. If we ever needed the pure light of Torah to energize us, to give us hope and guide us, it is today. And that light is forever within our grasp. We need only seize it and it will illuminate our path on the bumpy road of life. Let us make a commitment to illuminate our minds, hearts, and souls with the eternal light of Sinai.

---

31. Ibid. 27:21.

Garments That Are More Than Clothing

In this *parashah*, the Torah discusses in great detail the laws concerning the eight garments worn by the Kohen Gadol (High Priest) and the four garments worn by an ordinary Kohen while performing their service in the Temple.[32] Why does the Torah go into such great detail in discussing seemingly insignificant items such as the clothing of the Kohanim? After all, many would argue, "What difference does it make what one wears?" By that logic, why should it matter whether a soldier or a police officer is in uniform? Or if a doctor wears a white coat? And more, is there no difference between jeans and formal attire? Between modest and immodest clothing? Can anyone truly claim that what one wears does not influence his/her conduct or lifestyle? So it is that every part of the Kohen Gadol's vestments had a teaching of its own, all with one purpose: to remind the nation of its Divine calling — the covenant sealed at Sinai.

Since the destruction of our Holy Temple, we can no longer gaze upon these holy garments. Just the same, we are *Mamleches Kohanim* — a Priestly Kingdom — and we have our own special uniform to keep us anchored: the yarmulke, the tzitzis, the tefillin, our modest garments, and the head-covering of married Jewish women. All serve as reminders of who we are and what our responsibilities are. Let us not take for granted these tools with which God entrusted us in order to keep us connected to our *Yiddishkeit*. Indeed, one reason we were worthy of redemption from Egypt was that we did not abandon our special mode of Jewish dress.

---

32. Ibid. Chapter 28.

Bells and Pomegranates

Affixed to the hem of the robe of the Kohen Gadol were bells and pomegranates.[33] There are many beautiful and inspirational explanations for this, but allow us to share just one with you.

As the Kohen Gadol walked, the bells would tinkle, announcing his presence. From this we learn a basic rule of Torah etiquette. We are never to just barge into a room or a house, even if it is our own, for we have a responsibility to inform those who are inside that we have arrived, rather than take them by surprise.

Our father of blessed memory, HaRav Meshulem Jungreis, z"tl, was always careful to fulfill this precept. How, you might ask, did he announce his arrival? Did he knock or rattle the doorknob? No, he did not employ any of the conventional means, but we always knew when our father was at the door, because he never entered the house without singing. A survivor of the concentration camps, a pioneering Orthodox rabbi in Long Island, he certainly had undergone his share of challenges and tests, but no matter how stressful his day may have been, he never entered our house without singing.

What a wonderful lesson for all of us. Consider for a moment how different our relationships in our family life would be if we would only learn to smile and sing.

Sacrifices: The Path to Commitment and Love

The concept of *Korbanos* — sacrificial offerings — is greatly misunderstood in modern culture. The word *"korban"* is derived from the word *"karov"* — to come close, teaching us that in order to really build a relationship, sacrifice is a pre-

---

33. Ibid. 28:33.

requisite, and this holds true for all relationships, not only those between man and God, but also those between man and his fellows. Unfortunately, however, ours is a generation that is more interested in receiving than in giving, in indulging rather than in abstaining, in luxuries rather than sacrifice.

In the Megillah of Purim, we read about a terrible edict that was enacted against our people and placed the very existence of our nation in jeopardy. Haman, the archetypical anti-Semite, came up with a plan for the "Final Solution" from which there was no escape. Esther and Mordechai, however, saved the nation. What was their secret? How did they bring about this miracle? The answer is *sacrifice*.

"Go, assemble all the Jews that are to be found in Shushan," Esther decreed, "and fast for me; do not eat or drink for three days, night or day."[34] And Esther herself fasted and undertook an even-greater sacrifice — *she put herself on the line*. Without being summoned, she went to plead the cause of her people before the king, knowing full well that the penalty for such an infraction was death. But precisely because of that, precisely because she was prepared to forfeit her own life for the sake of her nation, she succeeded.

Mordechai, too, had put his life on the line. By refusing to bow down before Haman, he demonstrated his total, unflinching loyalty to Hashem.[35] But Mordechai did not stop there; he went further. He donned sackcloth and called upon all the Jewish people to pierce the Heavenly Gates with their cries and prayers.[36] He assembled the schoolchildren and dressed them in sackcloth as well. He called upon them to fast, pray, and study Torah, The children wept, and their tears and prayers reached the very Throne of God.

Once again, in our time, we are confronted by a Haman, and even as Haman of old, this 21st-century Haman is also a son of Persia–Iran. And even as Haman of old was determined to annihilate and exterminate all our people, so this modern-day madman has publicly proclaimed that he plans to wipe Israel off the

---

34. *Esther* 4:16.
35. Ibid. 3:2.
36. Ibid. 4:1.

map. And even as Haman had many willing accomplices, so this modern-day Haman has his cohorts and his deadly scheme. But even as Haman perished, so, too, will this evil man and his followers. We need only follow the example of Esther and Mordechai: Turn to our God in prayer, repentance, and sacrifice, and He will do the rest.

PARASHAS KI SISA

Measure Your Worth

Sometimes we wonder whether such puny individuals as ourselves can make an impact on world events, whether we can make a real difference in God's universe. Most of us would give a negative response to such questions. *Parashas Ki Sisa*, however, comes to challenge that view. This *parashah* impresses upon us that not only is it possible for us to make a difference, but it is our imperative to do so. The portion opens with the words "*Ki sisa* ... — When you take a census of the Children of Israel ... *v'nasnu* — every man shall give Hashem an atonement for his soul .... This shall they give — everyone who passes through the census, a half-shekel ...."[37]

---

37. Exodus 30:12-13.

At first glance, this commandment to count the Jewish people appears puzzling. Surely the Almighty God knows our number, so what purpose is there in a census? Moreover, why should the people be counted through a "half-*shekel*"? Herein is to be found a profound teaching, which, if absorbed properly, can be a life-transforming experience through which we can make that difference. *Ki sisa* — the words with which the Torah commands the census — does not literally mean "counting," but rather *"the elevation of one's head,"* impressing upon us that when we realize that we *count*, our *heads are lifted up* and we are elevated, The realization that we can impact on the destiny of the world, that our words and deeds have significance, charges us with responsibility and allows us to grow and become better people.

Our Sages offer many explanations as to how we may best achieve this elevation. When we make a spiritual accounting by carefully scrutinizing our lives, then we transcend ourselves and grow spiritually. By having to contribute *half a shekel* rather than a full *shekel* to the census, we are challenged to realize that we are *all only halves* and that our nation is strong only when its individual parts join in unity. It follows, then, that when we make a decision to pray with greater intensity and devote more time to Torah study, to be more scrupulous about the observance of Shabbos and kashruth, to make an effort to control our tempers and to desist from *lashon hara* (gossip and slander), to reach out with *chesed* (loving-kindness) and patience, then we are not only elevating our individual selves, but *we are actually tipping the scales in favor of our people and the world.*

The half-*shekel* that we are called upon to donate is also symbolic of a *heart broken in half*, which results from the awareness that sometimes we fail in our mission of fulfilling God's commandments. That realization is in and of itself a measure of atonement for our souls. As King David proclaimed in his psalm: "God is close to the broken hearted ...."[38]

Finally, the word *v'nasnu* — "and they shall give" — is a Hebrew palindrome, a word or phrase that reads the same backward and forward, reminding us that *that which we give always comes back*

---

38. *Psalms* 34:19.

and enriches us. When we give, our souls expand and our world becomes larger and more meaningful, bringing blessing to ourselves and to our people.

Only When We Lose It Do We Appreciate It

As Moses came down from Mt. Sinai and beheld the people dancing around the Golden Calf, he took the two tablets on which the Ten Commandments were engraved and threw them down, smashing them. It was only at this moment, just before the two tablets are about to be destroyed, that the Torah goes into great detail describing the beauty of the tablets.[39] "Tablets inscribed on both their sides were God's handiwork."

In Chapter 31, verse 18, however, the first time the tablets are mentioned in the Torah, the tablets are not depicted in such an elaborate manner. The Torah is teaching us a profound lesson in human behavior. Unfortunately, most people only appreciate that which they have when it is about to be taken away from them. Throughout their lives, when they can enjoy and appreciate God's blessings, they take those blessings for granted. So, when we gather with our family members and loved ones, let us pause for a moment and think how truly blessed we are right now, and not wait until those blessings are no longer with us to express our appreciation.

Torah for Everyone

We find an interesting occurrence in this *parashah* which may seem puzzling to even a seasoned scholar. Moses ascends Mt. Sinai, enters the heavens them-

---

39. *Exodus* 32:15.

selves, and for 40 days and 40 nights he neither eats nor sleeps, but devotes every moment to learning and understanding the Torah so that he night teach it to us, his beloved people. And yet, despite all this sacrifice, upon beholding the nation celebrating around the Golden Calf, he has no choice but to shatter the tablets.

The pain, the suffering, the disappointment is overwhelming, but Moses, the loyal shepherd of the Jewish people, doesn't give up, and once again ascends the mountain — once again he spends 40 days and 40 nights there in order to receive a *second set of tablets*, identical to the first.[40] And herein lies the paradox: Why did Moses have to learn the Torah a *second time*? What could he have possibly learned that he didn't already know?

Torah study is different from any other wisdom. It speaks to every individual in accordance *with his needs*. It purifies, it elevates, it is life transforming. But now that the sin of the Golden Calf had taken place and the nation had fallen from its exalted height, it would have to be taught on a different level. So it is not that something was, God forbid, lacking in *Moshe Rabbeinu* that made it necessary for him to re-learn the Torah, but rather, something was *lacking in the people*. Therefore, *Moshe Rabbeinu* once again spent 40 days and 40 nights learning the Torah so that he might better meet the needs of a nation that had fallen from its pristine state.

Herein lies a lesson for all of us. We should never consider it beneath us to teach someone who is not on our level. If *Moshe Rabbeinu* was willing to spend 40 days and 40 nights just to learn how to best explain the Torah to us in our fallen state, how much more must we reach out to our brethren who are distant from Torah. Let us remember that no matter at what station in life we might find ourselves Torah is always there to heal us and elevate us.

In the end, however, our Sages teach us that God gave the Torah to Moses *as a gift*.[41] So even when a person doesn't quite understand, if he demonstrates a sincere desire, a yearning, a passion to learn, God will do the rest and give the Torah to him as a *gift*.

---

40. Ibid. 34:1.
41. Ibid. 31:18.

This lesson is true. However, after the sin of the Golden Calf, the capacity of everyone — including Moses — was diminished spiritually. This notwithstanding, Moses had to adjust and assimilate Torah to the new level — with greater effort.

PARASHAS VAYAKHEL

WE NEED ONLY WILL IT AND IT SHALL BE

> Every man whose heart inspired him came; and everyone whose spirit motivated him brought the portion of Hashem for the work of the Tent of the Meeting, for all its labor and for the sacred vestments.
>
> *Exodus* 35:21

The previous *parshiyos* have dealt with the construction of the Tabernacle and all the various vessels and furnishings therein. God commissioned these articles with specific measurements and designs, and the people were responsible for their execution. The question that must occur to all of us is how it was possible for a nation of slaves who for generations had been in bondage, and who had no artisans among them, to create such an intricate and magnificent structure as the Tabernacle. Where did they gain the know-how and the experience?

The answer is to be found in this *parashah*: "Every man *whose heart inspired him* came ...." If we truly desire to fulfill the will of God, if our hearts burn with fervor for His sake, then God will remove all obstacles from our paths, and enable us to achieve the impossible. We have an enormous power within ourselves of which we are not even aware, and that is faith. Indeed, if we have faith in our Heavenly Father and seek to fulfill His will, He will enable us to tap energies and abilities that we didn't even know we possessed. We need only act upon our dreams and they may well become reality.

We see this throughout history. Consider Bitya, the daughter of Pharaoh, who went to the Nile to bathe.[42] She saw the basket in which the infant Moses was hidden, floating in the water. She attempted to save him, but her arms couldn't reach the basket. Nevertheless, she extended her hand, and when God beheld her genuine yearning to save the infant's life, He miraculously allowed her arms to extend and bring the basket to shore.

In the days of King Saul, the malevolent Philistine giant Goliath came to menace the Jewish people.[43] The nation froze in terror. King Saul offered his personal armor to anyone who would battle the monster, but no one had the courage to take up the challenge except David, the young shepherd. Saul was much taller than David, and it was ludicrous to imagine that he could wear Saul's armor, but miraculously, when David donned that armor, it fit like a glove! There are many more such examples, but the teaching that we must absorb is that if our hearts soar with faith and love of God — if we truly desire to serve Him — miracles can take place and God will enable us to achieve that which only yesterday appeared impossible. Let us never feel intimidated when undertaking mitzvos. If we truly desire it, God can give us wings to soar and energy to accomplish our task.

---

42. *Exodus* 2:5ff.
43. *I Samuel*, Chapter 17.

Converting Liabilities Into Assets

In the opening verse, *"Vayakhel Moshe* — Moses assembled,"[44] Moses gathers the entire congregation of the Jewish people. The word *"Vayakhel"* gives us pause. Usually the text reads "Moses spoke" or "Moses commanded." However, *"Vayakhel"* was the rallying cry calling the people to fashion the Golden Calf, and now the time had come to make *tikun* — to rectify that grievous wrong. *The very same words* that enticed the nation to sin are now used to summon them to perform the sacred task of constructing the Tabernacle. Thus, the *"Vayakhel"* of the Tabernacle comes to make atonement for the *"Vayakhel"* of the Golden Calf; that is the true essence of *teshuvah* — to convert our sins into mitzvos and to harness all our energies in the service of God. For example, if one was in the habit of speaking *lashon hara* and has an awakening — a moment of truth — he should not retreat into silence, but rather now use the very same energy with which he formerly maligned others to convey words of Torah, *chesed*, kindness, and blessing.

Your Name and Your Faith

Bezalel was chosen to be the master architect of the Tabernacle. He had expertise in all crafts, and in speaking of him, the Torah states, "See, Hashem has proclaimed **by name** Bezalel, son of Uri, son of Hur, of the Tribe of Judah."[45] What is the significance of that list of names?

Every person has three names: one given to him by his parents, one by which others call him, and the third, which he earns for himself ... **and that third name surpasses them all**. Bezalel was filled with such an all-consuming desire to build the Tabernacle, to serve God, that he was able to master every craft that was required

---

44. *Exodus* 35:1.
45. Ibid. 35:30.

for its construction. His name, which means *"B'tzeil Keil* — In the Shadow of God," reflects this desire. When a man truly yearns to fulfill Hashem's Will, he will transcend himself and achieve that which at first appears impossible. Through his own efforts, Bezalel earned his name.

Similarly, if we place our trust in God, if we truly wish to grasp the wisdom of the Torah and not allow those desires to remain unfulfilled, we will succeed in mastering the wisdom of Torah and convert our homes into sanctuaries of peace and harmony from which God's light shall shine forth.

We find this concept of faith reinforced throughout the *parashah*. In regard to the commandment of observing the Sabbath it is written, *"Six days work shall be done."*[46] It would seem to be more appropriate for the text to state, *"For six days **you** shall work ...,"* but the Torah teaches us a profound lesson: If we have faith and we place our trust in the Almighty, then, indeed, our work will be done in six days. God will make it happen. But if we lack that faith, then we will never know the sweet freedom of Shabbos; our minds will never be at rest because we will always be worried that we are forfeiting some great opportunities ... always feeling that there is still more work to be done.

This obsession with "more" is one of the great dilemmas of modern man. We have become slaves to our needs and have allowed greed to rob us of our peace of mind. The Torah teaches us that our work, our success, come from *above*. We are very much like a toddler who sits in his daddy's car with a toy steering wheel and believe that he is actually driving.

Now, it's one thing for a toddler to believe this, but it's pathetic when adults entertain such illusions. The success or failure of our livelihoods is preordained by God, so we should never consider that keeping the Sabbath might diminish our income. Indeed, just the opposite is true. God promises: "Keep My Sabbath and the work shall be done."

---

46. Ibid. 35:2.

PARASHAS PEKUDEI

Reinventing Yourself

There are many levels on which we can perceive the construction of the Tabernacle. In a sense, we are all sanctuaries in microcosm, for within each of us there is a spark of God. Therefore, we must study every aspect of the construction of the Tabernacle so that we may realize our spiritual potential.

It is written, "And Moses erected the Tabernacle."[47] Our Sages teach that the dedication of the Tabernacle lasted seven days, during which time, Moses *erected and dismantled* the Tabernacle every day. It was only on the eighth day that he allowed it to stand. At

---

47. Ibid. 40:18.

first glance, the reason for this may be difficult to understand, but therein is to be found a life-transforming teaching. Every time Moses went through the process of erecting and dismantling, he invested us with the strength to *rebuild ourselves*: *to learn from our failures* and *reinvent ourselves* so that we might reach our spiritual potential. *Moshe Rabbeinu* imparted to us a most powerful lesson: *Failures* can be converted into *growth* and *weaknesses* can be transformed into *strengths*, and that's what life's challenges are all about.

Further study of the building of the Tabernacle calls our attention to the fact that every time an activity was carried out for the Tabernacle, it is followed by the phrase, "As Hashem commanded Moses."[48] If we truly desire to live as Jews, we must commit ourselves to do that which God *commanded Moses*. Our Torah is a perfect instruction manual which addresses every detail of our lives, and if we follow it, we will be insulated from the corrosive influences of our society and culture. It's very much like finding an oasis in a hostile desert or discovering an island in a turbulent sea. Building a Tabernacle within ourselves assures our Jewish survival and fulfillment.

No Coincidences: Our Prayers Are Rooted in the Sanctuary

It is not by coincidence that the "Silent Devotion" that we recite thrice daily is called *"Shemoneh Esrei* — Eighteen Benedictions," for 18 times the phrase, "As Hashem commanded Moses" is repeated, and it is upon this foundation that our Sages built the *Amidah* — the Silent Meditation, which is comprised of 18 blessings. But the question remains: Why was it necessary to say, "Hashem commanded *Moses*"? Would it not have sufficed to say, "The Jewish people did as Hashem commanded"? Why the emphasis on Moses?

---

48. Ibid. 39:1 et al.

Herein lies the key to Jewish survival. Moses symbolizes *Daas Torah* — faith in our Torah Sages. The knowledge had to be transmitted through Moses so that, for all time, we should seek guidance from our Torah teachers, for that is the only way in which authentic Torah can be transmitted from generation to generation.

This concept is reinforced throughout the *parashah*: Verse 40:18 states, "Moses erected the Tabernacle." Why was it specifically Moses who had to fulfill this sacred task? Moreover, no one, not even Moses, knew how to erect the Tabernacle. Hashem Himself had to show him, and here again, is a lesson for us: *Only Moses, our Torah leader*, could invest the Tabernacle with sanctity. Similarly, in every generation, it is our Torah leaders who have the responsibility to impart to us the sanctity and eternity of the Torah. This is not to say that we cannot be innovative and use our ingenuity, *but that ingenuity must also be in consonance with the teachings of Daas Torah —* **the Torah of Moses as transmitted through our Sages.**

ONE HUNDRED BLESSINGS

We are called upon to pronounce 100 blessings each and every day, for there were 100 sockets that held up the planks of the Sanctuary walls. Even as the sockets formed the foundation of the physical Tabernacle, so too the 100 blessings that we say in our prayers are the foundation of our internal Tabernacle. The word for *socket* in Hebrew is *adon*, which also means "master." When we recite our blessings, we proclaim God as the Master of our lives and of the universe.

We might wonder how it is possible to make 100 blessings every day, but if we recite our daily prayers, if we makes a conscious effort to bless God prior to and after eating and drinking and for the performance of our bodily functions, we will discover that the 100 blessings are easily reached. And now, just consider how blessed we are to have within our reach a way of elevating our lives through 100 blessings and thus converting ourselves into a sanctuary, and what a pity it would be to live our lives unaware of this privilege.

WE NEED NEVER FEAR

We live in a menacing and uncertain world, a world which our Sages foretold and described as *Ikvesa D'Meshicha* — the Footsteps of Messiah (the period preceding the Messianic period). Our Sages predicted that during this time, all our cherished icons would fail us and our world would crumble before our very eyes. Nationally and internationally, we will be plagued by political and economic chaos. Internally, our families will become fragmented and, in place of serenity and love, turbulence and factionalism will prevail. But if we build a sanctuary within ourselves, we will be insulated from these plagues.

Thus, the concluding passage of the *parashah* teaches us that "the cloud of God would be on the Tabernacle by day and fire would be on it by night ...."[49] This teaching reminds us that if we make our lives into sanctuaries, the cloud of God will always protect us by day, and the fire of God — the light of Torah — will illuminate our darkness ... so we need never fear.

NEVER TAKE ANYTHING FOR GRANTED

It is written that when the Jewish people completed their work, Moses *blessed* the nation.[50] Here again, we witness the eternity of Moses' words, for the blessing that he proclaimed is familiar to us from *Psalms* 90:17 — a prayer that we say every night before we go to sleep, a prayer that is forever on our lips:

---

49. Ibid. 40:38
50. Ibid. 39:43.

"*Vi'hi noam* — May the pleasantness of the Lord our God be upon us …." We also learn from Moses' blessing that we must express *hakaras hatov* (appreciation), for a blessing is also an expression of gratitude.

We might ask, however, that since the Jewish people were only fulfilling God's commandments, carrying out their responsibilities, why was it necessary to thank them? Here, again, is a teaching to guide us for all time. We are not to take anything for granted. Every deed, every act must be acknowledged with thanks and blessing. So, for example, when the Kohen completes his blessing of the congregation, we say to him, "*Yasher Koach* — Thank you," although that is his responsibility and he is required to do it. Saying thank you enables us to develop a greater appreciation for life and to acknowledge the fact that we are *indebted* and *must give back to the world*.

This awareness is critical in our entitlement-oriented culture, in which we have come to believe that everything is coming to us. Our Torah's emphasis on indebtedness sensitizes us to our responsibility to give back. Indeed, the words *modim* and *l'hodos*, both meaning *thanks* in Hebrew, have a double meaning. They also connote "admission," for *thanks* is an *admission*, an acknowledgment of our dependence on the kindness of others. For many, it is difficult to concede their vulnerability. They convince themselves that they are "self-made" and not beholden to anyone. Such an attitude is self-destructive. It inhibits meaningful relationships, destroys marriages, and bars people from coming close to God.

ספר ויקרא

THE BOOK OF
Leviticus

PARASHAS VAYIKRA

THE MEANING OF SACRIFICE

In discussing a man's obligation to offer sacrifices, the Torah departs from its usual expression of referring to *man* as "*ish*"; and instead uses the word "Adam." The passage also begins with the singular verb, "*yakriv* — [he] brings," and then continues with the plural form, "*takrivu* — you shall bring." There is a profound reason for these word choices, for when a person brings a sacrifice to God, he must follow the example of the very first man, Adam, whose offerings were unblemished, free of the slightest taint of dishonesty. Since he was the only person in the world, there was no one he could have deceived or taken advantage of.

There are many ways in which we attempt to rationalize deception and dishonesty. When we allow arrogance to take hold of us and we feel superior to others, we also convince ourselves that our needs are greater than theirs and, therefore, we are entitled to that which belongs to them. That is yet another reason why, when the Torah instructs us regarding sacrifices, it refers to the individual as "Adam," evoking the memory of the first man, who, by virtue of the fact that he was the *first* and *only* one, could not have been guilty of such rationalizations. Even as Adam understood that everything that he possessed came from God, so we, too, must be aware of that fact and approach Him with clean hands. As the psalmist wrote: "Who may ascend the mountain of God ...? One with clean hands and a pure heart ...."[1]

The word for sacrifices is *"korbanos,"* derived from the word *"karov* — to come near," teaching us that if we wish to renew our relationship with our Heavenly Father, we must be prepared to sacrifice for His sake, and if we do so, we will discover that the more we give of ourselves, the closer to God we will feel.

MAKE HIS WILL YOUR WILL

In today's self-focused culture, we have been led to believe that our priority must be to ensure our own happiness. Sacrifice — renunciation of self — has become an alien concept. Many people live for themselves and focus on their own needs. All too often, such parents do not sacrifice for their children and such children do not sacrifice for their parents. And this holds true for all their relationships, including those between husband and wife. It is most blatantly evident, however, in their relationship with God. People make demands upon Him, but are not prepared to give back. "Why, why?" they ask when things do not turn out as they had anticipated ... and it never occurs to them that God may also be asking *Why?* "Indeed, why have you failed to fulfill My commandments? Why have you abandoned My Torah?"

But they never hear the "Why" of God and hear only their own cry.

---

1. *Psalms* 24:3-4.

So, let us search our hearts and ask, *How does God see me? How do I measure up? How much have I sacrificed for His sake? Have I made His will my own?* And if you do not feel as close to Him as you would like, if you do not feel faith motivating your life, ask yourself, *Have I offered Him my heart? Have I sacrificed?*

WE CAN ALL MAKE A DIFFERENCE

The question still remains: Why is there a change from the singular to the plural when the Torah discusses bringing this offering? Here, too, is an instructive lesson for all generations. The passage starts out in the singular because, when a man sins, he believes that his transgressions impact only upon him. But the Torah teaches that that which we do as individuals impacts on everyone and everything around us. Therefore, our Sages compare our predicament as a nation to passengers on a ship. If one should bore a hole under his seat, in vain does he protest, "This is *my* business; the hole is under *my* seat!" His "personal" hole will cause the entire ship, with all its passengers, to sink. The reverse is also true. Repentance and mitzvos not only elevate us as individuals, but they also enrich our community, our nation.

Thus, the passage starts with the singular and ends with the plural, reminding us that our families and our communities are only as strong as the individuals who form them. This is a lesson that can help us in our search for meaning and can validate our lives. We all have a need to make a difference, but we often feel futile in our anonymity and wonder what possible impact we can have. *Parashas Vayikra* reminds us that through our every word, our every deed, we have the power to either elevate or diminish the world. If we bear that in mind, we will find it easier to meet life's challenges with honor and dignity.

In Humility We Find True Greatness

The *parashah* opens with the words, "*VAYIKRa el Moshe* — "And He [God] called to Moses ...." In a Torah Scroll, the letter *aleph* in the word *vayikra* is written in a smaller size than the rest of the Torah, teaching us that Moses was keenly aware of his unworthiness in being summoned by God. The word *vayikra*, without the *aleph*, means that God *chanced* to speak to Moses, not that God called him lovingly. Because of his humility, Moses wrote the *aleph* small, to imply that he was less than worthy. Moses was *the most humble of all men*, but, paradoxically, he was also the greatest. True humility does not imply lack of confidence or unawareness of our God-given talents; rather, it is an affirmation of those Divine gifts. The realization that everything that we possess was given to us by the Almighty and therefore must be wisely used and returned to Him unblemished is most humbling.

A great Sage once illustrated this concept by comparing a person to an impoverished woman who borrows a magnificent gown to wear to a wedding. She cannot be arrogant about the dress, lovely as it is, for she knows that it is not hers and she will soon have to return it in perfect condition. Similarly, the gifts with which God endows us were given to us on loan, and that realization is a very humbling experience. Moses never lost sight of that awareness and it is that which rendered him the humblest of all men. We must bear in mind that the gifts with which we were endowed were not bequeathed to us for our own self-aggrandizement, but for the benefit of mankind. If we realize that unfortunately we have misused or abused those gifts, we will also realize how misplaced and foolish are all feelings of arrogance.

THE CALL OF GOD IS THE CALL OF LOVE

This portion commences with God teaching Moses all the laws concerning the service in the Tabernacle and Temple. In the very first verse, before Hashem speaks to Moses, the Torah teaches that the Almighty first *called* to Moses; *only then* did He *speak* to him.[2] We might ask, why did Hashem first have to call Moses? In most cases, the verse simply announces, "And God *spoke* to Moses ...."

The Torah is demonstrating a very important lesson here. Teaching Torah must always be preceded by a *call* that is an expression of love, concern, and closeness. Only when such a relationship has been formed, only when such bonding takes place, can the Torah teacher have a positive impact on his disciples. Thus, this passage teaches us a basic principle of imparting wisdom: The Torah teacher, whether a professional or a parent, must convey God's word with *love*, warmth, and kindness. Only thus will he succeed and only thus will the child/student absorb the teaching and make it a permanent part of his life's mission.

---

2. *Leviticus* 1:1.

PARASHAS TZAV

What You Wear Matters

In this *parashah*, we learn that after the Kohen separated the ashes of the burnt-offering from the Altar, he had to change out of his priestly garments before removing the ashes from the camp.[3] This imparts a lesson in *derech eretz* (respect and proper conduct). The Kohen is not to wear the same clothing when he carries away the ashes as he does when he performs his service of God. We are not to serve our God in the very same garments in which we do menial chores. So, for example, women should change their attire before lighting candles in honor of the Sabbath and holidays. This is a teaching for all of us: We must all make a conscious effort to dress respectfully when occupied with prayer. This rule applies

---

3. Ibid. 6:3-5.

not only when we enter the synagogue, but also in the privacy of our homes. "Know before Whom you stand ..."[4] is the teaching of our Sages. Even as we would be appalled at the thought of visiting royalty in work clothes or in an unkempt manner, so should we refrain from approaching God when inappropriately dressed. Such discipline will help us to keep focused on our prayers.

THE POWER OF LOVE

The last chapter of this *parashah* contains a puzzling passage, "This is the thing that Hashem commanded to be done ...,"[5] which refers to the commandment to inaugurate the Tabernacle. We suggest that the previous verse sheds light on what is needed to sanctify the Tabernacle and Jewish life in general. God instructed Moses to gather the entire assembly of the Jewish people "to the entrance to the Tent of the Meeting," and herein lies the explanation, which, in and of itself, is paradoxical. Although the area at the entrance was very small and could not contain many people, nevertheless, miraculously, there was ample room for everyone.

Through this phenomenon, the Torah teaches us a lesson that speaks for all time: When true love prevails among people, no room, no place is too small. On the other hand, when contention and animosity fill hearts, then no space is big enough. The most majestic palace cannot accommodate those who are not at peace with one another. Thus, the meaning of the passage becomes clear: "This is the thing that Hashem commanded to be done" — *to reach out with love, kindness, and understanding. If we do so, then even the smallest, most limited space will miraculously expand. That is the power of love. But where love is missing, even a palatial villa will not suffice.*

---

4. *Berachos* 28b.
5. *Leviticus* 8:5.

Download a Miracle

We hear people express a secret wish: *If only I could download a miracle; if only God could help me; if only I could connect with Him.* Well, the truth is that we *can* connect with the Almighty. As a matter of fact, He is waiting for us to call. As for His miracles: They are all about us, if only we had the vision to see them.

In this *parashah*, we discover how to make that direct call to God, and we see this theme running throughout the *parashah*: "And Moses said, 'This is the thing that Hashem has commanded you to do — then the glory of Hashem will appear to you.'"[6] If we wish to have a connection with God, if we wish Him to respond to our prayers, if we truly desire those miracles, then we have to do that which God commanded. There is nothing revolutionary about this concept, but somehow, this simple truth seems to elude us, for while we profess belief in God, we want to follow our own inclinations and we expect God to comply with our desires. We convince ourselves that it doesn't matter to God what we do, so long as we are happy with ourselves, we are "good people," and our hearts are in the right place, but the Torah specifically states that, if we wish the glory of God to appear to us, then we have to do *that which God has commanded.*

In our interaction with people, we understand this basic principle. For example, were you to hold an open house on Sunday afternoon from 1 to 5 o'clock, and someone barged in on Monday morning, saying, "This is a more convenient time for me to visit," you would be furious, and rightly so. And yet, too often, that is exactly what we do in our relationship with God. We choose to ignore His wishes; we indulge our own desires and expect Him to be pleased.

---

6. Ibid. 9:6.

Would Hashem Approve?

Later in the *parashah*, we find yet another dimension to this concept of fulfilling the will of God that we would all do well to remember and act upon. Aaron asks a question that it behooves us all to ask: "Would Hashem approve?"[7]

Normally, when performing a mitzvah, the paramount question to ask is, "Am I performing this mitzvah in accordance with *halachah*, according to the letter of the law?" But Aaron, the High Priest, went yet a step further. He understood that not only must we fulfill the mitzvah according to God's Law, but we must do so in a manner that will be pleasing to our Creator. This teaching applies to every aspect of our lives. Before making decisions, before taking any steps, ask yourself that simple, but piercing question, *Would Hashem approve?* Is this the way God would want me to live? Would He be pleased with my actions? Would He approve of my words?

If we learn to do this, then our relationship with God will not be based strictly on obligation, but rather, on love. A child who truly loves his parents desires to please them and give them *nachas*. Should we not desire to give our Heavenly Father *nachas*? Should we not express our love for Him?

So if we wish to connect with God, if we wish to download miracles and have His glory bless us, we need only follow His commandments, fulfill them as He proscribed, go the extra mile and ask, *"Is the manner in which I am performing the mitzvos pleasing to my Creator, my God?"*

Three Little Words

Our mother, Rebbetzin Esther Jungreis, often relates the story of the *Maggid* of *Kelm* — the electrifying inspirational preacher of the *shtetl* of Kelm who lived in Lithuania in the 19th century. One day he challenged his congrega-

---

7. Ibid. 10:14.

tion with amazing questions. "If, by some miracle, God allowed all those who are buried in the cemetery of Kelm to get up for half an hour, what do you think they would do? Where would they go? What would they say?"

Consider these questions, ponder them, and ask yourself, *What would I do? Where would I go? What would I say if I had just half an hour in this world?* And what if, instead of half an hour, you were told that your wife or your husband had just six months to live. How would you relate to her or him?

On 9/11 we found out. For perhaps the first time in history, we have audio messages from multitudes of people who were trapped in the Twin Towers and knew that their last moments were near. Miraculously, these tragic victims were able to get through on their cell phones and call their families. What do you think they said? What was their last will and testament?

Amazingly, not one of them spoke about business, money, or any other such matters ... but they each said three little words: "I love you." "I love you, my husband"; "I love you, my wife"; "I love you, my children"; "I love you, Mom"; "I love you, Dad"; "I love you, Grandma"; "I love you, Grandpa" ... "I love you."

So, if we have more than half an hour on this planet, should we not say *I love you* before it's too late?

When you study Torah, you learn to value the preciousness of time and try to live each day as if it was your last. You learn to appreciate and safeguard the simple gifts with which God has endowed you, gifts like love, gifts that you come to realize are not so simple after all.

DEDICATE YOURSELF

Although we no longer have the Temple, the laws concerning the Service are as meaningful today as they were yesterday. Our Sages teach that each and every one of us is a Temple in microcosm. If we dedicate our lives to God and His commandments, we become holy, but if we transgress, we defile ourselves. When we repent, however, we recreate ourselves, and, in essence, rebuild the Temple within our souls. In that re-creation we touch sanctity.

Today, we no longer have Temple offerings, but we can offer sacrifices through acts of *mesiras nefesh* (self-sacrifice), tapping deep within our hearts and dedicating our lives to a higher purpose: to serve our people and to worship God. Self-sacrifice is the stuff of which goodness and greatness are made. This ability is not limited to the few, but is within reach of each and every one of us. We need only be determined to place our trust in God and obey His commandments.

THE MENIAL IS ALSO SACRED

The question still remains: Why didn't the Torah designate some priests to perform the service and others to remove the ashes from the camp, so that it would have been unnecessary for the Kohen to change garments?

The Torah wants to impress upon us that when it comes to serving Hashem, every mitzvah is sacred. Removing the ashes from the camp is no less holy a calling than performing the service. Within this teaching we once again find an important message, one that is especially valid during the pre-Passover season when we are called upon to thoroughly clean our homes — a task that can be very tedious. If we bear in mind that this menial chore is also the service of God, we will be energized and undertake our task with zeal and enthusiasm. However, it is not only before Passover that this teaching should sustain us, but throughout the year. There are always those who volunteer for glamorous jobs, for chairmanships that lend honor and distinction, but when it comes to nitty-gritty, menial tasks, there are all-too-few candidates. At such times, it is important for us to recall the Kohen who removed the ashes, and remember that that too was the service of God; all mitzvos are equally honorable.

PARASHAS SHEMINI

A SILENCE MORE POWERFUL THAN WORDS

On the very day that the dedication of the Temple took place, Nadab and Abihu, the two noble sons of Aaron the High Priest, suddenly perished. The Torah describes the reaction of Aaron simply as *"vayidom Aharon"*[8] meaning that Aaron remained silent. The word *vayidom* usually refers to a *domeim*, an inanimate object that is incapable of speaking. This teaches us that while we may be able to control our external responses, in our hearts we are often in turmoil, and our facial expressions betray our feelings. Aaron's faith in the justice and compassion of God and in the eternity of the soul was so all encompassing, that even as an

---

8. Ibid. 10:3.

inanimate object is silent, he too was silent in his heart. His trust in God was so complete that he found peace in the knowledge that his sons' deaths were the Will of God; thus, *vayidom Aharon*, Aaron was silent.

Aaron's faith was so powerful that it transcended the generations and speaks to us for all time. Whether we experience personal or national tragedy, we recall and are sustained by Aaron's *vayidom*. Our faith, even as Aaron's, remains constant. Consider only those who survived the unspeakable calamity of the Holocaust. We recall our own parents and grandparents: Our grandfather, Rabbi Avraham HaLevi Jungreis, *zt"l*, who saw his entire family wiped out in the gas chambers of Auschwitz, remained the only surviving son of his noble rabbinic family. Upon arriving on these shores in 1947, he built a yeshivah, saying, "We will rekindle the light of the Torah that the Nazis tried to extinguish." Our father, HaRav Meshulem HaLevi Jungreis, *zt"l*, saw his entire family perish, but continued their lifework by teaching Torah to new generations of American Jews; and our mother, Rebbetzin Esther Jungreis, may she have length of days, founded Hineni at a time when the concept of Jewish outreach was virtually unknown in the world.

This same story was repeated by countless survivors, and today, the Torah academies of the *shtetls* of Europe are to be found in the United States, England, and Israel. Yes, the faith of Aaron the High Priest has transcended the generations and has infused us with strength and the ability to go on.

WHOSE WILL?

The question still remains: Why did this terrible calamity befall Aaron's two sons?

The explanation that the Torah offers is that they (the two sons) "brought before Hashem an *alien fire* that He had not commanded ...."[9]

---

9. Ibid. 10:1.

The strength of our people, our ability to triumph against all odds, can be found in the fact that we never deviated from the Divine commandments. While Nadab and Abihu were most sincere in their desire to serve God, they nevertheless desired to do so *in their own way* and bring *their own fire* rather than the one commanded by our Torah. Through their tragic deaths, the Torah warns us of the terrible consequences that can result from departing from God's commandments. No matter how lofty our intentions may be, if our service does not conform to God's Will, it is unacceptable. Our God is One, our Torah is One, and our worship must mirror that Oneness. It cannot be based upon our personal needs or emotions. Precisely because our Torah is from God, it reflects *His Will* and *not ours*. The Torah is not a set of laws that can be tampered with or altered to suit our desires or to accommodate our weaknesses.

This teaching is of special significance to our generation. In our egalitarian society, we have come to believe that we have the right to fashion *our own* mode of worship, to contrive *our own rituals*, and to author *our own* ceremonies. We have come to believe that *our sincerity makes everything right*. But if our service does not reflect God's Will, *whom are we worshiping? Are we not worshiping ourselves rather than our Heavenly Father*? Had our ancestors fashioned their own mode of worship, there would, God forbid, have been no faith for us to inherit. The strength of our people is to be found precisely in the fact that the very same fire that illuminated our souls at Mt. Sinai continues to shed light for us today.

Very often, we encounter people who challenge us, saying, "If you can give me a good reason why I should keep the commandments, I'll consider it." *What better reason can there be than that God commanded us to keep them?*

PARASHAS TAZRIA-METZORA

THE POWER OF SPEECH: DEATH AND LIFE ARE IN THE TONGUE

This week's *parashah* deals with the illness of *tzaraas* (spiritual leprosy), which in Biblical times afflicted those who spoke *lashon hara*. Most people are under the impression that *lashon hara* connotes speech containing fabrications regarding others, but that is erroneous. *All evil, derogatory talk falls under the category of lashon hara,* even if it is the truth.

Our Torah regards the sin of *lashon hara* as so heinous that those who were guilty of it succumbed to a skin disease known as *"tzaraas."* Since this was a spiritual ailment (albeit with physical manifestations), the afflicted had to be brought before Aaron the High Priest or his descendants, rather than to a physician, for examination and healing.[10]

The question that must occur to us is why the person must be brought, specifically, before Aaron the High Priest. What was so special about him that enabled him to examine and cure the individual who spoke *lashon hara?*

Lashon hara creates divisiveness; it generates animosity and contempt, forces that are antithetic to harmony and well-being. Aaron the High Priest loved people with such intensity that he was able to neutralize those negative forces. *Ethics of the Fathers* 1:12 states, "Aaron loved peace and pursued peace." When he saw two people in conflict, he would approach each of them individually and say, "You know, your friend truly regrets this altercation. As a matter of fact, he beseeched me to approach you on his behalf. He loves you and wants to make peace with you." He would then repeat the very same message to the other party involved and thus would appease them and make peace. To appreciate the awesomeness of Aaron's deed, contrast his way to that which has unfortunately become the norm in our society, in which people are only too happy to repeat gossip and thus further incite and deepen conflicts between others. Throughout his life, Aaron was determined to cement ties and bring harmony and love to fragmented families and broken relationships. When Aaron died, all of Israel, the entire nation, wept and mourned, for at one time or another, everyone had been touched by his awesome love and his passionate commitment to peace, and they realized that that gift was irreplaceable.

AARON'S LEGACY

Perhaps now we can better appreciate why Aaron's descendants were designated to bless the Jewish people through *Bircas HaKohanim* (the Priestly Blessings). Prior to pronouncing these benedictions, the priests are commanded to say,

---

10. Ibid. 13:12.

"Blessed are You, O Lord our God, Who has *sanctified us with the holiness of Aaron* and commanded us to bless His people, Israel, with *love.*" What is the holiness of Aaron? It is the total devotion and commitment that Aaron felt for each and every Jew, a commitment summarized in one little word: *b'ahavah* — with love. It is Aaron's love that is the unique hallmark of all his descendants, and it is that love that is the most vital qualification for imparting blessing.

CAN *LASHON HARA* EVER BE JUSTIFIED?

There are those who would justify speaking *lashon hara* by claiming that they are just being honest and forthright and telling the *truth*. But Aaron taught us that there are times when truth must take a back seat, for we can not and dare not put others to shame. We do have specific laws regarding giving honest information concerning *shidduchim* and business partnerships so that people are not misled. However, even in such cases, we must know how to phrase our words ... what to reveal and what to hold back ... and a Torah authority should be consulted before information is shared.

Lashon hara is such a serious infraction that there are 14 positive commandments and 17 negative commandments regarding it. The great sage, the Chofetz Chaim, warned that *lashon hara* is the most destructive of all sins, for it literally destroys people. Indeed, "*death and life are in the tongue.*"[11] God created us in such a way that our own organs serve to remind us to be aware of the potential danger inherent in our tongues. Our organs are either external (eyes, ears, etc.) or internal (kidneys, heart, lungs, etc.). The tongue is the *only* organ that is both internal and external. To protect it from misuse, God gave us two gates to guard it: our teeth and our lips, reminding us that, before we use our tongues, we should shut the gates

---

11. See *Proverbs* 18:21: "Death and life are in the power of the tongue ...."

and carefully consider whether we should allow our tongues to speak or whether it would be wiser to remain silent and keep the gates closed.

Guard That Which Enters and Leaves Your Mouth

Parashas *Tazria* and *Metzora* are usually read together. The word *metzora* is a combination of two words, *motzei* and *ra*, meaning, *to speak evil of others*. The juxtaposition of these *parshiyos* to *Parashas Shemini* is very instructive, for in the previous *parashah* we studied not only the dangers of speaking *lashon hara*, but about forbidden, non-kosher foods as well. By placing these two *parshiyos* — forbidden food and *lashon hara* — next to each other, the Torah reminds us that not only must we be careful about that which *enters* our mouths (that which we eat), but we must be equally careful about that which *comes forth* from our lips (that which we say). We must be ever on guard not to cause pain to anyone with our words. Since this is no small achievement, we pray for God's help and guidance. Therefore, we conclude every *Amidah* service with those awesome words, "My God, guard my tongue from evil and my lips from speaking deceitfully."[12]

Lashon hara is the equivalent of all three cardinal sins, a concept that might be difficult for us to absorb. In the 21st century, gossip has become a profession. Newspapers employ gossip columnists. Gossip columnists have social cachet and are very much sought after by hostesses and the media, and some of the biggest bestsellers are based on gossip. Our Torah laws are like a beacon of light that illuminates our path and reminds us of our higher calling. Speech is a Divine gift, given only to man. To abuse that gift is to betray that trust.

To what extent we must go to avoid *lashon hara* can be learned from Miriam, the prophetess, who in good faith criticized her

---

12. See *Psalms* 34:14.

younger brother Moses, and for those seemingly innocent words, was afflicted with *tzaraas*. The Torah commands us to *remember* what happened to Miriam and be cautious with our words even when we believe that we are speaking for the benefit of another.

THE HEALING EFFECTS OF THE TORAH

This shall be the Torah [Law] of the *metzora*."[13] A *metzora* is someone who sins by speaking *lashon hara*. Interestingly, the word "Torah" is invoked five times in this regard, teaching us that he who speaks evil about others is considered as if he had transgressed all Five Books of the Torah. Surely, this should impress upon each and every one of us the severity of this transgression.

Contrast this to the childish rhyme that is so popular in our culture: Sticks and stones may break my bones, but words will never harm me.

Regarding this rhyme, our mother, Rebbetzin Esther Jungreis, would often say that reality proves just the opposite. To mend broken bones, one can always consult an orthopedist, but where can one go with a broken heart? Who can heal scars on the soul?

REMORSE: INDICATION OF TRUE SINCERITY

"This **shall be** the law of the *metzora*" is written in the future tense, teaching us that feelings of remorse and a resolve to refrain from speaking *lashon hora* must characterize the *metzora* even **after** he goes through his purification process. In time

---
13. *Leviticus* 14:2.

of crisis and pain, it is easy to make commitments of *teshuvah*, but maintaining those commitments once the crisis has abated and healing has taken place is the true test of one's sincerity. How can a person hold on to his resolve and keep his promises? The answer is Torah study, the best maintenance program.

When Torah study is undertaken with purity of heart, it elevates, heals, and protects from spiritual malaise. God assures us of this, "I created the *yetzer hara* (the evil inclination), but I created the Torah as an antidote to it."[14]

---

14. *Kiddushin* 30b.

PARASHAS ACHAREI MOS– KEDOSHIM

Acharei Mos–Kedoshim focus on sanctity. We, the Jewish people, are not only mandated to adhere to God's commandments, but through these commandments, we sanctify ourselves and become holy. In these two *parshiyos*, which are usually read together, the Torah gives us specific instructions as to how we might attain that lofty goal. It is not only what we must *do* that is of concern; equally significant is that which we must *avoid* doing.

"Do not imitate the practice of the land of Egypt in which you dwelt, and do not imitate the practice of the land of Canaan to which I bring you, and do not follow their statutes."[15] And this applies to all lands of our sojourns.

It is always tempting to be part of the group — to follow the

---

15. *Leviticus* 18:30.

masses and to adopt that which is in vogue. Therefore, at the very outset of our history, Hashem warns us that if we are to survive as Jews, if we are to retain our faith, then we cannot imitate the ways of the nations among whom we dwell. Our morals, our ethics, are all rooted in Sinai and are not given to change, but the rules that regulate the lives of the nations, the laws by which they live, are in a constant state of flux. That which only yesterday was considered immoral may very well be accepted today, and this holds true for every aspect of life. Just consider the language that has become politically correct, the manner of dress that is termed "high fashion," the entertainment that is regarded as "culture," the manner in which the young are permitted to address their elders, the breakdown of our families, and you will see for yourself the wisdom of this prohibition.

But what if we don't see it? What if we are comfortable and have no objection to what society advocates? Then remember the concluding words of this passage: "Do not follow their statutes." The only way in which we, the Jewish people, have survived centuries of exile, the only way that we have maintained our Jewishness in a hostile world, the only way we have resisted the onslaught of assimilation was to cling tenaciously to our Torah laws and divorce ourselves from even those statutes to which at first glance we may have been drawn. Our way of life, our values, our morals and ethics are all rooted in Sinai and that Divine Voice from Sinai binds us eternally in every culture, in every century.

TRUST:
THE BASIS OF ALL RELATIONSHIPS

One of the mitzvos mentioned in this *parashah* is, "You shall not place a stumbling block before the blind."[16] This statement is not meant to be taken only literally; it also means that we must be careful not to give misleading advice.

---

16. Ibid. 19:14.

We also have to insure that we do not have hidden agendas and that our motivations for giving advice are pure. The question that must arise, however, is, why the Torah doesn't simply state that we are not permitted to mislead others. Why use this figure of speech, "place a stumbling block before the blind"?

The Torah wants to impart to us the seriousness and the importance of trust. Even as no sane individual would countenance tripping a blind person or allowing him to step in front of a moving vehicle, so too, misleading someone who is unaware is equally deplorable. We all know how painful it is to discover that we have been betrayed by people in whom we placed our trust, so we should take care not to do this to others. All relationships are built on trust. Neither individuals, nor families, nor societies can survive when trust is missing. When we come to this understanding and realize that deceiving or misleading someone is no different than allowing a blind person to walk into traffic, we will surely be more sensitive to every word that we pronounce.

THE GOLDEN RULE

Love your neighbor as yourself."[17] Rabbi Akiva proclaimed that this is a fundamental principle of the Torah, from which we learn how to relate to our fellow man. The question is asked whether it is possible to love another as we love ourselves. The great Chassidic master, the Baal Shem Tov, responded by reminding us that, even as we are aware that we have many faults and yet still love ourselves, similarly, we should feel kindly toward our fellow man and love him despite his faults.

Rambam (Maimonides) teaches that this commandment instructs us to love every Jew as ourselves, by acting lovingly toward them and being as careful of their feelings, their possessions, their money, and their dignity as we would our own. On the other hand, Ramban (Nachmanides) teaches that the Torah does not demand

---
17. Ibid. 19:18.

that we literally love someone as we love ourselves. As a matter of fact, we have a ruling that, in times of danger, our own lives take precedence. What God *does* demand is that we desire for others that which we desire for ourselves, and we *treat them with the same respect and consideration* as we want for ourselves.

Hillel the Elder paraphrased this commandment, saying, "What is hateful to you, do not inflict upon others," and instructed a would-be convert, "That is the entire Torah. Go and study it. The rest is commentary."

The Path to Holiness

Many people will tell you that while they may not be observant, they are spiritual. What exactly does that connote? Does it mean meditation? Vegetarianism? Jogging? It is none of the above, for all the aforementioned are focused on the self. In this week's *parashah*, we discover the meaning of spirituality. "*Vehiyisem li kedoshim, ki kadosh Ani Hashem* — You shall be holy for Me, for I Hashem am holy …"[18] is God's proclamation.

But can ordinary man aspire to holiness? Is that realistic? Yes, the Torah states, not only is it possible for him to attain such a goal, but *he has a mandate* to do so. Our *parashah* does not present this command as a theoretical concept, but it details the exact steps that we must take to realize that goal. As a result, most of the essence of the Torah is mentioned in this *parashah,* for it is through the adherence to these mitzvos that we can become holy. These mitzvos range from revering parents to loving our fellow man as ourselves; from refraining from taking vengeance to being on guard against gossip; from being kind to the stranger to paying the day worker his wages on that selfsame day; from keeping the Sabbath to not worshiping or fashioning idols, and many more; every aspect of life is addressed.

---

18. Ibid. 20:26.

Moreover, God commanded Moses to teach these commandments to the entire nation: *"Kol Adas Bnei Yisrael"* — every Jew had to be present to underscore the fact that sanctity cannot be attained through a hermitlike existence, nor through self-abnegation, meditation, or climbing the Himalayas, but only through reaching out to others in *chesed*, justice, consideration, and love, thereby bringing them and ourselves closer to Hashem.

ROAD MAP TO SANCTITY

The Torah never leaves anything to speculation, but provides us with a clear road map that shows us how to attain our goals. Our Sages outlined several paths, each leading to sanctity:

1) Separate yourself from that which is immoral and sinful.

Obviously, our Torah's definition of immorality and sin is a far cry from that which our 21st-century culture has come to accept as the norm. As responsible Jews, it behooves us to study exactly what "immoral and sinful" connote.

2) Sanctify yourself with that which is permitted.

Thus, we are charged to temper all our actions and words with discipline; i.e., we are permitted to eat, but not to be gluttons; we are permitted to shop, but not to be shopaholics; we are permitted to drink alcohol, but not to become drunk. Thus, we sanctify wine by making *Kiddush*.

3) To make God beloved through our deeds and words.

As Jews, we are charged with the responsibility of being ambassadors of God. Thus, we have a mandate to inspire people so that they might praise and love Him. By demonstrating kindness, refinement, and consideration, we bring honor and glory to God's Holy Name. And this does not only pertain to major world-shaking events, but to our everyday interactions as well, such as saying "thank you" to a clerk in a store or to a flight attendant, giving someone the right of way when driving, and not grabbing someone else's parking space — and there are myriad other examples.

4) Even as God is compassionate and forgiving, we must be compassionate and forgiving.

We must strive to emulate God's attributes of mercy and forgiveness in our interpersonal relationships, for therein are to be found the essence of holiness.

At first glance, this may appear to be the most difficult of all, but if we bear in mind that we want God to forgive us for our trespasses, then surely, we must also be capable of saying those two powerful words, "I forgive."

PARASHAS EMOR

Reaching Beyond Yourself

In the opening verse of our *parashah*, God instructs Moses, "Say to the Kohanim …"[19] and, in *that very same verse*, God once again repeats the command, "Say to them …."

Since there is no redundancy in the Torah, we must try to decipher the meaning of this repetition. The Torah is teaching us that once Moses taught the Kohanim the special commandments that only they were permitted to perform, God tells Moses to repeat the other mitzvos to them, because through the performance of mitzvos, the soul is elevated and attains a new, enhanced state. It therefore follows that when one grows spiritually through the performance of mitzvos, one is not simply performing the same mitzvah, but because of one's new, heightened spiritual state, one

---
19. Ibid. 21:1.

brings oneself and the very same mitzvah to a much higher level.

Mitzvos actually have the power to change us, so if we are consistent in our observance we can attain a much higher level today than we enjoyed yesterday. Herein lies the secret of the miraculous transformation that enabled us, a nation of slaves, to become a Priestly Kingdom in only 49 short days after our Exodus. Every day, we were commanded to count, and as we did so, we shed the dross of Egypt and filled the vacuum with the mitzvos of our God until we came to that awesome moment: the giving of the Torah on the holiday of Shavuos, when God sealed His covenant with us. From this seminal experience, we learned that when we perform commandments, we are not simply adding mitzvos to our portfolios, but *we are creating a change in the essence of our beings*. What an amazing opportunity for spiritual growth! What a tragedy not to avail ourselves of it.

Imparting a Life Lesson to the Young

Our Sages teach us that this double language of "say" has yet another meaning, and that is that the adults must instruct the young. What is puzzling, however, is that this command is given to the Kohanim specifically when the Torah is discussing *contact with the dead*.

Once again, there is a special lesson to be derived from this. When we are overcome by grief at a death, it becomes easy to abandon our responsibility to teach the young; it becomes easy to fall into a depression and forget that little eyes are watching us. Therefore, the Torah teaches us that even in the face of pain and suffering, our responsibility to serve as an example to our children can never be abandoned. Our commitment to passing on Torah knowledge must transcend all other considerations.

We have personally witnessed this in the homes of our revered parents and grandparents, who, despite the pain of their Holocaust experiences, devoted themselves to imparting the light of Torah to a new generation. Upon arriving on these shores, our grandfather, HaRav HaGaon Avraham HaLevi Jungreis, *zt"l*, built a yeshivah. Every morning, our grandmother, Rebbetzin Miriam Jungreis, *a'h*, stood at the entrance to the yeshivah, greeting every child with a home-baked cookie and asking him to make a *berachah* — to say a blessing over the treat.

Our father, HaRav Meshulem HaLevi Jungreis, *zt"l*, was a pioneering Orthodox rabbi in Long Island. Our mother, Rebbetzin Esther Jungreis, may she have length of days, established the Hineni organization to inspire a new generation to Torah commitment. In the spirit of the teaching of our *parashah*, they did all this despite their personal pain and the suffering that they experienced in the concentration camps.

But life's tests are never quite over. When our father learned in the course of a routine checkup that he had what appeared to be a malignant tumor, his immediate reaction was to go to his grandchildren and teach them Torah. Only then did he call our mother to inform her of the painful news. This, indeed, has been the imperative of our Jewish people. No matter how difficult or painful our personal situation might be, our commitment to teach Torah remains unswerving.

Let us then never succumb to the forces of darkness, but rather, let us bear in mind that we have a mission to elevate ourselves and those who are near to us to God's Divine calling.

AN ONGOING COMMITMENT

In this week's *parashah*, we study the special mitzvos pertaining to the Kohanim as well as to the Kohen Gadol. A High Priest is different from the ordinary priest in that even in the midst of the pain of losing one of his closest relatives, he must still carry on and perform the Temple service and minister to the Jewish people. The Torah states, "And he shall not leave the Sanctuary."[20] This commandment calls upon the Kohen Gadol to bear in mind that his responsibility to the community is so great that he must repress his personal suffering and continue his service to the people.

From this we learn the level of commitment required of our leaders. A leader of the Jewish people must find the strength to transcend his own pain for the greater welfare of the community. The teachings of the Torah are timeless; thus, this level of commitment applies to each and every one of us, for our entire nation is described as "*Mamleches Kohanim* — a Priestly Kingdom." Thus, in a sense, we are all *Kohanim* — we are all leaders, for there is always someone in our lives who looks to us for strength and must be fortified.

This lesson applies to every parent, grandparent, rebbi, and teacher. We must always bear in mind that one day, our children, our students, will remember that in time of crisis we remained steadfast in our faith; of course, the converse is also true. If we succumb to despair, that too will be etched in their memories. So let us ask ourselves, *What legacy are we imparting to future generations? Will we be remembered for the darkness that we allowed to envelop us or for the faith and hope that we inspired?*

It's all in our hands; the choice is ours to make.

---

20. Ibid. 21:12.

PARASHAS BEHAR

TOTAL TRUST IN GOD

Our *parashah* begins with the commandment of *shemittah* (the Sabbatical year), which means that every seventh year in Israel, the land must lay fallow. Interestingly, the Torah introduces this commandment by stating that God commanded this mitzvah at Mount Sinai, which, at first glance, appears rather enigmatic, for we know that *every* mitzvah — *all* the commandments — were given at Sinai, so why should the Sabbatical year be singled out for special mention? In the answer to this question is to be found the foundation upon which our Jewish faith is built, and that is total trust in God.

Ancient Israel was an agricultural society. The nation's survival was totally dependent upon the produce of the land, but the laws of *shemittah* required that after every seven-year cycle, the land be allowed to rest; no tilling, no planting, no harvesting of the earth was to take place, which in essence meant that the harvest of the sixth year had to last for three years (the sixth, the seventh, and the eighth, since no work was done in the seventh). For an entire nation to come to a standstill demanded complete and utter trust in God. Just try to visualize what would happen if, in our contemporary world, we were told that we had to shut down our businesses, our farms, etc. every seventh year and *rely upon income from the sixth year to sustain us for three years*! There would be total and utter chaos. Panic would break out, and this, despite the fact that many of us have some savings and our government has reserves to fall back on, and we have the wherewithal to preserve food, so that famine would not become an issue. Therefore, the very fact that our forefathers accepted this mitzvah unquestioningly testifies that it had to come from Sinai, for such a demand could only be made by God, Who sustains us in all seasons. Hence, that is the the reason for the mention of Sinai in connection with the Sabbatical year.

Additionally, when we observe *shemittah*, we declare to the world that the true owner of the land is God, and it is only with His permission that we till the soil and reap the harvest. Such an admission makes us keenly aware that it is our Heavenly Father Who is in control and not we who are in charge — an admission that renders us humble and compassionate, mindful of that which is of paramount significance in life.

No Explanation Required

From the very genesis of our history, it is this *total trust* that shaped our relationship with God. At Sinai, we proclaimed, "*Na'aseh v'nishma* — We will do and we will obey,"[21] without really knowing what would be demanded of us. Our unequivocal response was based totally on *trust*, and it is this trust that is the basis for the observance of all our 613 mitzvos. More than logic

---

21. *Exodus* 24:7.

and reason, our commitment is rooted in the knowledge that God is there, that it was He who spoke, so no commandment can be too difficult, even if at times the challenge might appear to be so. We rely totally upon God, trust Him implicitly, and know that, since He created us, if He commanded it, we have the ability to deliver.

The Jew who is imbued with this faith does not need any explanation as to why he should observe a mitzvah; the very fact that God spoke is reason enough, and he does not need any better rationale than that. Over the years, we have seen science catch up to us and substantiate many of our commandments, pronouncing them medically sound. Society has also come to appreciate the wisdom inherent in our ethical and moral laws, but whether science or conventional wisdom verify our commandments is irrelevant. Ours is a commitment of *total faith and trust*, for the voice of God forever reverberates in our hearts. This faith and trust are at the root of our survival. We are a minuscule minority and by every law of logic, we should have long ago disappeared.

Nor is our situation different today. Our brethren in Israel are surrounded by a sea of hostile nations who seek her destruction. How can we possibly survive? The Passover Haggadah gives us the answer: In every generation our enemies seek to annihilate us, but the Almighty God always saves us.

Take Care Not To Inflict Pain

Our *parashah* coincides with preparations for the holiday of Shavuos, when God gave us His Torah. Therefore, most appropriately, this *parashah* imparts mitzvos that teach us how we may best prepare ourselves for this awesome day. Not only are we called upon to intensify our faith and place our trust in the Almighty God, but we are also reminded how to be more sensitive toward our fellow man:

"Each of you shall not aggrieve his fellow,"[22] meaning that we

---

22. *Leviticus* 25:17.

must be very careful with our *words* and with our *comments* so as not to embarrass or hurt others. The use of derogatory language or offensive nicknames is not permissible under any circumstances, nor are we allowed to remind people of their past misdeeds, even if we claim that we are just joking.

In our society, "ranking out people" and "telling it like it is," regardless of how much pain is inflicted, has become the "norm." Taunting, hurling insults, name-calling start at a very young age, and many children are psychologically destroyed by their peers in school or in summer camp. The use of abrasive, cutting words continues throughout life. It mars our marriages and our relationships; it is at the root of our broken homes and our angry, bitter personal lives. Our *parashah* speaks to us with great urgency and reminds us that basic to a stable, harmonious society and family life is the art of communicating with kindness and love.

Do Not Overburden Others

The verse, "For the Children of Israel are servants to Me,"[23] teaches us that we must be ever so careful not to burden anyone to the point where he no longer has energy for the service of God or for the fulfillment of their higher calling and mission.

The eminent sage, Rabbi Moshe Feinstein, *zt"l*, expounded on this commandment and taught that we must be cautious not to impose tasks on others that would inhibit them from living a life of mitzvos, and we must apply these same concerns to our own lives as well. We live in a culture that is obsessed with the pursuit of success; in doing so, we all too often lose sight of our priorities: our obligations to our family, to our people, to our God. Our Torah calls upon us to live with these priorities by first and foremost remembering that we, the Children of Israel, are the servants of God.

---

23. Ibid. 25:55.

PARASHAS BECHUKOSAI

COINCIDENCE OR THE HAND OF GOD?

The Book of Leviticus ends with a somber warning. God admonishes us to beware of the terrible fate that will befall us if we abandon His covenant. One word that stands out in the *parashah* is repeated again and again: *"keri* (casualness),"[24] an attitude that implies lack of causality, coincidence. The Torah warns us that our undoing will come about as a result of *keri*, a feeling that everything that befalls us is *happenstance* — merely an accident of fate.

---

24. Ibid. 26:27 et al.

Maimonides taught that when suffering is visited upon us, we are commanded to cry out and awaken our people by sounding the *shofar*. Everyone must be alerted to examine his or her life and commit to greater adherence to Torah and mitzvos. Most significantly, Maimonides warned that to regard tragedies as natural happenings — the way the world does — is to be guilty of cruelty.

At first glance, it is difficult to understand why Maimonides chose the term *"cruelty"* to describe those who view tribulations as "natural occurrences," We may regard such people as being guilty of apathy, obtuseness, or blindness, but why *cruelty*?

The answer is simple. If we regard our pain and suffering as mere coincidences, we will feel no motivation to examine our lives, abandon our old ways, and change. So yes, such an attitude is cruel, for *it invites additional misfortune upon ourselves and others*.

Thus, when we obstinately refuse to see Divine Providence in our daily lives, when we believe that things happen simply because they "happen to happen," we allow the suffering to continue unabated and we create a wall between ourselves and our Heavenly Father. So yes, it's cruelty to relegate God's wake-up call to *"keri"* — mere coincidence.

Rediscovering Yourself

At the end of the *parashah*, after enumerating all the calamities that will befall us, God makes a promise: "And I will remember My covenant with Jacob, and also My covenant with Isaac, and also my covenant with Abraham will I remember …."[25] This declaration is an eternal guarantee that no matter what, we, the Jewish people, will be redeemed in the merit of our Patriarchs.

There is one aspect of this covenant, however, that is rather puzzling. Why the reverse order? Why commence with Jacob? Why not commence with Abraham?

---

25. Ibid. 26:42.

At the opening of the *parashah*, when we are warned about the terrible curses that will befall us if we abandon the covenant, we are also told how it could have happened that we, the People of the Book, the nation who stood at Sinai and heard the voice of God, could have forgotten our Divine calling. Those curses are given in seven ascending steps of severity, corresponding to the people's continuing failure to take the punishments to heart and learn from them to repent.

To be sure, no Jew ever woke up one morning and suddenly decided, "I will forsake my Jewish faith." It is a slow, seven-step process and our *parashah* delineates it. The *first* step is the cessation of Torah study. The *second* is laxness in Torah observance, the *third* is mockery of those who do observe the commandments he abandoned, etc. One erosion leads to another until it culminates in the *seventh* and the covenant is forsaken. It is as a consequence of this abandonment that the *"curses"* befall us.

How do we redeem ourselves?

The answer is simple: Reverse the process, as Hashem reversed the names of the Patriarchs; reclaim that first step — Torah study — and the rest will follow.

Three Pillars

There are three pillars upon which our faith stands: Torah, *Avodah* (service, sacrifice), and *gemilas chassadim*. Each of our Patriarchs personified one of these pillars. Abraham represents loving-kindness; Isaac, service and sacrifice; and Jacob, Torah. And because the tragic process of Jewish defection commences with the abandonment of Torah, the revitalization of Jewish life must commence with the re-acceptance of Torah as symbolized by Jacob. And so it is that God's promise in this instance is given by mentioning the names of the Patriarchs in reverse order.

The Way to Study Torah

The opening verse of this *parashah* commences with "In My statutes you shall *walk* ...." The use of the word "walk" is rather odd. It would seem to be more appropriate to use the verb *observe* or *study*. But the Torah is teaching is how to safeguard our spiritual lives and preserve our *Yiddishe neshamos*.

Walking connotes constant movement, teaching us that we never graduate from Torah study; as long as we are alive, we must continue to delve into its deep secrets. Our Sages further explain that this "walking" implies "*ameilus* — toiling in Torah," putting heart and soul into our study, for it is only when we study and teach with passion, with every fiber of our beings, that we will reap the full benefits of this toil.

Walking also implies that we Jews are charged with the imperative of following the well-trodden path of our ancestors, for it is only by following their path that we can be true to our calling, our mission.

ספר במדבר

THE BOOK OF
Numbers

PARASHAS BAMIDBAR

WE ALL COUNT

With *Parashas Bamidbar*, we commence the fourth of the Five Books of Moses. This Book is also known as *Sefer HaPekudim* — the Book of Numbers — for God commanded that a census of the Jewish people be taken. One might ask what the purpose of that census may have been, especially since the Jewish nation had already been counted in the Book of Exodus, and surely, God knew our numbers without a physical census.

The Hebrew term for census-taking, *s'u es rosh*, literally means "lift up the head." Through this counting, God reminds us how precious we are to Him, that we are all part of His master plan, and because of that, we all *count*. Each and every one of us is endowed with a special purpose that *only we can fulfill*. That awareness lends meaning to our lives, for it gives us a *tachlis* (a God-given purpose)

— a reason to *lift up our heads* and confront life's challenges with strength and dignity.

DISCOVER YOUR MISSION

At the beginning of the *parashah*, the Torah mentions that, starting from the second year after the Exodus from Egypt, whenever the Jewish people traveled they were arranged in a specific formation. The 12 tribes were divided into four groups of three, with each tribe stationed in a specific location — north, south, east or west — each carrying its own flag that identified its group. One might ask, why didn't the tribes travel in this formation when they left Egypt?

A flag symbolizes one's nationality, and if each tribe had had its own flag from the time the people left Egypt, it could have splintered the nation. Indeed, history is replete with examples of people going to battle under the banner of their national flags. Therefore, our tribal flags were given to us only after we constructed the Tabernacle that stood in the center of the camp. The Tabernacle, the symbol of our love and commitment to Hashem and His Torah, unified us and molded us into one nation.

Once we were unified in our service of God, our individual flags would no longer be a source of conflict, but rather, they would galvanize us and forge us into one. This not only pertains to our ancient past, but it speaks to us in every generation. In families where parents are strong, loving, role models, sibling rivalry is neutralized, for the children are unified in their commitment to their mother and father. Similarly, Jews who truly love God and His people will subdue their individual predilections, for the sake of the greater good of Hashem and His nation. Thus, while every one of the 12 tribes had a unique mission, for the sake of Hashem they all unified around the Tabernacle, *carried their flags*, and fulfilled their unique mission as one nation. In our contemporary world, in which broken homes are so prevalent and our people are fragmented, we would do well to absorb this lesson

You Are Special

God created all of us with eyes, noses, ears, etc., yet no two people look exactly alike. Similarly, no two souls are exactly alike. Every individual is *custom made by Him* and has a purpose that *only he or she can fulfill*. Therefore, he must carry *his own flag, know his own identity, and thus fulfill his/her task*. King David praises God Who counts the billions of stars and calls each and every one of them by *name*.[1] Our names are not merely names; they define us, imbue us with a sense of our past, charge us with purpose, and impart a legacy.

Now, let us consider for a moment: Since God is aware of each and every star and calls each one by name, He is most certainly aware of us and surely calls us by our names. He hears and knows the thoughts in our innermost hearts. He understands our hopes and aspirations, so we are never to despair; God, our heavenly Father, is guiding our lives, summoning us daily to fulfill our mission. We need only study His holy Torah and we will hear His voice and discover our flag and our own identity.

Counting: An Expression of Love

Let us consider some further insights regarding counting. As we explained, *"S'u es rosh"* literally mens *"Lift up the head."* When something is precious to us, we count it. The very fact that Hashem wanted us to be counted testifies to the love that He harbors for us, and that awareness is, in and of itself, uplifting. The first time Hashem mentioned the number of the Jewish people was when we departed from Egypt[2]; that was an awesome, uplifting experience, because it demonstrated our miraculous

---

1. *Psalms* 147:4.
2. *Exodus* 12:37.

growth. From the 70 people who had descended to Egypt, we became millions strong, a phenomenal growth that could only be explained by God's miraculous intervention and love.

We were counted once again after the sin of the Golden Calf, when we felt despondent and worthless at the memory of that perfidious act. "Count them, lift their heads," Hashem commanded Moses, and this time, we were counted through the half-*shekel* that we were commanded to contribute for the Tabernacle.[3] The knowledge that God did not reject us, that we still counted, that we still had a share in the creation of the Tabernacle, imbued us with purpose. Our half-*shekel* served to remind us that we are all halves in the greater mosaic of God's plan.

In our *parashah,* the counting took place after the Tabernacle was completed. The counting was done in accordance with our *families,* our *tribes,* and our *names.* There are many ways to understand this. One explanation is that a person might think that since the Tabernacle had been completed, individual contributions of the half-*shekel* were no longer critical. He might think that the service would go on, regardless of new contributions or lack of them. The Torah comes to remind us, however, that our task is never over: The Tabernacle and the Jewish people are only as strong as their individual *families,* as their *individual tribes,* and as *we, ourselves.* We dare not lose sight of that knowledge.

Lastly, there was a *head count* once again through the half-*shekel.* From this we learn that while it is important for everyone to recognize his own strengths and ideals, he must always bear in mind that God gave him his gifts so that he might enhance his family, his tribe, his community, and fulfill the unique mission inherent in his name. However, because it is forbidden to literally do a head count of the Jewish people, they were counted once again by counting half-*shekels.*

---

3. Ibid. 30:12-15.

Essential Tools for Torah Learning

Parashas Bamidbar is always read prior to the great festival of Shavuos, which commemorates the day that God gave us the Torah. And that in itself is instructive. *Midbar* can be defined as *wilderness* or *desert*; the word *bamidbar* means "*in the Wilderness,*" teaching us that if we wish the Torah to impact on us and elevate us, we have to make ourselves like a desert. Even as a desert is barren, so too must we divest ourselves of all preconceived notions and allow the Torah to re-shape us. Even as in a desert there are no diversions, so we cannot allow anyone or anything to distract us from our Torah study. Even as in the Wilderness of Sinai everything was free, so we must make Torah study available to one and all.

The backdrop for the giving of the Torah is equally significant. The Torah was given at Mount Sinai, a lowly mountain, and while logic would dictate that it would have been more impressive had God proclaimed His words on a tall, majestic mountain, He nevertheless chose Sinai for His revelation, teaching us that a prerequisite for Torah study is humility. At Sinai, the people saw flames and clouds dripping water; flames symbolize fiery passion, while clouds dripping water are symbolic of clarity. The verses teach us that if we wish Torah to enter our hearts, we must study it and transmit it with fiery passion; we must tackle our studies with discipline and stay with them until we have *full clarity*. All this is a reminder that Torah study cannot be undertaken casually. It is our very life and the length of our days, and must be accorded the seriousness and respect it deserves.

PARASHAS NASSO

The Threefold Priestly Blessing: Blessings for All Eternity

In this *parashah*, the Almighty God imparts to us the Threefold Priestly Blessing. These blessings have accompanied our people throughout the centuries, through all the lands of our exile. They are forever sealed in our hearts, engraved upon our lips, and passed from generation to generation.

> May God bless you and safeguard you.
> May God illuminate His countenance for you and be gracious to you.
> May God lift His countenance to you and establish peace for you.[4]

---

4. *Numbers* 6:23-26.

God conferred upon our Patriarch Abraham the privilege of bestowing blessing, as the verse states, "And you shall be a blessing."[5] That honor was passed on to Isaac and then to Jacob. In this *parashah*, Hashem instructs Moses to bequeath this privilege to Aaron and all his descendants, the Kohanim, in perpetuity. In the Land of Israel, the Kohanim bless the congregation daily. Outside of Israel, the Kohanim pronounce the blessings on the holidays. However, no matter where we reside, the blessings are part of our daily prayers. We recite them during the morning service as well as during the bedtime *Shema*, and the cantor chants these blessings during the repetition of the *Amidah*. If we stop to consider for a moment that these blessings have survived the centuries and are as a part of us today as they were thousands of years ago when God first proclaimed them at Sinai, we must be struck by the awesomeness of it all.

It is not only during our formal prayers that we pronounce these blessings, but on the eve of every Sabbath. In the glow of the candlelight, prior to making *Kiddush*, parents impart this blessing to their children. How fortunate we are that we are able to bless our children with the very words that were given to us by God Himself, words that are inscribed in the Torah. Moreover, when we pronounce these blessings, we connect with the millions of souls who preceded us, with our *zeides* and *bubbies* who are no longer on this planet, but who whisper the words with us. To this very day, we can hear the voices of our father and our *zeides* whose *berachos* we were privileged to receive. They forever accompany us — and so it goes, from generation to generation.

The Meaning Behind the Blessing

The blessing is composed of three parts. The first contains three words, in memory of the three Patriarchs; the second, five words, anchoring us to the Five Books of Moses; the

---

5. *Genesis* 12:2.

third, with seven words, reminds us of the seven heavens, and asks God to shower us with His bounty.

Prior to imparting the blessing, the Kohanim themselves have to recite a prayer, the last word of which is *"ahavah"* (love), teaching us that a pre-condition to imparting a blessing is that one's heart be *overflowing with love*. A person may have Torah wisdom, but one who is not a likeable individual will not be able to share these treasures with others and the blessing will remain incomplete.

However, you don't have to be a Kohen to give a blessing. The power to bless is in the domain of all of us, the only prerequisite being that *our hearts overflow with love*. Blessings are so much a part of our lives that in the holy tongue, we extend a welcome by saying *"Baruch HaBa* — Blessed is the one who comes," and in Yiddish, the folk language of our people, we bid farewell with *"Zei gebencht* — Be blessed."

FURTHER INSIGHTS INTO THE BLESSING

The first blessing is for *health and sustenance*, but, once attained, those gifts can easily be abused and taken for granted, so we conclude the blessing with the word *"Yishm'recha* — May God protect you" so that you may be forever aware of this gift and treat it with great care.

The second blessing requests that God illuminate our minds with the holy teachings of His Torah, and we conclude that blessing with the word *"V'yechunecha* — May He cause you to find favor in His eyes" and in the eyes of others. As stated above, a person may possess Torah wisdom, but if he or she is not likeable, he/she will not be able to share these treasures with others and the blessing will remain incomplete.

The third blessing is that God look upon us with compassion, forgive our sins, and grant us *shalom* — peace. In this blessing, the concluding word is *shalom*, teaching us that without peace, everything else is worthless and pointless. You can live in a palatial home, but if you do not have peace in your relationships, all your blessings will be for naught. Our Sages teach, *"Im ein shalom, ein kloom* — if there is no peace, there is nothing." We, the Jewish people, are so aware of the all-importance of *shalom* that we conclude our most important prayers — the *Amidah* service and the *Kaddish* — with a prayer for *shalom*.

KNOW YOURSELF

"And they shall confess their sin that they committed."[6] The question is obvious: One can only confess a sin that one has committed, so why is there the redundancy of language ("that they committed")?

The Torah teaches us here that the mistakes we make in life, the sins that we commit, are not born in a vacuum. They stem from deep roots, so if we are to confess and make a real change in our lives, it's not just verbal platitudes that are required, but genuine soul-searching. The *parashah* teaches us that if we really want to elevate ourselves, if we really want to be transformed and become better, more spiritual individuals, we have to go through this process honestly, without rationalizations, as painful as it may be. We must focus not only on the sin just committed, but must ask ourselves, *What led me astray? How is it that I have become so lost?* Once we come to grips with that concept and discover the answer, it will become easier for us to uproot the negativity from our hearts and to embark upon a new course. That's what *teshuvah* is all about. To be sure, this is not a simple path. Most of us are quick to see the faults in others but are slow to recognize them in ourselves. How often does it happen that when we read a book or hear a message, we say, "That's just for my sister, brother, friend, etc.," and it never occurs to us that the message was meant for us. So, know yourself.

---

6. *Numbers* 5:7.

WE ALL HAVE A GOD-GIVEN MISSION

This *parashah* reminds every individual that he/she has a unique mission in life. It opens with the words, "Count the children of Gershon *as well*." The phrase "as well" is jarring. What does it mean? The children of Gershon had the responsibility of carrying the curtains and other heavy objects of the Tabernacle. At first glance, one might think that to be charged with such a menial task is to be labeled a *schlepper*, a mere porter. Therefore, the Torah tells us, "Count them *as well*," reminding us that the children of Gershon were as important as those who had the responsibility of carrying the Holy Ark itself.

It's not *what* we do but *how* we do it that counts. It's the love and dedication that we invest in a task that make all the difference. In the homes of our parents and grandparents, we saw our father and *zeide*, eminent rabbis, waiting upon and serving all those who crossed their threshold. No task was too menial for them; and of course, our grandmother, of blessed memory, and our mother, may she live and be well, never tired of attending to the needs of others. The knowledge that they were of service, that they were helping others, lent meaning to their every deed. So, when we are challenged with tasks that we may consider being beneath our dignity, let us remember these words from the Torah: "Count the children of Gershon as well." Whether you carry the curtains or the Holy Ark, you count, and in the end, that's the only thing that matters.

The awareness that we are fulfilling our mission empowers and elevates even the most menial task in the service of God.

Custom-Made by God: It's Not What We Have, But Who We Are

This *parashah* is the longest in the Torah: 176 *pesukim* (verses). It is the longest because, at the end of the *parashah*, the offerings that each of the princes brought to the Tabernacle are enumerated separately.

What is puzzling is that although each of the princes brought *exactly the same gift*, instead of enumerating the components of the first contribution and then stating that the other princes each brought the same gifts, the Torah lists each offering individually. This is all the more difficult to understand since there are no redundancies in the Torah. Every word, every letter, every punctuation mark is carefully measured. The Torah never repeats anything without a deeper purpose; what, then, is the significance of the repetition of "the offering of [the name of the prince]"?[7]

Consider what would happen if a group of friends became engaged at the same time, and after the first was married, the others copied the wedding exactly, ordering exactly the same menu, flowers, bridal gown, music, etc. Such an eventuality would be virtually unheard of in our society for two reasons: First, the bride and groom of the first wedding would be resentful that the other couples were copying them and would object vehemently. Second, the other couples would not wish to copy them because our culture is rooted in competitiveness and therefore we have a need to be better and to be more than the other. The 12 princes of Israel, however, were happy to bring identical gifts because jealousy, resentment, and a desire to outdo others were foreign to them. They understood that it was not the gift, but the manner in which it was offered that made the difference. God Himself gave His seal of approval by enumerating the gifts of each separately, teaching us that what is special about each person is his spiritual essence — the spirit in which he gives rather than the gift itself.

---

7. Ibid. 7:17, et al.

This is a lesson that we would do well to implement. Ours is a generation that often measures a person by that which he possesses rather than by that which he is. The story of the tribal princes comes to remind us that we are each custom made by Hashem, with unique souls and unique missions and that it is not having more but being more that matters. God does not look at our possessions, but rather at the manner and spirit in which we give them away. So, instead of focusing on the physical and the material, let us try to develop our inner selves.

PARASHAS BEHA'ALOSCHA

Elevate Your Life

In this *parashah*, Aaron is commanded to kindle the lights of the Menorah, but a most unusual expression is used in this connection. *"Beha'aloscha"* literally means "when you elevate," rather than *"l'hadlik,"* the word used in connection to kindling the Shabbos and festival lights.[8]

There is a profound teaching therein. The Menorah is symbolic of the Torah and we must at all times bear in mind that studying the Torah is not just undertaking another study; observing the mitzvos is not just another lifestyle, but it is the very essence of our lives, the very fiber of our beings, through which we are *elevated* and realize our purpose in life. Therefore, the word that is used is "elevating" rather than "kindling."

---

8. Ibid. 8:2.

There is yet another teaching found in the Menorah. The Book of Proverbs states, "The soul of man is a candle of God."[9] Buried deep in the crevices of our *neshamos* is the light of God — a love of Torah and mitzvos. We need only kindle it. So, if we seek elevation, meaning, and purpose in life, we need only kindle the light of Torah in our souls. It's as easy as that.

A Jewish Litmus Test: When Do You Feel Deprived?

The mitzvah of kindling the Menorah was given to Aaron after the princes of the tribes brought their contributions for the dedication of the Tabernacle. The Midrash[10] teaches us that Aaron was *distressed* that the leaders representing the tribes were called upon to offer gifts, while he and his tribe were not invited to do so.

This should give us all pause. In our world, very few people would feel deprived or distressed if they were exempt from making a contribution. They would be more than happy to be overlooked when it comes to solicitations. When honor is dispensed, however, when gifts are given, then, of course, it's a different matter. Let's ask ourselves: When do we feel deprived?

Aaron taught us proper priorities. To him, it was not what he *possessed* that counted, but what *he was able to give away*. Aaron felt deprived when he was not called upon to give. His message transcends the centuries and speaks to us, loud and clear. It's not what we *have*, but what we *give* that is significant. Aaron gave with a full, loving heart and because of that, the Almighty assured him that his gift — the kindling of the Menorah — would be eternal. Indeed, to this very day, even the most alienated Jew kindles a Chanukah menorah, although he may not know the significance of that act.

How do you rate on this litmus test? When do you feel deprived?

---

9. *Proverbs* 20:27.
10. Rashi, *Numbers* 8:2.

The Menorah and Its Many Dimensions

There are many dimensions to this mitzvah of kindling the Menorah, for as we pointed out, it is not just a physical light, but it is symbolic of our spiritual light, the Torah. Therefore, every aspect of the kindling is significant and imparts a lesson. The oil used for the Menorah must be pure olive oil, free of sediment, teaching us that when we study Torah, we must take care not to allow foreign influences to infiltrate our minds and hearts, nor should we adulterate our studies with alien concepts.

Throughout the year, whether the nights were long or short, the same measure of oil was used to kindle the Menorah, impressing upon us that we have to invest the same energy, the same love in each child, whether he/she is bright or dull, strong or weak. Moreover, Aaron himself had to cleanse the Menorah, from which we learn that a Torah teacher has to help his disciples put their lives into order, and he himself must be vigilant about his conduct so that he may be an inspiration to others. Although the Menorah was only five to six feet high, the Kohen had to ascend a step to kindle it, teaching us that you have to "step up to Torah" and study it with proper *derech eretz*.

How Will You Be Remembered?

Aaron himself was commanded to kindle the light, telling us that the most effective way to impress upon our children the importance of Torah study and the observance of mitzvos is by being an example, a proper role model. It is not what we *preach*, but what we *do* that counts, for that is how our children will remember us. If they see our commitment, then they will follow suit and walk in our footsteps.

It was through his dedication and love of the mitzvah of the

Menorah that Aaron merited that the miracle of Chanukah would come about through his descendants, Mattisyahu, the son of Yochanan the High Priest, and the entire Hasmonean family. From this we learn that the merit of performing a mitzvah with love and devotion has no bounds, and its impact has the power to transcend centuries. Let us ask ourselves: What example are we imparting to our children? How will future generations remember us? What is written on the legacy that we will leave behind?

Maintaining Our Enthusiasm: A Key to Meaningful Living

Following the instructions regarding the commandment of the Menorah, the passage goes on to say, "*Va'yaas kein Aharon* — And Aaron did so ...."[11]

Rashi states that this verse is in praise of Aaron, who fulfilled the command exactly as instructed. This is difficult to understand, for even a lesser person than Aaron would not have deviated from God's command. How much more so, Aaron?

But once again the Torah teaches us an important lesson. It is easy to be enthusiastic when we undertake a new project; to keep that enthusiasm going, however, when the novelty wears off, is the real test of character. We all have visions and dreams when facing new challenges. We go under the *chuppah* certain that we will be the best husbands and wives. When we become parents, we are confident that we will be the best mothers and fathers; when we start a new business, we are ready to invest all our energies. But very soon, our dreams fade, our enthusiasm wanes, and we become habituated and perhaps blasé, taking our lives for granted. Aaron, however, was different. Throughout his 39 years of service, he retained the same enthusiasm as on the day that he first received the command. Indeed, "Aaron did so ...."

Complacency is a terrible detriment to meaningful living. Not

---
11. *Numbers* 8:3.

only does it sap our energy, but it makes us neglectful of our responsibilities. This holds true in all areas. When we take our relationships with our spouses or our children for granted, when we become complacent in our businesses, we underwrite our own undoing; be it the breakdown of our families or the erosion of our enterprises. This same truth applies to our relationship with God. When we become sloppy in our Torah study, in our prayers, in our observance, we go into a downward spiral that too often tragically leads to alienation from our faith and a lonely godless existence. But how are we to maintain that early enthusiasm?

Each and every time we commence our studies, we must strive to view ourselves as we stood at Mount Sinai, when we declared *"Na'aseh v'nishma,"* which can be interpreted, "We will fulfill the Torah and study it." If we adopt this attitude, we will discover that absolutely nothing can dampen our spirit or limit our spiritual growth.

A SECOND CHANCE

The concept of feeling deprived because of an inability to give is reinforced in the *parashah*, when a group of men approach Moses and state that they feel *diminished* because they were unable to bring the *pesach* offering.[12] Herein we see the greatness of soul of our forefathers. They agonized over the fact that they were not able to participate in a mitzvah. They approached Moses and asked to be given a second chance and be allowed to bring the *pesach* offering. Moses told them that he would have to consult Hashem for guidance. Moses was unable to respond, for this declaration had to come from God Himself, so that we might know for all eternity that if we will it, God grants us a second chance and we can start anew.

The holiday of *Pesach Sheni* was not decreed as were all our other holidays because it is one holiday that God could not legislate until the people themselves desired it: A second chance must

---

12. Ibid. 9:6.

spring from the sincere yearning of those who wish for it. Thus, our *parashah* teaches us that, if we feel diminished because we didn't participate in the service of God, if we agonize over it and beseech the Almighty to grant us that *second chance*, He will give it to us.

LIFE-TRANSFORMING LESSONS FROM *PESACH SHENI*

We have a mandate to emulate God. Even as God is merciful, so too must we be merciful. Even as God is forgiving, so too must we be forgiving. It follows then that if God is willing to give us a *second chance* and even allows us to create a holiday to celebrate this concept, should we not give ourselves and our brethren that same opportunity? If we examine our relationships, we will surely come up with some people whom we have written off, but who should be given that second chance. And if we take a good look at our own personal lives, we are bound to discover situations in which we have given up on ourselves, in which we are convinced that we lost it and it's too late for us to change. But Torah reality teaches that a second chance is always possible, so why shortchange ourselves? Why deny God's miraculous healing gift of a *second chance*?

Pesach Sheni testifies that no matter how far we may have strayed, no matter what distant road we may have traversed, God will always accept us if we indicate our yearning to come home. This then, is our choice: We can reinvent ourselves, or we can remain mired in our failures. It's all up to us.

PARASHAS SHELACH

NOT AFFLICTION, BUT CORRECTION

Very often we experience what we believe to be the punitive hand of God, but the Almighty is our Heavenly Father Who created us and loves us with infinite paternal devotion and Whose mercy and compassion always encompass us. His punishments are not *afflictions*, but *corrections*. This teaching is blatantly obvious in this *parashah*. The people are guilty of an act of perfidy. They spurn God's magnificent gift, Eretz Yisrael, the Holy Land. They demand that scouts be sent on a reconnaissance mission, which, in and of itself, betrays a hidden agenda. As anticipated, the spies return with a most disheartening, blasphemous report. They inject fear into the hearts of the people, a fear that results in a call for a return to Egypt.

The Almighty God, Who knows the machinations of the hearts of men, foresaw the future and protected His people, even in their time of disgrace. He allowed these ill-intentioned spies to scout out the entire land in a *mere 40 days* — an impossible feat for those times. God gave the spies good speed so that the punishment might be minimized, since for each day that they spied out the land, the nation had to spend a corresponding year in the desert. The 40 days of scouting became 40 years of wandering. During this time, the nation was reborn and made atonement for the sins of the spies; herein lies profound lessons for us to remember.

When difficult and challenging days come upon us, and we find ourselves wandering in our own "desert," we should *recognize that this experience is a call from God* ... a challenge to grow and realize our higher purpose, our life mission.

Our mother, Rebbetzin Esther Jungreis, has often advised people struggling with life's many tests not to ask "Why?" "Whys" have no answers and leave people bitter, angry, and cynical. "But," she would advise, "do ask 'why' in the holy tongue, for Hebrew is God's language and every word is definitive. The Hebrew word for 'why,' *madua*, is the contraction of two words: *mah dei'ah* — what is the wisdom; that is, what can we learn from this?"

There is yet one more Hebrew word that means "why," and that is *"lamah."* That word, too, is the contraction of two words, *"le mah* — to what end." That is, what is the higher purpose of this challenge? Thus, the Hebrew "why" transforms a question that can leave one cynical and bitter into an inspiring, self-motivating quest.

The second lesson that we can learn from this 40-day journey of the scouts is that even as God wanted to minimize the punishment of the nation and allowed scouts to travel the length and breadth of the land in a mere 40 days, similarly, we too should make it easy for those who wronged us or departed from the path of Torah to make amends, re-enter, and become part of our families and the greater Jewish community.

IT ALL DEPENDS ON HOW WE SEE IT

Through the sins of the spies, we gain a glimpse of the complexity of human nature. We become painfully aware that if the mind is twisted and the heart is crooked, then no matter how many miracles God performs, no matter how much kindness He extends, His actions will be misinterpreted and maligned, for *a man sees and hears only that which he wants to see and hear.* Thus we find that when the spies entered the Land of Israel, God made a miracle on their behalf and arranged that just on that day, Job, the righteous citizen of the land, should die. Job was respected and revered; therefore, his death signaled a national day of mourning. Everyone attended his funeral, and this great outpouring of people permitted the spies to go undetected. No one paid attention to them, no one hampered their movements, and they were able to return safely to their camp.

However, instead of being grateful for this miracle, instead of recognizing God's protective care, the spies had the chutzpah to pervert God's kindness and gave a slanderous report: "The Land … is a land that devours its inhabitants!"[13] "People are dying all day — there are constant funerals," they declared.

This jaundiced response to God's benevolence reinforces the sad reality that even open miracles are of no avail if people have hidden agendas. Commentators discuss what motivated the spies to be so fearful of entering Eretz Yisrael, but whatever their rationale, it perverted their judgment. *They will see only that which they want to see and hear only that which they want to hear.*

The reality of this painful portrait of human nature should prompt all of us to self-scrutiny. Before making a decision, let us ask, *Am I looking at the situation truthfully or do I have a hidden agenda? Am I motivated by personal bias or by emes?*

---

13. Ibid. 13:32.

The Power of Prayer and the Power of a Name

What was the power of Joshua and Caleb? How did they resist the evil counsel of the spies? How did they remain immune to the pressure?

Prior to their departure, Moses blessed Joshua and prayed that he might be protected from the counsel of the spies. In his prayer, Moses changed the name of Joshua, who had formerly been known as Hoshea, to Yehoshua, meaning, "May God save you." Our Sages teach us that this change of name shielded Joshua from the poisonous influence of the other spies.

There is an amazing Midrash[14] that tells us that the *yud* that Moses added to Joshua's name came from our Matriarch Sarah. That little letter *yud* complained before God's Throne, "Why was I removed from the name of that holy woman?"

At first glance, this may appear to be a strange Midrash. After all, do *yuds* talk? And again, why was there a need to take the *yud* from Mother Sarah's name? Certainly Moses could have given Joshua a new *yud*? And if a change of name could be so powerful, why didn't Moses change the names of all the spies? Let us address all these questions.

Everything that God created speaks on its own level, even if we do not understand it. And this is even more valid in regard to the Hebrew *aleph-beis*. The letters of the *aleph-beis* are alive and have profound dimensions. As a matter of fact, it was with the *aleph-beis* that God created the world. As for the *yud* having its roots in Mother Sarah's name, there too lies a basic principle of Judaism. We are a nation that is sustained by *zechus avos* — the merit of our ancestors. Our wisdom and our vision are gifts bequeathed to us by our Patriarchs and Matriarchs. It was specifically the *yud* of Sarah Imeinu's name that had the power to endow Joshua with the understanding and foresight to guide the nation to its destiny.

Sarah was the first to discern the brutal, savage character of

---

14. Tractate *Sanhedrin* 107a.

Ishmael, who would shoot his arrows and kill for sport. It was Sarah who told Abraham to send Ishmael and his mother Hagar away, for she recognized that it would be disastrous for Ishmael to inherit the land with Isaac. Thus, Moses prayed that Joshua might be guided by the wisdom of Sarah and would lead the people to their ultimate calling, establishing the Kingdom of God in the Land of Israel, where righteousness and truth would prevail and evil would be banished. In such a society, there is no room for terror and brutality — the murderous acts of Ishmael.

Caleb, on the other hand, was saved by the power of *prayer.* As soon as they entered the land, Caleb departed from the group and made his way to Hebron, the city where our Patriarchs and Matriarchs are buried, so that he might pray at their gravesite. Those prayers protected him, infused his heart with faith, and enabled him to resist the conspiracy of his comrades.

The eminent Rabbi Yaakov Kamenetsky, *zt"l,* explained that Caleb did not require a change of name, for he was married to Miriam, the righteous prophetess, and if a man is married to an *eishes chayil* (woman of valor) that, in and of itself, affords protection.

As to why Moses did not change the names of all the other spies: Blessings work only for those who desire and appreciate them. In vain does one bless someone or change his/her name if he/she chooses to spurn and defile that blessing and that name. Sadly, these spies all had their preconceived bias: They were determined to reject the Land even before seeing it. Blessings are potent when we truly desire them, appreciate them, and act upon them

How Do You See Yourself?

When the spies gave their report to the nation, they related that there were giants in the land of Canaan, and they felt like grasshoppers next to them.[15] Herein is to be found the roots of the demoralization of these scouts.

---

15. *Numbers* 13:33.

Parashas Shelach / 227

How is it possible for members of a nation that stood at Sinai, that heard the voice of God, to view themselves as grasshoppers?

Time and again, our parents related to us how, even in the brutal, dehumanizing darkness of Hitler's concentration camps, Jews of faith never forgot their calling and thanked God every day for the gift of the Torah. No matter how many epithets the Nazis hurled at them, they stood proud and strong with *Shema Yisrael* on their lips.

We live in a generation in which people are lacking Jewish pride. Even as the spies of old, many of us see ourselves Jewishly as grasshoppers, unaware of the Divine spark in our souls and the gift of Torah that is our rightful legacy.

How do you view yourself as a Jew ... and how do your children view themselves?

PARASHAS KORACH

The Root of All Evil: Jealousy, Lust, and the Thirst for Honor

Korah, a cousin of Moses from the distinguished tribe of the Levites, falls prey to two of the three sins which our Sages teach are the source of all destructive character traits: *jealousy* and the *thirst for honor*. (The third character trait is lust.) In his obsession, Korah foments rebellion and tries to unseat Moses and Aaron.

"*Vayikach Korach* — And Korah took"[16] are the opening words of the *parashah*, and our Sages explain that he "took," i.e., seduced, people with persuasive words. He duped them and managed to incite 250 leaders of the nation to join him.

---

16. Ibid. 16:1.

Those who participated in Korah's rebellion all had their own hidden agendas. First and foremost among them were Dathan and Abiram, who had a long history of attacking Moses and who harbored a desire to return to Egypt. Then there was the neighboring tribe of Reuben. Korah convinced them that Moses was guilty of nepotism. stating that it was not by the command of God that Moses had appointed Aaron as High Priest, but rather, by his own ambition to keep all the high honors for his own family. Korah's arguments fell on willing ears since, following the sin of the Golden Calf, Reuben lost his privileged position as the firstborn. Reuben's vulnerability also lay in his close proximity to Korah, reinforcing the warning of our Sages, "Woe to the wicked, woe to his neighbor." We must be careful when choosing a place of residence, for our neighbors can influence us without our even realizing it.

Accusations, Libels, and a Formula for Peace

There are times in life when accusations are leveled that are so outrageous, so egregious, that one is left stunned and unable to respond. Moses — lovingly referred to as "Ro'eh Ne'eman, the loyal shepherd" — who sacrificed his entire life for his people, who wrestled with God and put himself on the line by declaring, "If You forgive them, good, and if not, erase my name from Your Book,"[17] is now put on trial by this pretender and accused of nepotism and greed.

One can only imagine the pain that Moses must have felt at this senseless accusation. We gain a glimpse of his suffering when the Torah tells us that he "fell on his face" in prayer,[18] for what could he have possibly said when confronted by such ingratitude and betrayal?

---

17. Cf. *Exodus* 32:32.
18. *Numbers* 16:4.

How would you have reacted in Moses' place? What can we learn from Moses to help us when we are unjustly accused by those for whom we sacrificed and gave our love?

By all rights, Moses would have been justified in reacting furiously and demanding the obliteration of the insurgents, but instead, he tried to reason with them: "In the morning (*boker*) Hashem will make known ...," he said.[19] The word *"boker"* does not only mean "morning," but is related to the word *"bikores,"* meaning "to clarify, to investigate." By telling them to "sleep on it, to wait until the morning," Moses hoped that they would examine their own motivations and re-think their malevolent plans. Sadly, however, they remained adamant and refused to concede their evil intent. So lesson number one that we learn is not to act hastily or precipitously. Before speaking, before acting, before condemning, try to make peace. Tell you opponent to "sleep on it, to wait until morning" in the hope that he/she will investigate and find clarity. Unfortunately, in the case of Korah, it did not work. Korah and his followers remained blind and obdurate. Nevertheless, Moses' example is here to guide us.

Despite it all, however, Moses did not give up. He sent for Dathan and Abiram and tried to make peace with them but once again, they arrogantly refused, so Moses, the prophet of God, the leader of Israel, the beloved rabbi of all the Jewish people, did not hesitate to humble himself, but personally went to Dathan and Abiram in a final effort to make peace.[20]

Once again, we are given a profound lesson. If strife and contention plague our families or community, let us not stand on ceremony, but let us be the first to extend the hand of peace. If Moses didn't feel that he compromised his honor by humbling himself, how can we? Even if our overtures are rebuffed, we should not give up, but try and try again.

Our Sages admonish us not to keep a quarrel going and gave us a threefold formula to achieve peace: "Be like a teakettle, be like a bird, and be like a river."

---

19. Ibid. 16:5.
20. Ibid. 16:25.

- A teakettle makes peace between fire and water, even though it becomes scorched in the process.
- Try to catch a bird: It will fly away. Someone took your seat, your parking place? Instead of being angry, learn from the bird: Fly away.
- The banks of the river keep the waters from overflowing. Learn control and do not permit the floodwaters of your temper to take over.

Let us take to heart Moses' example: Pursue peace and make every attempt at reconciliation.

The Disastrous Consequences of Jealousy

Korah possessed everything to which a man could aspire: He was brilliant, came from a noble family, was majestic in appearance, and was the wealthiest man of his time. But all his attainments were for naught because he had no peace; his heart was consumed by jealousy. His obsession came to a tragic climax in the controversy he fomented, resulting in his death and that of his family as well as of many others.

Jealousy is the ugliest trait a person can harbor, so how can we protect ourselves from its deadly sting? Whenever we feel it invading our hearts, let us bear in mind that jealousy is pointless and also self-destructive. It is pointless because the venomous feelings that envy generates will not alter our situation; if anything, it will make it worse. What we covet will not become ours, but it will prevent us from enjoying what we *do* have, and worse, it will transform us into bitter, cruel individuals. Thus, Korah — who at first had everything — in the end had nothing. All his accomplishments, all his wealth, had no meaning because, in his mind's eye, all he saw was *the crown of the priesthood on his cousin's head*.

The story of Korah speaks to us in every generation. Alas, jealousy has been the undoing of man since the beginning of tin when Cain rose up to kill his brother Abel. *Baruch Hashem*, in our own generation, we enjoy so many blessings, and yet we are discontented and ungrateful. Somehow, we always feel that our neighbor, our relative, our friend, is better off than we, that the grass is greener on the other side, Thus, we rob ourselves of our peace of mind, make ourselves miserable, and are unable to enjoy those blessings that we *do* have. So, instead of looking enviously at others, we would do well to focus on our own lives and develop our own potential.

The great Chassidic leader, the Rebbe Reb Zisha, was once asked if he would have preferred to have been born the Patriarch Abraham. To which he responded, "What would the Almighty God gain from that? There would still be only *one* Abraham and *one* Reb Zisha." This teaching of Reb Zisha's is one that we would do well to contemplate. We must realize that each and every one of us has a special task and that, throughout our lives, we must strive to fulfill the purpose for which God created us. Instead of trying to imitate others, we should probe our own souls and become our own unique selves. Genuine joy can only be found in the knowledge that we are standing at the post to which we were assigned by God, and are fulfilling His Will. On the other hand, self-aggrandizement and an envious eye can only lead to frustration and destruction. The sooner we realize this, the sooner we will know peace of mind.

In living a purposeful life, it is important to remember the very first passage of this *parashah* in which it is related that Korah took it, which means that the life of Korah centered on *taking* rather than *giving*. Takers are never content, since genuine happiness can only be found in giving. Had Korah realized that, he would have understood that the very essence of life is to help others and create a relationship with Hashem; that realization would have enabled him to rejoice in the achievements of his fellow man.

PARASHAS CHUKAS

Voids Left by Those Who Die

In this *parashah*, we encounter the deaths of two of our spiritual giants, Aaron and Miriam. With their deaths, calamity befalls the nation. After Aaron's death, it is written, "And the Canaanite king of Arad heard ... and he warred against Israel."[21] Our Sages ask: What exactly did the king hear that prompted him to do battle against our people? And one answer given is that he heard of the death of Aaron the High Priest and the subsequent departure of the Clouds of Glory that accompanied the Jewish people in his merit. But the question still remains: Why did the death of Aaron render the nation vulnerable to attack and cause the Clouds of Glory to depart?

---

21. Ibid. 21:1.

Ethics of the Fathers describes Aaron as "loving peace and pursuing peace, loving people, and bringing them closer to the Torah."[22] So we find that Aaron was forever involved in resolving all sorts of quarrels. Whenever he heard that two people were at odds, he would approach one of them and say, "Your friend said that the quarrel was all his fault, and he deeply regrets it." Aaron would then go to the second party and tell him the same story. Thus, when the two met again, they would embrace and become friends again. It is for this reason that the entire nation wept when he passed away.[23]

So it is that, with the passing of Aaron, a terrible void was left. Who would make peace between brother and brother, neighbor and neighbor, husband and wife? Thus, when Aaron died, arguments erupted again, and that caused the Cloud of Glory, which represented the spirit of Hashem to depart, rendering the nation vulnerable to attack.

The reading of *Parashas Chukas* falls in the month of Tammuz, the month that foretells disaster for our people; the month in which the walls of Jerusalem were breached, culminating in the destruction of the Holy Temples. At the root of this tragedy and all the subsequent tragedies that have befallen our people is baseless hatred. It is *baseless hatred* that caused the Clouds of Glory, the presence of God to abandon us, and it is love — exemplified by acts of *chesed* — between Jew and Jew that merits God's presence in our midst.

This simple and yet complex message of Aaron is desperately needed in our fragmented, torn families and communities. If we would only follow Aaron's example, we could dissipate the anger that has created ugly walls of animosity that destroy us.

GRATITUDE

In contrast to Aaron, whom the Torah testifies was mourned by the entire nation, at Miriam's passing, which took place earlier, there is no mention of mourning. Rather, it states

---

22. *Ethics of the Fathers* 1:12.
23. *Numbers* 20:29.

"there was no water for the congregation."[24] Sometimes silence speaks louder than words, and the silence that should give us pause is the absence of mourning and weeping. God denied the nation water so that they might be ever-cognizant that the fresh sweet water of the well in the desert was all in the merit of Miriam. During the long, bitter years of Egyptian bondage, Miriam was responsible for imbuing the nation with faith. She put herself on the line to save the lives of doomed Jewish babies; she lovingly stood guard over the infant Moses while he was floating in a basket on the Nile; and she courageously convinced Pharaoh's daughter to entrust the baby to the care of Jochebed, Moses' mother. At the Splitting of the Reed Sea, Miriam inspired the women to call out to God in praise, dance, and sing songs of thanksgiving.[25] How could the people have forgotten her? Unfortunately, human nature is such that with the passage of time, it is easy to forget. There is an all-too-familiar adage that speaks in every generation, "What have you done for me lately?"

Therefore, with the death of Miriam, Hashem reminded the people of one of the main pillars of Jewish life: *hakaras hatov*. They had to remember that it was in the merit of Miriam that they had been granted the gift of water in the desert; to drive the lesson home, with her death, her well was lost. The people had to search for it so that forever after, they — and we, their descendants— might bear in mind this basic principle of *hakaras hatov*.

We are never to forget any kindness that was extended to us, even if it occurred centuries ago. To this day, we gather at our Seder tables and recall with thanksgiving that time so long ago when God brought us forth from Egyptian bondage. We chant *"Dayeinu"* and enumerate in great detail every blessing that God bestowed upon us. However, it is not only on Pesach night that we are enjoined to thank God for His manifold blessings, but in our daily prayers as well. There is no aspect of life that we can ignore, from the most physical to the most spiritual, from the most simple to the most complex; we thank God for it all.

---

24. Ibid. 20:2.
25. *Exodus* 15:20.

Unfortunately, too often, these expressions of thanks are just empty words, mouthed without thought or feeling. We would do well to take a few moments every day to consider God's manifold gifts, as well as the kindnesses that our families, friends, and many others have extended to us. The well of Miriam is an eternal testimony to our indebtedness. We dare not take anything for granted, but must count our blessings. If we would only absorb this simple teaching, our lives would have much more meaning; people who realize that they have been blessed are content and happy. In contrast, those who are ingrates know no peace, for instead of appreciating their own gifts, they are forever gazing enviously at others. If we think about it, we will quickly realize that to live by Torah values is to our benefit, and negating them is to our detriment and misfortune.

UNWAVERING FAITH

The *parashah* begins, "This is the decree of the Torah ... and they shall take unto you a *parah adumah* (*Red Heifer*) ...."[26] The obvious question is, why does the text preface the commandment regarding the Red Heifer with those puzzling words, "*This is the decree of the Torah* ..."? It seems that the text should simply state, "*This is the decree of the parah adumah — the Red Heifer.*"

But herein is a very profound teaching. Even as the laws of the *parah adumah*, which can simultaneously purify and contaminate, are beyond our human comprehension, similarly, all the laws of the Torah (even *mishpatim* — those laws that appeal to our human intelligence, such as "Thou shalt not steal") have elements that are inexplicable.

King Solomon was the wisest of all men and he proclaimed, "All this I tested with wisdom; I thought I could become wise; but it is beyond me."[27] Solomon was not speaking only of the laws pertain-

---

26. *Numbers* 19:2.
27. *Ecclesiastes* 7:23.

ing to the Red Heifer, which he could not grasp; rather, he stated that *all of the Torah* is above man's reason. And *that is precisely why it is Torah* — the Word of God. We finite beings cannot possibly hope to understand the infinite.

One might argue however, that we have entire responsa on *ta'amei hamitzvos* — reasons for the mitzvos — but *ta'amei hamitzvos* doesn't really mean "reasons for the commandments"; rather, it means a *taste* for them. For example, when a mother encourages a child to eat, saying, "Taste it — it's delicious," does she want the child to eat the food because it tastes delicious, or does she want him to benefit from its nutritional content? The answer is obvious. Similarly, our Sages gave us *ta'am* — a *taste* for the mitzvos, but that is not the ultimate reason for observing them.

Through the wisdom of our Sages, through our studies, we can better appreciate the majesty, the sanctity, and the blessings of the Torah, but we have to bear in mind that the *definitive* reasons for the mitzvos are beyond our reach.

Ultimately, if our relationship with God and our observance of the commandments are to survive the vicissitudes of time, they must be rooted in unwavering faith. Most of life is baffling; death, illness, sorrow — the ups and downs of daily existence — are very much like the Red Heifer; they are beyond the scope of our understanding, but our faith sustains us and keeps us going.

Even as a toddler cannot comprehend why his parent takes him to a physician, makes him go to sleep, and disciplines him, we cannot possibly know why certain things befall us. Next to God, we are not even toddlers. But despite this lack of understanding, the toddler trusts his parents implicitly and would panic if they were absent. Similarly, should we not have as much trust in our Heavenly Father as the toddler does in his parents? At Sinai, we accepted the Torah and proclaimed *"Na'aseh v'nishma."* We will observe the mitzvos and study the Torah. This unequivocal declaration of observance and study laid the foundation for our relationship with the Almighty.

The moment we attribute our own reasons for the observance of the commandments, we also place them at risk, for "reasons" are debatable. Moreover, that which appeals to us today may lose its attraction tomorrow. Our commitment must be *above* our human reasoning. It must be constant, immutable, and steadfast. So, why do we observe? Because *"Zos chukas HaTorah* — This is the decree of the Torah." This is God's decree.

Unequivocal Faith

The need for this unequivocal faith is evidenced throughout the *parashah*: Miriam the prophetess and Aaron the High Priest die, and Moses, the loyal shepherd of the Jewish people is denied the right to enter the Promised Land. Our human reason might rebel against these apparently harsh decrees, but who are we to question the will of God? So, yes, the entire Torah is like the laws of the Red Heifer, beyond the bounds of our finite reasoning. But how else can it be, since it is God's Word?

This teaching is especially relevant to our generation, for while we pride ourselves on our intellectual acumen, we fall pitifully short on faith. We lack spiritual stamina and at the slightest crisis collapse and become angry, bitter, and alienated. Foolishly, we close the door on our only source of help — God — and feel that we are forced to walk alone through life's dark, treacherous valleys.

PARASHAS BALAK

WAKE-UP CALLS: HOW WELL DO WE LISTEN?

Time and again in this *parashah* we encounter the infinite compassion and loving-kindness of Hashem, who never gives up on anyone. Balak, the king of Moab, consumed by hatred of the Jewish people, is very much aware that the secret power of the Jews lies in their prayers, in their devotion to God. To counteract this energy, he appoints a delegation to invite Bilaam, the heathen prophet, to curse the Jews. Bilaam sanctimoniously answers that he would have to ask God for permission, which, at first glance, appears to be a righteous response, but which in fact, is an indictment of his character, for how could a decent human being even consider undertaking such an evil deed? What sane man would ask God for permission to do evil?

Just the same, God, in His boundless mercy, does not punish Bilaam, but sends him his first *wake-up call*. In a dream, God speaks to him and asks a simple question: "Who are these men with you?"[28]

This question is difficult to understand, for surely God knows who these people are; but throughout the Torah, we find that God sends His wake-up calls by prodding man with similar gentle questions. For example, when Adam and Eve sin, God asks, "*Ayekah*? — Where are you?"[29] When Cain kills his brother, Abel, God asks, "Where is Abel, your brother?"[30]

These questions are meant to challenge man, to make him realize how low he has sunk, and to motivate him into taking control of his life before it is too late and he perishes. What God is really asking Bilaam is to consider what has happened to him. "Who are these people with you? How do you come to associate yourself with such evil? How low can you sink?"

WHOSE FAULT IS IT?

Bilaam just doesn't get it! He is so full of his own self-importance that he never hears the deeper question of God. Again and again God sends messages to Bilaam to prevent him from following this disastrous course. Sadly, however, when a man is bent upon evil, God's warnings fall upon deaf ears. Man has this uncanny ability to rationalize, to twist and turn reality to suit his desires. As obvious and as pointed as God's messages may be, they are all to no avail if a person chooses to disregard them. So it is that, despite God's warnings, Bilaam sets out on his journey. Still, God doesn't give up on him and places obstructions in his path. Perhaps as a result of these hardships, Bilaam will re-think his malevolent plan and come to realize the catastrophic consequences of his undertaking. But Bilaam continues on his blind course, and when he encounters new difficul-

---

28. *Numbers* 22:9.
29. *Genesis* 3:9.
30. Ibid. 4:9.

ties, he blames outside forces and strikes the donkey he is riding, believing that the donkey is at fault.

At this point God performs an open miracle that cannot possibly be taken for coincidence. The donkey actually opens its mouth and *speaks*, an occurrence that would shock any normal person! "What have I done to you that you struck me these three times?" the donkey asks.[31] But Bilaam remains obstinate and continues to ignore God's call.

There are several lessons that we can learn from all this. The most important message that we should absorb is how disastrously self-destructive human nature can be. This realization should give us all pause. How sensitive are we to God's wake-up calls? When difficulties befall us, do we search for scapegoats? Like Bilaam, do we blame the "donkeys" in our lives? Do we hold others responsible for our failings and difficulties, or do we have the courage to examine our own hearts and determine where and how we strayed? These are painful questions, but if we are to lead meaningful, purposeful lives, we must answer them candidly.

NEVER GIVE UP ON ANYONE

An additional lesson to be gleaned from this story is that we should try to emulate the ways of Hashem and never give up on those who are bent upon a disastrous course. Despite everything, Hashem continues to appeal to Bilaam to change his ways. Similarly, we too must try to persuade people whom we see embarking upon a ruinous path to come to their senses before it is too late. We are never to give up on anyone.

WE CHOOSE THE PATH

In a dream, God tells Bilaam not to go with those who want him to curse the Jewish people, but when a second delegation arrives, God gives His permission. A superficial reading

---

31. Numbers 22:28.

of this text would suggest that God is sending contradictory messages.

At first glance, this appears rather paradoxical. Does God change His mind? Of course we realize that changing one's mind is a human trait, so how are we to understand this passage? There is a Talmudic teaching that "the path that a man chooses to follow is the path on which he is *led*."[32] God grants us free will: There is life, there is death; there is blessing, there is curse; there is good, there is evil. It is for us to choose the good, but God cannot force us to do so without depriving us of our free will and rendering us robots. If we will it, there are no external forces that can prevent us from choosing the right path. If we will it, there is nothing to inhibit us from becoming better and kinder people. It's all in our hands, and we can't blame fate or the stars for our actions. *We are all responsible!*

God warns Bilaam not to go with Balak's emissaries, but when he insists on doing so, God gives him permission to *accompany* them, but at the same time, Bilaam is warned not to join them in their evil scheme. This warning is evidenced in the use of the Hebrew word, *itam* — with. In the Hebrew language, there are no redundancies; thus, the two words for "with" have different connotations. *Imahem*, derived from the word *"am* — nation," implies a common ideology, while *"itam"* is more objective, implying being physically in the same place as others (i.e., on a plane or a train with many passengers) but having no common purpose with them.

In Bilaam's first dream, God warns him not to go *"imahem"*[33] — "Do not be one in purpose with them." In the second dream, when Bilaam persists in his desire to go, God gives His consent with the word *"itam,"* meaning that if Bilaam was determined to go, he could *physically* accompany them, but he *could not* join forces with them.[34] But once again, despite God's clear warning, Bilaam refuses to listen and he goes *"im,"* joining them in heart and mind.[35] Later, when he was already on the way, God warned him again that he

---

32. *Makkos* 10b.
33. *Numbers* 22:12.
34. Ibid. 22:20.
35. Ibid. 22:21.

could go only to pronounce what he would be commanded to say.[36]

The sad lesson that we learn from this incident is that even when God gives us a specific warning, even when His messages are crystal clear and cannot possibly be misinterpreted, even then, man can pervert and twist God's command.

But the sad lesson does not end there. There is a kabbalistic teaching that Bilaam was a *gilgul* of Laban, the treacherous father of Rachel and Leah. Like Bilaam, Laban was bent upon destroying the Jewish people. He too was warned by God in a dream to stay away from Jacob and refrain from speaking either good or bad to him — informing us that even his apparent good was bad. However, just as Laban refused to heed God's warning, Bilaam repeated the same evil. Generations may pass, conditions may change, but man's perverse nature remains the same. How very sad!

THE SECRET POWER OF THE JEW

Bilaam was bent upon cursing the nation, but God placed a blessing on his lips. When Bilaam beheld the beautiful, modest family life of the Jewish people, despite himself he proclaimed the timeless prayer that has become the identifying characteristic of our people throughout the centuries: *"Ma tovu ohalecha Yaakov ...* — How goodly are your tents, O Jacob, your dwelling places, O Israel."[37] This is the first prayer that we pronounce upon entering the synagogue, and it is the prayer that some people chant under the *chuppah* as a new Jewish home is created.

What is the significance of this blessing? What exactly did Bilaam see? Indeed, there are many dimensions to this prayer. Bilaam was awed by the sanctity and modesty of Jewish family life, as evidenced by the manner in which the tents of the Jewish people were placed. To assure the total privacy of each family, the doors of the tents were set up so that no one had a view of the other.

The "tents" and the "dwelling places" are also references to

---
36. Ibid. 22:35.
37. Ibid. 24:5.

the synagogues and the study halls. It is this threefold bastion of strength that guarantees the Jewish people's invincibility and eternity:

- The modesty and sanctity of Jewish family life.
- The nation's devotion to prayer and the service of God.
- The people's commitment to Torah study.

These three pillars guarantee our Jewish survival, but if they are compromised, then the very life of our nation is at risk. Bilaam intended to invoke a curse on our Jewish people by declaring that our study halls and synagogues be empty and that our homes and family lives be infiltrated by foreign influences. But despite himself, he had to declare praise, for God granted him vision, and he saw that for all of eternity there would be Jewish people who would cling tenaciously to these three foundations upon which Jewish life is built.

Indeed, no matter to what corners of the earth destiny may have propelled us, no matter how much suffering, pain, and persecution we may have experienced, no matter how the ravages of assimilation may have eaten away at us, there have always been and shall always be committed Jews who are prepared to sacrifice and adhere to this threefold formula: the sanctity of the Jewish family, devotion to prayer and the service of God, and our study of Torah.

Indeed, "how goodly are your tents, O Jacob, your dwelling places, O Israel."

PARASHAS PINCHAS

Love of God

This theme of love, commitment, and passion runs throughout the *parashah*. In the opening verses, Phinehas, the grandson of Aaron, is awarded the covenants of priesthood and peace. What rendered him worthy of such an awesome honor? When God's Name was desecrated through acts of immorality and idol worship,[38] Phinehas rose like a lion and put himself on the line; he jeopardized his life to champion the cause of God and thus restored sanctity to the nation. Phinehas rose from *amid* the assembly,[39] teaching us that he could have waited on others to take action, but chose to act himself. If we truly care, if we are sincere in our love and faith, we will not be content to remain passive;

---

38. Ibid. 25:6.
39. Ibid. 25:7.

we will find the strength to raise our voices and act. We live in a generation in which, for many, it is politically correct to be casual about everything. Yes, we protest, we love our Judaism, but how deep is our love? How *committed* are we? How much are we ready to sacrifice? How much are we prepared to give of ourselves?

There is an apt analogy to this: Imagine a sport that has only fans and no players. Even if those fans are devoted, the sport will eventually die out. Alas, too many of us have become fans. Too many of us are content to be passive spectators. But if our nation is to thrive, we need players who are ready to take the ball and run. Let us consider for a moment the single-minded commitment with which athletes train for the Olympics. Should we not at least invest the same energy in the greatest Olympics of all: our lives here on Planet Earth?

So, as Jews, the question that we must ask ourselves is, are we players or spectators?

STAND UP TO THE PLATE

In the opening verses of the *parashah*, we find that Hashem bestows His covenant of *peace* on Phinehas and promises him the priesthood for all time. And indeed, all the Kohanim Gedolim were the descendants of Phinehas.

In explaining why Phinehas was worthy of these two sacred gifts (peace and priesthood), the Torah states that "he took vengeance *for his God.*"[40] The unusual wording, "... *his* God," should give us all pause. After all, isn't the Almighty the God of everyone? In order to understand, it is important that we review the background against which this story unfolds.

Our Exodus from Egypt shook up the world. The Ten Plagues, the Splitting of the Reed Sea, manna falling from the heavens, water flowing from a rock, and later, the giving of the Torah, made the entire world aware of the existence of God. And yet, incredibly,

---

40. Ibid. 25:13.

with the exception of Jethro, the father-in-law of Moses, no one reacted. No one came to Sinai to declare his/her faith. Rather, the response from the nations was one of hatred and jealousy.

Balak, the king of Moab, could not contain his venom. He schemed to destroy our people. Knowing, however, that he could never defeat us on the battlefield, he commissioned the heathen prophet, Bilaam, to rain curses upon us. But God would not allow him to curse; when Bilaam witnessed the beautiful family life of the Jewish people, despite himself he proclaimed blessings.

Having failed to execute Balak's diabolical plan, Bilaam suggested that there was only one way to defeat the Jews, and that was to entice them to sin. And so, the most beautiful girls of Moab and Midian were enlisted to seduce the men of Israel. A terrible calamity ensued. Zimri, the prince of the tribe of Simon, took possession of Kozbi, the Midianite princess, and publically desecrated the Holy Name of God. There was total chaos; the nation stood stupefied in shock, and the very survival of our people was in jeopardy. No one took action — but Phinehas arose *"from amid the assembly"* and put an end to that horrific defilement. And here again the question arises. Why does the Torah emphasize *"from amid the assembly"*?

Very often, we gauge our action or inaction by comparing ourselves to others. If everyone is passive, we feel justified in being passive as well. Phinehas, however, did not allow the passivity of others to affect him. He rose to the occasion and acted on behalf of God, proving that indeed, God was *his* God.

We can all learn from Phinehas, and emulate him, even if it be in a small way. Peace cannot be attained through the Chamberlain tactics of appeasement and looking away. The Hebrew word for peace, *shalom*, comes from the word *"shalem* — complete," teaching us that peace can only be achieved if we give of ourselves completely and are willing to sacrifice to combat injustice. Phinehas reminds us that we *must get involved*, that we must protest when we behold debauchery, corruption, and evil; that we must learn to raise our voices and *"stand up to the plate,"* for, in the end, we are all responsible for one another, and we all have to testify that *God is our God*.

Converting Handicaps Into Assets

Moses takes the census of all the tribes, and we find that, strangely, the tribe of Dan has almost 20,000 more people than the tribe of Benjamin.[41] The remarkable growth of Dan is all the more astonishing since, initially, Benjamin had 10 sons while Dan had only one, Chushim, who also happened to be deaf.

Consider for a moment the thoughts and feelings that must have plagued Dan. How could his tribe equal the other tribes of Israel? He had only one son, and the boy was deaf. What would the future hold?

This week's portion teaches us never to despair and never to measure ourselves by others. We need only make a sincere effort, give of our best, and strive to fulfill our own unique mission; if we do so, the possibilities are limitless. Perhaps it was precisely because Chushim was deaf that he remained immune to the many confusing and misleading voices assailing the others. The Talmud teaches that, when the sons of Jacob came to bury their father in Hebron, Esau protested and demanded to see the deed to the Cave of the Machpelah, Naftali, noted for his swiftness, was commissioned by his brethren to return to Egypt for the deed. Chushim, who was deaf and not perturbed by Esau's bullying, was outraged by the lack of respect shown to his grandfather and attacked Esau, thus championing the honor of the Patriarch. The story of Chushim demonstrates that if we will it, our handicaps can become our assets and our burdens our inspiration. We need only have faith. And so it was that from that one son, Chushim, the tribe of Dan grew and multiplied and surpassed the others.

---

41. Ibid. 26:41, 43.

How Deep Is Our Love?

The five daughters of Zelophehad, of the tribe of Manasseh, the son of Joseph, approach Moses with a most unusual request.[42] "Our father died in the Wilderness … he had no sons. Why should the name of our father be omitted from among his family because he had no son? Give us a possession among our father's brothers." Moses brought their request to God, and God deemed it fitting and proper that the daughters of Zelophehad be granted their share in the land.

Many questions come to mind. Why were the daughters of Zelophehad so zealous about ownership of the land? Would it not have sufficed for them to have simply lived in the Holy Land? And why was it necessary for the Torah to trace their lineage back to Joseph?

The answers to both questions are one and the same. If you truly *love*, you will not be satisfied being passive about the object of your love; you will want to protect it, guard it, work for it, and if necessary, sacrifice for it. The daughters of Zelophehad, because they loved the Land of Israel, wanted to possess and cultivate it. They weren't content to be mere bystanders. From where did this fire in their hearts emanate? From their ancestor Joseph, whose love for the holy land was legendary. During his exile in Egypt, he never for a moment forgot his roots. Despite the fact that the Egyptians held Jews and their land in contempt, he never denied his origins. Whether in bondage, in prison, or in the palace, the Land of Israel remained uppermost in his heart and mind. Even on his deathbed, Joseph spoke of the Land and made his brethren swear that when the Exodus took place, they would not forget him but take his remains with them and bury him in the Holy Land.

---

42. Ibid. 27:1-4.

PARASHAS MATTOS

Your Word Is Your Bond

Parashas Mattos reminds us of the timeless values that have distinguished our people throughout the centuries. As the *parashah* opens, Moshe commands the leaders of the tribes, and, through them, the entire nation, regarding the sanctity of vows and the tragic consequences of not keeping one's word, *which the Torah regards as a desecration.*[43]

Our faith is linked to the sanctity of speech. It is through speech that we committed ourselves to an eternal covenant with God when we proclaimed *"Na'aseh v'nishma."* It is through speech, via prayer and Torah study, that we continue to connect with our God. It is through speech that we give expression to the Divine spark that God breathed into our beings. It is through speech that God

---
43. Ibid. 30:3.

created the world and it is through speech that we, in our own human fashion, send forth positive or negative energies. As stated previously, "Death and life are in the tongue."[44]

We have 14 positive and 17 negative commandments, all centering around speech. To protect us from using our tongues irresponsibly, God places them behind two gates, our teeth and our lips, so that before we speak, we may weigh and measure our words, for once they are spoken, we cannot easily undo them or take them back. The damage wrought by broken promises, curses, and painful or blasphemous words cannot be easily erased. The converse, of course, is also true. Kind, warm, loving words are balm for the soul and have the power to transform darkness into light and despair into hope.

ANOTHER FACE OF GRATITUDE

God instructs Moses to "take vengeance ... against the Midianites,"[45] but, strangely enough, rather than assume this responsibility, Moses appoints Phinehas to lead the people in battle. At first glance, it is difficult to understand Moses' reaction, for he was a loyal servant of God, ever ready to do His bidding, and this transfer of responsibility is totally out of character for him. But herein lies a powerful lesson to guide us on the road of life.

When Pharaoh discovered that Moses, the young prince, was a Jew, he was determined to kill him. Moses had to flee for his life and found refuge in the land of Midian. Many years had passed since that incident. The world scene had changed; the Midianites were an evil, immoral people, bent upon seducing and destroying the Jewish nation. Nevertheless, Moses could not do battle against them, for at one point in his life, he had benefited from the Midianites' hospitality. Similarly, when God brought the Ten Plagues upon Egypt, Moses was not permitted to strike the water

---

44. *Proverbs* 18:21.
45. *Numbers* 31:1.

of the Nile (Aaron struck the Nile), for, when he was an infant, the water had sheltered him. If Moses had to be grateful to a body of water, an incorporeal entity that had not made a willful decision to save him, how much more should it hold true for human beings? We are never permitted to forget or take for granted an act of kindness or a favor rendered.

This message is especially relevant to our generation, in which ingratitude is so commonplace. We easily forget benefits that we have enjoyed and rationalize our insensitivity by saying, "It's coming to me!" or "They owe it to me!" Let us guard against such rationalizations; let us never lose sight of the kindnesses that have been extended to us and let us work on developing our sense of gratitude.

A True Leader

God instructs Moses to tell the Jewish people to do battle against the Midianites who were the cause of the terrible plague that befell them. At the same time, however, God also informs Moses that following that battle he would die.[46] Knowing this information before the battle, Moses could have taken his time, especially since God did not give him a specific time frame in which to carry out his task. No one could have faulted him had he delayed this action in order to prolong his life. Moses, however, responds with alacrity to the call of Hashem and puts aside his own personal wishes. And that is the mark of true greatness, true leadership: to have the ability to think of the greater good of one's family and one's people rather than one's own narrow, selfish concerns.

Moses' example challenges us to examine our own actions, our own priorities. Are we prompted by selfish concerns? Do we come first, or do we see the needs of our families, our people, and the call of God as our first priority?

---

46. Ibid. 31:1-2.

Life's Battles

The soldiers of Israel return victorious from their battle with the Midianites, but, paradoxically, it is written, "who *came* to battle," rather than "who *returned* from battle."[47] From this we learn that after winning a battle, after tasting success, we may feel overly confident and arrogant, deluding ourselves into believing that we no longer are required to be vigilant. Therefore, the soldiers of our people are warned that the real battle is just starting, and that is the *battle of life*. The battle of life is a constant struggle against the *yetzer hara*, of which we must remain vigilant until the day we die.

In this same *parashah*, Elazar the priest proceeds to instruct the people in regard to the laws of *kashering* vessels by purging them. One may wonder about the connection between these two themes, and once again there is a message for us: The path to success in our ongoing life struggle is to purge ourselves of all that is "non-kosher," all that is antithetical to the Torah way of life. But what we should remember for all time, what should imbue us with courage and hope, is the deeper meaning of this teaching. If a pot, which is an inanimate object, can be made kosher, how much more so can a human being, who carries within him the breath of God, who has a holy *neshamah*, become holy again and be purged of even the most terrible failings.

How Much Do You Feel?

The Torah informs us that the tribes of Reuben and Gad had abundant livestock and requested permission from Moses to settle on the other side of the Jordan where the land "is a land for livestock, and your servants have livestock."[48]

Moses' response transcends the centuries and speaks to us in

---

47. Ibid. 31:21.
48. Ibid. 32:1-5.

every generation: "Shall your brothers go to battle while you settle here?"[49]

We, the Jewish people, are one family. If any one of us is hurting, we are all hurting. The heart of each and every Jew must beat with the heart of his people. Yes, Moses' question challenges us in every generation.

Our parents have often related how, in the concentration camps, they asked, "Can it be that our brethren in America are silent? Can it be that they are busy with their own lives while we are being fed to the ovens? Can it be that they don't hear our cry? Can it be that they don't see our tears? Can it be …? Can it be …?"

This question of Moses speaks to us, not only in times of Holocaust, but in our everyday family life as well. Can it be that you are buying jewelry while your sister can't pay her rent? Can it be that you are going on vacation while your father is lying alone in his hospital bed? Can it be that you are celebrating at your holiday table while your brother sits alone in his dark apartment? Can it be …? Can it be …?

Moses' challenge demands that we take a good look at our lives and examine to what extent we feel empathy for our families, for our people. When you read in the papers that there was another suicide attack in Israel in which our people were massacred, do you stop to shed a tear? Do you stop to pronounce a prayer, or do you move on? Is it business as usual?

JEWISH PRIORITIES

The tribes of Reuben and Gad hastened to assure Moses that they intended to join their brethren in battle. "Pens for the flock shall we build here for our livestock and cities for our small children. We shall arm ourselves swiftly in the vanguard of the Children of Israel …."[50]

---

49. Ibid. 32:6.
50. Ibid. 32:16-17.

Moshe Rabbeinu is not satisfied with their response and corrects them, saying, "Build for yourselves cities for your small children and pens for your flock."[51]

There is a profound lesson in *Moshe Rabbeinu's* correction that, once again, is relevant for all times. Even as the tribes of Reuben and Gad put their livestock before their families; even as the tribes of Reuben and Gad prioritized Israel — the Jewish people — over Hashem, there are those today who put business first and families second, and regard their commitment to Israel and the Jewish people above their faith in Hashem. They forget that love of Israel and the Jewish nation has meaning only if it is rooted in Torah and commitment to God.

---

51. Ibid. 32:24.

PARASHAS MASEI

LIFE'S JOURNEYS

The reading of *Parashas Masei* always coincides with the season that marks Jewish suffering and sorrow: the anniversary of the destruction of our Holy Temples. But our Torah never speaks of sorrow without imparting hope and consolation. So it is that this *parashah* imbues us with strength and faith, and the very fact that these tragedies occurred in the Jewish month of *Menachem Av*, which, literally translated, means "a comforting father," speaks volumes.

The *parashah* teaches us that we were launched upon life's journeys *"al pi Hashem* — at the bidding of God,"[52] and that knowledge, in and of itself, is the greatest source of comfort. We are fortified in the realization that our journeys are not just random happenings.

---

52. Ibid. 33:2.

There is a God above us Who directs it all, Who oversees our going forth and our coming in. Nothing, but nothing, escapes Him. He hears our cries, He sees our tears, and He never forsakes us. Yes, there *is* a purpose to our wandering, even though we may not understand it. We are strengthened in the knowledge that there is an ultimate destination to which God leads us.

To reinforce this teaching, the Torah reader chants this *parashah* to a special tune so that we may be ever mindful that we are not alone. Even as our forefather's journeys through the Wilderness were hazardous, but they arrived safely to their destination, Eretz Yisrael, just the same, so too shall we arrive in the Promised Land, no matter how difficult our journey may be. God is leading us.

The Torah speaks of 42 encampments along life's journey. Forty-two is a mystical number, comprising the letters in God's ineffable Name. There is a kabbalistic teaching that as a result of our sins, those letters in God's holy Name have become blemished, and so we embark upon our journeys to gather those holy sparks and return them to wholeness, to God's holy Name, which we have blemished through our sins. When our journeys become difficult, when they test our mettle and we wonder how we can possibly go on, let us remember that there is a purpose to our journeys. We need only stay the Torah course and God will guide us to our ultimate destination

THE LAND IS OUR DESTINY

Moshe Rabbeinu apportions the land among the tribes in accordance to a *goral* (drawing of lots).[53] The word *goral*, however, has a double meaning. It not only means "lot," but also "destiny." The land is our destiny for all eternity. Thus, the Torah teaches us that the Jewish people, Hashem, Torah, and the Land of Israel are forever intertwined. No matter what the political situation may be, no matter what the nations of

---

53. Ibid. 34:13.

the world or world leaders may scheme, that land is our Divine destiny, and no human being and no nation can ever negate that. Our history is testimony to that eternal truth. Indeed, there is no nation on Planet Earth that has been separated from its land for almost 2,000 years and yet remained loyal to that land. And moreover, there is no country on earth that, throughout the long centuries, rejected all its occupiers, all its conquerors, to await her children's homecoming. Over 3,000 years ago, our Torah proclaimed that Eretz Yisrael is our *goral*, the *destiny of the Jewish people*, and today, history testifies to it.

CITIES OF REFUGE: SPIRITUAL REJUVENATION

Moshe Rabbeinu instructs the nation in regard to the establishment of six *arei miklat* (cities of refuge),[54] three on either side of the Jordan. These cities belonged to the Levites and were to provide sanctuaries to those who were guilty of accidental murder. While their crimes may have been unintentional, nevertheless, blood was spilled and the perpetrator could not simply resume his life as though nothing had happened. Such a tragic deed required spiritual rehabilitation. Additionally, the guilty parties needed protection from the vengeful family members of the victim. So it was that the man who had blood on his hands relocated to a city of refuge accompanied by his family and his rabbi — his Torah teacher.

One might ask why it was necessary for his Torah teacher to go with him. After all, these cities were inhabited by Levites who were all well versed in Torah. But each rabbi, each Torah teacher, has his own unique approach, and when a soul is in crisis and carries the heavy burden of having murdered, albeit accidentally, the teacher who could best penetrate the depths of his soul must be there to teach.

---

54. Ibid. 35:11-15.

From this we learn that Hashem worries about each and every one of us, so we should never feel that we have been rejected or abandoned by Him or that we are beyond redemption. In the Torah, there is an *ir miklat* for every person. Now, if God has commanded us to make such provisions for those who committed a crime, albeit unintentional, then we too must extend love and concern to each and every person. Let us merit Hashem's mercy by being merciful to one another.

ספר דברים

THE BOOK OF Deuteronomy

PARASHAS DEVARIM

How To Criticize Without Offending

Deuteronomy, the fifth Book of the Torah, is also referred to as *Mishnah Torah* — a review of the Torah. Knowing that he will soon die, *Moshe Rabbeinu* reviews the Torah with his beloved people and admonishes them for their sins. He begins by alluding to those sins by recalling the *places* where they occurred, but he does not detail them explicitly until later in the Book. For example, instead of specifically referring to the grievous sin of the Golden Calf, he simply states, "*di zahav* — much gold."[1] Through this method of criticism, he not only preserves their digni-

---

1. *Deuteronomy* 1:1.

ty, but he also calls attention to the hazards of *too much gold* which, if uncontrolled, can lead to a person's downfall.

Our Sages teach that, sadly, the residue of the sin of the Golden Calf is evidenced in every generation. When greed and lust consume us and we compromise our commitment to Torah and mitzvos, we are, in a sense, fashioning our own "Golden Calves." Moreover, anything that takes priority over our God-given covenant becomes our Golden Calf.

THREE STEPS

Moses imparts to us three steps in the art of constructive criticism:

- When admonishing, be on guard not to put anyone to shame.
- Couch your admonishment in loving and positive terms.
- Remember: A few words are more effective than a deluge of badgering.

This teaching of Moses has served as our model for criticism throughout the centuries. Our Sages instruct those who would criticize to "push away with the left hand (the weaker one) and simultaneously draw near with the right hand (the stronger one),"[2] so that the person we are admonishing may come to realize that it is not *he* who is being censured, but his *actions*. Finally, Moses taught us that, when offering criticism, our words should not only be censorious, but also therapeutic, and they should demonstrate how to overcome weakness and temptation.

---

2. Tractate *Sanhedrin* 107b.

Less Is More

Too often, when we admonish members of our own families and friends, we have a tendency to fall into the trap of "overkill." We go on and on, and unfortunately, don't quite know where or when to stop. To be sure, we may be motivated by love and genuine concern, but, because of our heavy-handedness, by the time we finish, our words are interpreted as abuse rather than as loving, concerned guidance. Not only does such criticism fail to be instructive or helpful, but it will elicit just the opposite reaction. Instead of correction and improvement, it will generate resentment, disdain, and further rebellion.

Moses teaches us that, when it comes to criticism, *less is more*. There is a Talmudic dictum, "*Die l'chachima b'remiza* — for the wise, an allusion suffices."[3] Admittedly, there are those who are not wise and remain deaf to admonition, but such people remain obdurate no matter what, and even a sledgehammer won't move them. Harping on a subject is not only counterproductive, but it will generate contempt. Before criticizing, collect your thoughts and weigh your words carefully. King Solomon taught, "Don't criticize a fool, for he will hate you; criticize a wise man and he will love you."[4]

The Torah Speaks for All Eternity

The verse states, "Moses began explaining this Torah."[5] The Midrash teaches us that Moses translated the Torah into 70 different languages, encompassing all the languages of the nations.

At first glance, it is difficult to understand why Moses would go to such great lengths in translating the Torah. After all, our

---

3. *Midrash Shmuel* 22:22.
4. *Proverbs* 9:8.
5. *Deuteronomy* 1:5.

ancestors didn't speak these foreign tongues, but Moses reviewed the Torah in 70 different languages, for he foresaw all the different exiles that we would have to endure until the coming of *Mashiach*, and he wanted us to feel connected to our Torah no matter where fate took us. Moses also knew that in future generations there would be those among us who would argue that outside the Land of Israel, one need not live a life governed by Torah. Therefore, he taught us the Torah in all languages, so that it would speak to us in all situations, in every generation, and in every culture.

Our lives as individuals and as a nation, indeed our very survival, are contingent upon our connection to Torah. Through our Torah, we become a unified and cohesive people. This message of unity was critical for our people as they were about to enter the Promised Land. In our Torah, in our unity, is to be found our strength. Thus, the Torah speaks to us for all eternity.

It's Never Too Late To Start a New Life

Perhaps what is most telling is that even as Moses recounts the names of all the places where the Jewish people angered God during their 40 years of sojourning in the desert, he also demonstrated to them the extent of God's great love, for despite their rebelliousness, the Almighty always forgave, and the people flourished. Thus, Moses reminds the nation, "Hashem, your God, has multiplied you, and behold, you are like the stars of heaven in abundance.[6]

Herein lies another lesson that should not be taken for granted. We should never make someone feel that, because of his sins, he has become persona non grata. Similarly, we should never feel that, because of *our* sins, we have been cut off from God and can no longer come back to Him, Heaven forbid. If our repentance is sincere, God will always embrace us and enable us to start life

---

6. Ibid. 1:10.

anew. Nevertheless, we must be on guard not to abuse His love, rationalizing that sin will have no consequences because God will forgive.

Beware of Your Genetic Predisposition

We can understand *Moshe Rabbeinu* admonishing those who sinned, but what is perplexing in this *parashah* is that his criticism is leveled at those who never participated in those heinous deeds. Moses is bidding farewell in the 40th year of their long journey in the desert, and the generation that had sinned had already died, so he was actually addressing the *children of the rebels*. Why, then, did he castigate them? They had not sinned. It was their fathers who were guilty.

That which is spiritual can very often be best understood through the physical. If you go to a physician for a checkup, you are given a form to fill out on which you have to respond to a number of questions regarding any family history of cancer, diabetes, neurological and mental illness, etc. You might very well protest that you are feeling perfectly fine and are not suffering from any of those ailments. Why, then, must you respond to those questions?

The explanation is that if there is a family history of illness, the doctor has to be aware of it, for you might just have a genetic disposition that must be monitored. Similarly, we have spiritual dispositions to character flaws, and must be ever on guard regarding them. For example, if we were raised in a family in which tempers quickly flared, in which, instead of rationally communicating, people shouted abusively, chances are that we will repeat that same pattern of behavior, even though, logically, we find it reprehensible and reject it. Therefore, we must be ever on guard not to repeat the aberrations of past generations.

You Can Redeem Your Ancestors

By admonishing a new generation, Moses not only alerted us to be on guard against succumbing to the weaknesses of the past, but he also demonstrated how we can rectify the failings of our fathers and bring them merit in the heavens above. So while we, in the physical world, may inherit the possessions of our parents and grandparents, in the spiritual world, just the opposite holds true. Our parents and grandparents are elevated in the heavens above through our deeds, through our commitment to Torah, mitzvos, *tzedakah*, and *chesed*.

Our father, Rabbi Meshulem HaLevi Jungreis, *zt"l*, when officiating at funerals, would very often tell the bereaved members of the family to send daily "Torah–mitzvah care packages" to the departed. What an amazing challenge! Not only does the Torah enable us to start a new life of blessing, but through our Torah and mitzvos, we can also bring that blessing to those of our family members who are in the heavens above.

PARASHAS VA'ESCHANAN

The Power of Prayer

In *Parashas Va'eschanan* there are many of the pillars of our faith: the Ten Commandments, the *Shema*, the art of prayer, prophecy, and teachings that guarantee our Jewish survival. Just by reviewing this portion, we can gain an enormous insight into the essence of our Judaism. In the opening verses of the *parashah*, *Moshe Rabbeinu* prays to God,[7] but the expression he used is most unusual: *"Va'eschanan"* is derived from the word *"chein* — to find favor," or from *"chinam* — free," implying that even if we are undeserving, we beseech God to find favor with us, accept our prayers, and grant our request as a *free gift*.

---

7. Ibid. 3:23.

It is difficult to understand why *Moshe Rabbeinu*, the greatest of all men, would have to resort to such a form of prayer. If anyone was worthy, it was surely he. Never did Moses pray for himself. All his supplications were on behalf of the Jewish people, and now, for the very first time, he pleads on his own behalf and begs God to grant him the privilege of seeing the Promised Land. Moses certainly could have felt entitled to have his prayers answered.

The truly righteous understand, however, that before God, there is no entitlement. When we perform a mitzvah, when we live a righteous life, it is we who have to thank God for granting us that opportunity, that privilege. We are not doing God a favor when we fulfill the commandments; rather, it is *we* who become enriched and elevated. So, when we beseech God in supplication, we have no bargaining points, but are totally dependent on His infinite mercy. In effect, as stated above, we are asking that we may find favor in His eyes and be granted a "free gift."

This message is especially significant to our generation. Too many of us harbor feelings of "entitlement." In our foolish arrogance, we have come to believe that God "owes us one," never realizing that it is *we who owe everything to Him*. Were it not for His constant mercy, in a split second, we could lose our ability to function ... even our very lives. Therefore, we commence each and every morning with these simple, but majestic words, "*Modeh Ani* — I thank *You*" for returning my soul, and we proceed to express gratitude throughout all our waking moments. We thank God for the food that we eat, the water that we drink, for our bodily functions, for the wonders of nature, for the good, and even for the apparently bad — we take nothing for granted.

To be sure, it is not easy to focus on prayer. It is one of the most difficult mitzvos to fulfill. It is so easy to become distracted, to lose focus. Therefore, in earlier generations, pious people would meditate for a full hour prior to prayer so that they might properly direct their words to God. Obviously, we are not on their level, but just the same, we should all endeavor to pray with greater concentration and zeal.

Ours is a generation that is short on patience but long on expectations. If we feel that our prayers have gone unanswered, we are quick to give up in frustration and self-righteous indignation. Yet prayer is our only solution. Let us never forget that when problems overwhelm us, it is only God Who can help.

Our Sages teach that since the destruction of the Holy Temple, all the gates to heaven are locked, except for the gate of tears, which means that genuine, heartfelt, prayers can bring about many miracles. Let us never give up. Let us follow the example of Moses.

DOES GOD ANSWER ALL OUR PRAYERS?

The answer to this question is an emphatic "Yes!" As it is written, "God is near to all those who call upon Him, to all those who call upon Him sincerely."[8]

So why, we might ask, didn't God grant Moses' request to *see* the Promised Land? Upon closer study of the text, however, we will discover that God *did* fulfill Moses' wish. "*Alei rosh hapisgah* — Ascend to the top of the cliff," God commands Moses, "and raise your eyes westward, northward, southward, and eastward, and *see* with your eyes ...."[9] It was thus that Moses was granted his prayer. Not only did Moses *see* the entire Promised Land, but he also *saw* all of Jewish history pass before his eyes. So, yes, God does respond to all sincere prayer, but the manner in which He does so is His to choose, for only He knows what is to our benefit. So let us always approach God in prayer, and trust Him to lead us on the right path.

Our *Zeide* would often tell unmarried people who were searching for their life partners, "*Got zol firren oif gittins*: Rather than specify a specific person, *ask God to lead you to the right one*." Place your trust in Hashem, for only He knows what is right and good for you.

---

8. *Psalms* 145:18.
9. *Deuteronomy* 3:27.

Perseverance in Prayer

The expression *va'eschanan* ("and I implored," referring to prayer in our *parashah*) in *gematria* (numerology) totals 515, teaching that Moses prayed in 515 ways and never lost faith … so, surely, we must cling tenaciously to God in our prayers. This teaching is reinforced by King David in Psalm 27, which counsels us, *"Kavei el Hashem* — Hope to Hashem, strengthen your heart, and hope to Hashem,"[10] meaning that we must keep praying, for it is in prayer that we find our salvation. In Nusach Sefard, we recite this passage as we come to the conclusion of our daily prayers. One might have thought that it would be more appropriate to do so at the commencement of the service. Our *Zeide*, HaRav HaGaon Avraham HaLevi Jungreis, *zt"l*, explained that it is precisely at the conclusion of our prayers, when we may feel discouraged and wonder whether God will answer us, that we strengthen ourselves and proclaim our resolve to continue to pray.

Commitment to Mitzvos

Moses set up three cities of refuge on the bank of the Jordan River.[11] What is remarkable about this is that Moses knew full well that these cities of refuge would be ineffective until such time as three parallel cities were designated within Israel[12] — a task that Moses himself would be unable to fulfill because he was not destined to enter the Promised Land.

There is an inspirational lesson for all of us to learn from Moses' example: When it comes to fulfilling a mitzvah, we are not to make calculations, such as, *Will I be able to complete the commandment?* Rather, we must take on each commandment with full vigor and enthusiasm, even if we are convinced that we will not see the fruit

---

10. *Psalms* 27:14.
11. *Deuteronomy* 4:41.
12. See *Numbers* 35:11-15.

of our labor. We have to learn to transcend our selfish, limited world and think in terms of the greater good of our families and the greater good of our people. If we can do that, we will truly be worthy of God's blessing.

Hands Off

Moshe Rabbeinu admonishes us not to *add* or *subtract* from the commandments, saying, "… be careful to perform them [God's decrees and ordinances]."[13] This is a difficult challenge, since human nature is such that we like to write our own script and author our own mode of worship, but if we do so, we will *not* be upholding the commandments of God, but indulging our own whims and desires. To appreciate the audacity that tampering with the commandments connotes, consider only someone who, upon viewing a work of art — a Rembrandt or a Van Gogh — decides that the painting needs "a little bit more orange or a touch less blue." That painting was the creation of a human being, yet no one would dare touch it, but there are those who have no hesitation in rewriting God's Laws.

The Covenant

Moshe Rabbeinu reminds us of the eternity of our covenant and exhorts us to bear in mind that, "Not with our forefathers did God seal this covenant, **but with us — we who are here, all of us alive today.**"[14]

This teaching is at the root of our faith. It is a teaching that we must all engrave upon our hearts. Every person must, at all times, feel that he/she stood at Mount Sinai and that, yes, God sealed His covenant with him/her. It is in this spirit of accepting personal

---

13. *Deuteronomy* 5:1.
14. Ibid. 5:3.

responsibility that we transmit Torah to our children. Torah study is not the study of ancient documents; it is not "Bible stories." Rather, it is the living word of God which we all heard at Mount Sinai and that continues to resound in our *neshamos* for all eternity.

The Ramban expounds on this concept, teaching that, in addition to keeping the Torah and the mitzvos, it is our duty at all times to remember *"Ma'amad Har Sinai* — the Revelation at Sinai," all that we witnessed there, and transmit it to our children forever and ever.

Yes, the covenant was sealed with each and every one of us — even with those of us who are alive today. We dare not forget.

The Ten Commandments

The Ten Commandments were addressed to the entire nation, they are written in the singular, teaching us that God is our *personal God*, who sees and is concerned about every individual. He hears our cry and feels our pain. *He is our loving Father*. This teaching is reinforced by the first commandment, in which God introduces Himself as the One Who brought us forth from the land of Egypt, rather than stating that He is the One Who created the heavens and the earth. Our God is not a distant deity. Rather, He is the God Who is with us in our suffering, and even as He brought us forth from the land of Egypt, He continues to bring us forth from our personal "Egypts" in every generation, no matter how hopeless our situation may appear to be.

The *Shema*

Two letters in the *Shema* are written in an extra-large font: the *ayin* in the word *"ShemA"* and the *daled* in the word *"echaD."*[15] These two letters, when written together, spell *"eid* — witness." When we say the *Shema*, we are witness

---

15. Ibid. 6:4.

to Hashem's presence, and indeed, that is the task of every Jew, to be God's witness. As it is written, *"Atem eidai — you are My witnesses."*[16]

The *Shema* continues with the familiar words, "And you shall love the Lord your God with all your heart." Our Sages ask if it is possible for the Torah to legislate love. "Isn't 'love' an emotion?" they ask. But the Torah never demands anything without showing us how we may attain that goal. So, even as we are instructed to love, we are also immediately told to meditate, study, keep the word of God, and perform mitzvos. All those activities generate love, and indeed, the more we focus on the Torah, the more we probe its infinite depths, the greater will become our love for Hashem.

INTERMARRIAGE

In this *parashah*, we also have the prohibition against intermarriage:

> You shall not intermarry with them; you shall not give your daughter to his son, and you shall not take his daughter for your son, for he will cause your child to turn away from after Me and they will worship the gods of others; then Hashem's wrath will burn against you, and He will destroy you quickly.[17]

It is noteworthy that this is one of those rare instances in the Torah that God gives us a reason for the prohibition. Usually, we are commanded to observe for no other reason than that God spoke. These passages teach us that the Torah's opposition to intermarriage is not based on some blind bias against non-Jews, but rather, on the simple reality that, when intermarriage takes place, the survival of the Jewish people is at risk, for "they will follow other gods." Alas, our generation has only too painfully borne witness to this reality.

---

16. *Isaiah* 43:10.
17. *Deuteronomy* 7:3-4.

PARASHAS EIKEV

A MITZVAH LITMUS TEST

This *parashah* commences with the verse "This shall be the reward when you hearken to these ordinances ... Hashem, your God, will safeguard for you the covenant and the kindness that He swore to your forefathers."[18] On this verse, Rashi quotes a Midrash explaining that the Hebrew word *"eikev,"* which is translated "if" or "in lieu of," literally means **"the heel of one's foot."** Therefore, the question that we must ask is, "What is the deeper message herein?"

Rashi explains that mitzvos which we do not deem important we tend **to tread upon with the heels of our feet**. But it is in pre-

---

18. Ibid. 7:12.

cisely this area that we must be ever so cautious, for the Mishnah teaches that we do not know the value of a mitzvah. All our commandments were proclaimed at Sinai by God and therefore **are all equally important**. The Torah is not a supermarket in which we can pick and choose. And yet, we label certain mitzvos as unimportant and discard them. How do we justify such a betrayal of God's commandments?

Those mitzvos that we find burdensome or too demanding we tend to categorize as unessential, and after a while, we truly come to believe that they are of no consequence and regard those who do observe them as religious fanatics. Obviously, none of us always truly fulfills the letter of the law, but when we fail to do so, we should at least have the integrity to recognize our weakness, ask for God's forgiveness, and hope to one day attain the spiritual strength to fulfill the mitzvos as God commanded.

There is yet another reason why many take for granted or neglect certain mitzvos. It's easy to rise to the challenge when a mitzvah is observed only on special occasions, but maintaining a high level of commitment day in and day out is not so simple. That, however, is the "litmus test" of our Jewish commitment.

This passage in the Torah challenges each and every one of us to scrutinize our level of observance and ask ourselves, *Are we trampling on some mitzvos? Are there mitzvos that we consider "burdensome" and reject out of hand?* If our commitment to Torah is real, then we have to work on ourselves to refine and improve our observance.

God Does Not Punish

At one time or another, we are all challenged by difficulties and sorrow. At such times, we may ask, "Where is God? Why is He punishing us?"

Our *parashah* teaches that God never punishes, in the sense of meaning to inflict pain without a constructive purpose. As the verse states, "And you should know in your heart that just as a father will chastise his son, so Hashem, your God, chastises you."[19] So even in the midst of our pain, we have to know that God, our Father, is with us and has not abandoned us. And this knowledge cannot be merely cerebral, but must be "felt in our hearts," for only thus will we be able to stay the course. A father has only love for his children, and his intention is never to punish, but to correct. Even as a father longs for his children to come home to him, so our Heavenly Father awaits us. God sends us **wake-up calls**, but sadly, in our pain and anger, we don't hear His call.

The Almighty God, Who is our loving Father, does not take pleasure in our suffering. He would never wish to hurt us. He places difficulties in our paths so that we may come to realize that we are self-destructive and have lost sight of the higher purpose of our lives. In counseling people who are challenged and hurting, our mother, Rebbetzin Esther Jungreis, *tichyeh*, very often advises people not to ask "why," for "why" only leads to more anger and bitterness. But, she counsels, do ask *"madua"* or *"lamah"* — the Hebrew equivalents of "why," for in the holy tongue the word *madua* can be understood as a contraction of *"mah dei'ah* — what do I learn from this?" and *lamah* can mean *le mah* can mean, "to what end? How can I grow and mature from this?" If we keep this in mind, it will be so much easier for us to cope, come closer to our Heavenly Father, and realize our goal in life. King David reinforces this teaching in Psalm 23, "Your rod and Your staff shall comfort me," meaning that even when God's *rod* causes me pain, it *comforts me*, because I know His purpose is to help me improve me.

FORMULA FOR MAINTAINING CLOSENESS WITH GOD

Moshe Rabbeinu continues his farewell address and bequeaths to the Jewish people a formula for survival: "Now, O Israel, what does Hashem, your God, ask

---

19. Ibid. 8:5.

of you? Only to fear Hashem, your God, go in all His ways and to love Him, and to serve Hashem, your God, with all your heart and with all your soul ...."[20]

The Talmud in Tractate *Berachos* asks, "Is fearing God such a small thing then, that Moses uses the diminutive 'only'?" And our Sages answer, "Yes, for Moses who was so close to God, it was indeed that simple." Still, that response is puzzling, for, after all, how does that help us? We are not on Moses' level. Moreover, reverence for God is the responsibility of every Jew, so obviously, we have all been mandated to fulfill that imperative — but how, you might ask. The Talmud teaches that if we surround ourselves with God-fearing people, then our awareness and reverence for Hashem will be easily attained. Our prayers, our Torah learning, our observance, will all *soar* in the company of the righteous. Many times, people ask, what can I do to improve myself as a Jew? How can I elevate my observance of mitzvos, my prayers, and my Torah studies? The answer is simple: Surround yourself with people who are proficient in those areas, people who truly believe. Cling to them and their faith will become infectious.

Prescriptions for Faith

Moses, our teacher, gives us many more prescriptions as to how we may best maintain our close relationship with Hashem. We will cite just a few: The portion opens with "*V'hayah eikev* ..." — "And it shall be when — because — you hearken ...."[21] As we explained above, however, literally translated, the word "*eikev*" does not mean "if" or "because," but "heel," to teach us that *life is made up of steps*, and if we realize that *every little step leads to a bigger one that can define our lives*, we will automatically be more careful about the steps we take. Those who do not give forethought to their steps can easily find themselves at a destination at which they never wanted to be. If we take this teaching to heart, we

---

20. Ibid. 10:12.
21. Ibid. 7:12.

can avoid the pitfalls that lead to unfortunate consequences, so let us remember that every step that we take on the road of life leads us to a destination ... but what that destination may be is for us to decide.

Eikev — footsteps — also remind us that reverence for God comes easily to us because we all had *bubbies* and *zeides* who made a path for us. We need only *follow in their footsteps.* As a matter of fact, the entire Book of *Genesis* can be described as "footsteps" that our Patriarchs and Matriarchs blazed for us on the highway of life. They experienced every trial, every tribulation ... they passed every test so that we, their descendants, might follow in their well-trodden path and walk in honor, unafraid, on the highway of life.

Finally, when we are overcome by sadness, when we feel *"eikev,"* our feet dragging us down, then we must remember that the word *eikev* is preceded by *"v'hayah,"* which is a code word for happiness. As Jews, we must strive to be in a constant state of *simchas hachaim,* which means that we must work on developing a positive, joyous attitude toward life. We can't afford to give in to our dark moods. We can't indulge our feelings of depression. We simply have too much to accomplish during our short sojourn on this planet. But how, you might ask, can we achieve happiness? How can we control our moods? Once again the Torah gives us the answer and it is to be found in the remainder of the passage: If we "hearken to these ordinances," if we study and observe the Torah, our spirits will carry us, and God will help us to lift our feet with positive energy, enabling us to tackle even the most difficult tasks.

THE TORAH: ONE BIG MITZVAH

"The entire commandment that I command you today you shall observe ...."[22] The expression, *"Kol hamitzvah* — the entire mitzvah,"* teaches us that we are to view the entire

---

22. Ibid. 8:1.

Torah as *one big mitzvah* — all commandments contained therein are equally important.

There is yet another lesson to be learned from this expression, "*Kol hamitzvah* — the entire commandment."

Very often, when we embark upon a new program, we are full of enthusiasm and zeal, but then, in midcourse, something happens. We run out of steam and become lethargic. We rationalize and convince ourselves that what we have already accomplished is quite sufficient. The *parashah*, however, teaches us that we can't give up in midcourse, but must persevere in our task and fulfill the *entire* commandment. We have to remember that he who is credited with the mitzvah is the one who completes it.

Some of us might feel overwhelmed by such a responsibility and wonder whether such a goal is realistic. The answer is "Yes!" The mitzvos are all within our reach. God would never charge us with a responsibility that is beyond our reach. Let us consider for a moment the literal meaning of the word "mitzvah," the root of which implies "connection," teaching us that every mitzvah is designed to make our connection with God closer and more powerful. As we connect more and more, we will also discover that we are invigorated with new spiritual energy, and with each mitzvah, our bond with Hashem will strengthen and grow. So it is that our Sages taught, "... one mitzvah leads to another mitzvah ...."[23]

GRACE

"And you will eat and you will be satisfied and bless Hashem, your God ...."[24]

This is the mitzvah of saying Grace After Meals. But by stating, "... you will be *satisfied*," it might appear that the Torah qualifies the mitzvah and requires saying Grace only when we feel satiated.

Our mother has related how, in the Bergen-Belsen concentration

---

23. *Ethics of the Fathers* 4:2.
24. *Deuteronomy* 8:10.

camp, our *Zeide* would eat a very small portion of his daily ration of bread and hide the rest for his children for Shabbos. Was he satiated by these few morsels? Was he satisfied? Hardly! Nevertheless, he said Grace and thanked God. Similarly, we tell Hashem that even when He is not satisfied with us, just the same, He should bless us with His gracious kindness.

WHAT DOES GOD REQUIRE OF US?

Now, O Israel, what does Hashem, your God, ask of you? Only to fear Hashem, your God ...."[25] From this passage, our rabbis conclude that everything is in the hands of Hashem, except our fear of Him. In the end, it is this fear — reverence — that will define our lives. Contrary to conventional wisdom, it is not the situation in which we find ourselves, nor the profession or business in which we work, that is crucial, but what we make of them; and all that depends on the measure of our reverence for God. For example, a person may find himself confined to a hospital bed, but whether he reacts with anger or expresses faith will depend on his reverence for God. Whether he is rich or poor is not the determinant, but what he does with his wealth or how he accepts his poverty will define his life, and all that will depend on his reverence for God. We experienced the reality of this teaching during the illnesses of our beloved grandparents, Rabbi Avraham and Rebbetzin Miriam Jungreis, *zt"l*, and of our father, Rabbi Meshulem HaLevi Jungreis, *zt"l*. They never allowed their pain to confine their spirits. Their faith was so powerful that whoever visited them went forth elevated and wiser, and it was all due to their deep reverence for God. But how do we develop this reverence?

A good first step is to pray. If we ask that God inspire us with reverence for Him so that we may properly fulfill His commandments, we may be confident that He will fulfill our wishes. Thus,

---

25. Ibid. 10:12.

we are never to feel discouraged in our observance of mitzvos, in our Torah studies, or in our daily prayers. We need only ask for God's help and it will certainly be forthcoming.

PARASHAS RE'EH

Free Will: It's Up to Us!

"See, I present before you today a blessing and a curse."[26] We are granted free will to choose between the good and the bad, between a blessing and a curse. It is all in our hands. We can chart our own course; we can change our paths.

There are some puzzling grammatical discrepancies in this passage. The word *"re'eh* — see" is written in the singular, while *"lifneichem* — before you" is written in the plural, and the word *"nosein* — give" is in the present rather than in the past tense, even though Moses was referring to commandments that had already been given. All this is to remind us that God made the blessings of the Torah available to *the entire nation*. We *all* stood at Sinai; we

---

26. Ibid. 11:26.

all heard His voice, but it is up to us as individuals to act upon it. God can send us wake-up calls; He can even chastise us, but He cannot coerce us, for if He were to interfere with our free will, we would become robots and the entire concept of spiritual growth, of reward and punishment would be negated. Whether we choose to follow God's instructions or ignore them depends entirely upon us and is at the root of our undoing as well as our happiness.

The good news, however, is that the word "give" is in the present tense, meaning that God is willing to *give* us a new chance every day ... more, every minute of every day. We may have failed a thousand and one times, but in His infinite mercy, He does not lose patience with us and makes *teshuvah* possible at all times, under all conditions. As King Solomon said, "Though the righteous one may fall seven times, he will arise ...."[27]

How does a man become righteous? By standing up and starting all over again, even seven times, symbolic of the seven days of the week. But how do we make that fresh start? Every mitzvah that we undertake, every prayer that we pronounce, every page that we study in the Torah, every act of *chesed*, is a step in the right direction, a step that will lead us to a new life of blessing.

You Need Only Open Your Eyes and See

The Torah invites us to choose between blessing and curse, and most telling is the word that the Torah uses in extending this opportunity is *"re'eh* — see," which is somewhat puzzling, for one would have imagined that a word such as "consider," "study," or "contemplate" would have been more appropriate and descriptive. The Torah, however, is teaching us that the difference between blessing and curse is so sharp, so obvious, that it doesn't even require contemplation. One need only open one's eyes and **see**. Yes, *see* how beautiful is the family life of those who

---
27. *Proverbs* 24:16.

observe Shabbos: parents and children sitting around the table in the glow of candlelight; parents placing their hands upon the heads of their sons and daughters and pronouncing the timeless blessings of the Patriarchs and Aaron, the High Priest; parents and children exchanging words of Torah and singing hymns in praise of God. The TV, the phone, the computer, the iPods are all silent — the tumultuous outside world is shut out; serenity and peace descend upon the family. No one is rushing off someplace. It is Shabbos, a day laden with blessing and peace.

Now contrast that scene with homes where Shabbos is not observed, and you will *see* the difference between blessing and curse. This holds true in regard to all mitzvos. Just *see* the marriages of those who live by the laws of the Torah, which require that husband and wife not only *love* each other, but *respect* each other. *See* children who have been taught the Torah laws of honoring parents; *see* how they communicate with their mothers and fathers, and *see* how others do. No, you do not require any special wisdom to discern the difference between blessing and curse — you need only open your eyes and *see*.

How Well Do We Listen?

"The blessing: that you *hearken* to the commandments of Hashem, your God, that I command you today."[28] The Torah teaches us that the very first step in acquiring blessing is to learn the art of *listening*. If you have ever had the frustrating experience of talking your heart out to a family member or friend in an attempt to direct them on the right path, and even as you were talking, you saw that your words just rolled off their backs, then you will concur that the art of listening is not a simple one. God has given us the message, but how many of us have listened? God has provided us with a perfect GPS system to guide us on the highway of life, but whether we will listen to the instructions and

---

28. *Deuteronomy* 11:27.

follow them or chart our own course is a decision that only we can make, but it is a decision that will lead to either blessing or curse.

King Solomon, the wisest of all men, was a young lad when his father David died. Solomon was charged with the awesome task of sitting on his father's throne ... a responsibility that, to say the least, would intimidate anyone, but how much more so a young boy.

God appeared to Solomon in a dream, assured him that He would be with him, and invited him to make a wish. Solomon could have wished for many gifts — wealth, longevity, a great empire ... but even as a young lad, he was filled with wisdom. Solomon's request was for "A *listening heart*," for he understood that, if you know how to listen, not only with your ears and mind, but also with your heart, then you will discover the blessing of life, and it is that blessing that our *parashah* invites us to take possession of.

THE LAWS OF TZEDAKAH

In Jewish life, there is nothing ambiguous about giving *tzedakah*. The laws of *tzedakah* are not a matter of personal preference, of likes and dislikes. We have definite obligations, and they are spelled out in this *parashah*. Significantly, in the holy tongue, *aseir*, the word for *tithing*,[29] used in the commandment to separate a portion for the needy, also spells *asher*, wealthy, assuring us that when we give *tzedakah*, we are never diminished. On the contrary, we become enriched.

The Torah teaches us that we should not harden our hearts or close our hands to the indigent; that it is not only giving charity that is significant, but also the manner in which we offer it.

This is most unusual, because in most cases, the Torah focuses on the fulfillment of the mitzvah rather than on the manner in which it is being performed. But when it comes to *tzedakah*, we

---

29. Ibid. 14:22.

must be sensitive to the feelings of the needy, who are humiliated by the fact that they have to beg. Therefore, the words *"Paso'ach tiftach es yad'cha* — Open your hand," literally, "open, you shall open your hand,"[30] repeats the word *open*, teaching that we are required to give again and again, and always with a gracious, full heart, as seen in the previous verse, "… you shall not harden your heart or close your hand against your destitute brother."

The *parashah* teaches us that, in addition to monetary gifts, we must offer words of encouragement to the poor. Asking for help is a humbling experience, so we should do our utmost to lift the spirits of those in needs. Our Sages teach that for the monetary gifts that we offer, we receive six blessings, but for words of encouragement and comfort, God gives us 11, impressing upon us that to revive broken spirits and to imbue them with hope and confidence is of the highest priority. Charity is such an integral part of our people that, throughout our long history, even the most impoverished community established charity funds, free-loan societies, and *hachnasas kallah* (helping poor brides) and *bikur cholim* (visiting the sick) groups.

TZEDAKAH: NOT AN OPTION BUT AN OBLIGATION

The Hebrew word *tzedakah* means something far deeper than *charity*. *Tzedakah* is derived from the work *tzedek*, which means "justice" or "righteousness," telling us that to give is an obligation to do justice. The word *tzedakah* reminds us that what we have is not really ours but has been given to us in trust by God for distribution.

"For Mine is the silver and Mine is the gold …."[31] It all belongs to God, and when we give, we are only returning that which He gave to us. Charity, on the other hand, is a totally different concept. It

---

30. Ibid. 15:8.
31. *Haggai* 2:8.

is derived from the Latin word *caritas*, meaning "love," suggesting that we have an option: to give to those we love and to withhold help from those we dislike.

In the world of *tzedakah*, such options do not exist. Whether we like someone or not, we have a responsibility to give, for that is the correct thing to do, and we should not feel that we deserve any special credit, even as we deserve no reward for paying our taxes.

Why Does God Allow the Poor To Be Poor?

A Roman nobleman once challenged Rabbi Akiva, "If your God is so concerned for the poor, why did He create them?"

"For the same reason that He didn't create bread trees," came the answer. "God wants us to join Him in partnership to continue the work that He began. Through the act of giving, we become kinder and better people and can make *tikun olam*; we can participate in the process of perfecting the world.

"Can you imagine what the world would look like if we were all self-sufficient and never needed one another? Can you imagine the selfishness, the greed, and the baseness if no one ever felt compassion or gratitude? Therefore, the Torah teaches that 'destitute people will not cease to exist within the Land; therefore I command you, saying, "You shall surely open your hand to your brother, to your poor, and to your destitute in your Land."'[32]

Indeed, it is through the act of giving that humanity is elevated and the spark of God lying dormant in the soul becomes visible. The Torah teaches that that which we give away is the only thing we really have.

---

32. *Deuteronomy* 15:11.

IF WE TRULY SEEK HIM, WE CAN FIND HIM

The *parashah* states, "… there shall you seek out His Presence and come there."[33] There appears to be a discrepancy in the passage. It would seem that the correct way for the Torah to phrase the sentence would have been to first mention the coming there (going to the Temple in Jerusalem), and there, in the midst of sanctity, to find Hashem. The Torah is teaching us, however, a very profound lesson, one which we should incorporate into our everyday lives. If we are bent upon finding God — no matter where we may be, no matter how far we may have distanced ourselves from Him — if we truly seek Him, we will find Him.

God is waiting for *all* of us to return to Him. God's Court is open, but whether we will have the wisdom to enter therein depends on us. So let us seize the moment: Let us intensify our Torah study; let us accelerate our prayers, and let us commit to the observance of mitzvos. Even one small step toward God can launch us on the path of Jewish fulfillment. We need only take that step.

---

33. Ibid. 12: 5.

PARASHAS SHOFTIM

Road Map for Spiritual Growth

"Judges and officers shall you appoint in all of your cities [literally, gates]."[34] There are many levels on which we can understand this passage. A simple reading reveals that even thousands of years ago, in every hamlet, in every town, and in every city of Israel, there was a functioning judicial system. Judges, men of enormous integrity and moral excellence, were not only knowledgeable in the laws of the Torah, but more importantly, lived by them and led the people in truth and sanctity. A "Dodge City," in which anarchy reigned, was never tolerated in our history. This, in and of itself, is quite remarkable when we consider the evil and

---

34. Ibid. 16:18.

corruption that were prevalent in those days and which continue to plague us to this day. Only Divinely ordained laws could have endowed us with such a righteous judicial system as mandated in this *parashah*.

On yet another level, this passage can serve as a road map for personal spiritual growth. The *gates* at which we must place judges and officers are our *personal gates* through which we receive impressions and through which we impact on others. All told, they number seven. They include our eyes, ears, nostrils, and mouth. We must place judges at these gates; we are required to be judicious as to what we allow ourselves to see, hear, smell, and say, and we have to have "officers" — strong convictions — to enforce our decisions. Of all our gates, our lips are the most powerful. As we have noted before, King Solomon declares, "Life and death are in the tongue."[35] Therefore, nature has provided us with two gates to safeguard the tongue: our lips and our teeth. Before we speak, we must close those gates and consider carefully whether that which we say will be helpful or damaging. Let us remember that what we do not say, we can always say later, but that which escapes our lips, we cannot retrieve.

There is yet another interpretation of this passage. Before judging others, we should judge ourselves. People have a tendency to overlook their own foibles while demanding perfection of their fellow man. Therefore, if we place judges at our personal gates, then we will succeed in overcoming our negative traits.

God Our King

Each passage in the *parashah* can be understood on many different levels. We are told that when our forefathers came to the Land of Israel, they were to "set a king over [themselves]."[36] But everything written in the Torah is eternal, for all generations, so how are we to understand this command-

---

35. See *Proverbs* 18:21: "Death and life are in the power of the tongue ...."
36. *Deuteronomy* 17:15.

ment? In our contemporary world, how can we appoint a king to reign over us? We, the Jewish people, have only One King — the Almighty God. During the High Holy Days our *Shacharis* commences with the awesome word **HAMELECH — THE KING**. Our Sages would actually tremble when the cantor pronounced those awesome words declaring that God is our King Who reigns over us.

Whether we are in the privacy of our homes, in the workplace, or on vacation, we must always remember to *set the King — God — over us*. "*Shivisi Hashem l'negdi samid* — I have set Hashem before me always,"[37] is the teaching of King David.

Strangely enough, however, when the people settled in the Land of Israel and petitioned Samuel, the prophet, to appoint a king for them, Samuel reacted with anger. It was not their *request* that upset Samuel, but rather, *the manner* in which it was made. "*Appoint for us a king to judge us, like all the nations*,"[38] the people said. The problem was that they meant it literally; they wanted to imitate their heathen neighbors. It was not the *words* that mattered. Their *intention* should have been, "Give us a king who will inspire us to greater commitment to God, who will lead us in our Torah life."

Once again, herein is a lesson for all of us. Our aim should never be to emulate the nations among whom we reside, but to walk on our unique path, to live by the light that was given to us at Sinai — it is to this end that we must strive, so that all that we acquire will be committed to the higher service of God.

Never Think You Are Smarter

God gave three commandments that pertain specifically to kings. He advanced *reasons* for these disciplines, which is most unusual, for the Torah seldom puts forth reasons for observance. The very fact that God commanded is reason enough. This is not simply a matter of faith. There are other

---

37. *Psalms* 16:8.
38. *I Samuel* 8:5.

considerations as well: Once a reason is given for the observance of the mitzvah, the commandment is at risk, for the temptation to tamper with and second-guess the command is too difficult for man to resist. And indeed that was the undoing of the wisest man, King Solomon. For example, God prohibited kings from having too many wives and the reason He gave was "so that his heart not turn astray."[39] Solomon rationalized that he could handle it, that he would not allow anyone to corrupt him. In his old age, however, his many wives brought tragedy upon his kingdom. Now, if this was the case with King Solomon, who had the distinction of being the wisest man on earth, what can we anticipate if we try to outsmart the Torah?

All this teaches us that we should never be overly confident; that we should never believe that the disciplines of the Torah are not applicable to us, that we can handle the many temptations of our 21st-century society and not succumb. It is easy to lose our way, but very difficult and painful to find our way back. If ever this message was relevant, it is today. Our world is in chaos and we stand humbled before our Creator. Let us not try to be smarter than His Torah.

Lessons To Be Learned

The Torah does not abide arrogance. "There is no room for Me in the arrogant heart," says God. Arrogance, however, is a monarch's occupational hazard and continues to be the undoing of many of us in every generation, even today. To immunize himself from the disease, the king was commanded to write two Torah scrolls,[40] one of which had to be carried at all times on his right arm, and the other kept in his treasury. Those Torah scrolls were there to remind him that as august as his position might be, and as much wealth as he might have in his treasury, he is bound by the Torah's commandments, for above all, he is a servant of God.

In our own generation, in which it is easy to become caught

---

39. *Deuteronomy* 17:17.
40. Ibid. 17:18.

up in success and in all the enticements of our culture, we must remember that, even as the Torah enabled the king of Israel to fulfill his mission with humility, so we too, by remaining focused on the Torah, can fulfill our purpose, and not become drunk with arrogance. We must learn from this law of the king to keep the Torah forever in our sight so that we never forget our higher calling, the true purpose of our lives, and the source of our success.

WE ARE ALL STEWARDS OF GOD

When referring to the king sitting on his throne, the text uses the expression *k'Shivto*, which can be understood as "**like** he was sitting,"[41] meaning that at all times, even when sitting on his throne, the king of Israel had to be aware that he was but a steward of the Almighty God and had no inherent right to occupy the throne, for that was a privilege reserved for the One and only One — the Almighty. Similarly, we must remember that we are all stewards of God and are here to fulfill His charge.

WE ARE ALL RESPONSIBLE

At the end of our *parashah*, we find the most perplexing commandment. If a corpse is found abandoned in the field, the elders of the city closest to where the body was found must go forth and declare, "Our hands have not spilled this blood and our eyes did not see."[42]

At first glance, this declaration of the sages seems absurd. Can anyone imagine that the elders murdered this man? But the Torah is teaching us a profound, timeless lesson. The leaders *are* responsible. To be a leader in Israel is not a matter of honor or prestige.

---

41. Ibid.
42. Ibid. 21:1-7.

Rather, it is an awesome charge which holds the leader accountable for everything that occurs on his watch. Similarly, parents are responsible for their children, teachers for their students, and we are all responsible for one another. Thus, if a man is found dead and abandoned, and no one had offered him food, shelter, or an escort to see him on his way, then something was drastically wrong in that community. The leaders must scrutinize themselves, their community, and their society to determine whether they have been guilty of neglect.

Now, if this be the case when a man's physical life is at risk, how much more does it hold true when his spiritual life is on the line? In our contemporary world, multitudes of our people are disappearing through assimilation, but what are we doing about it? How many of us can truly testify that we offered them the spiritual nourishment and shelter of our Torah?

Yes, we are all our brothers' keepers. Yes, we are all responsible for one another.

PARASHAS KI SEITZEI

SENSITIZING YOUR HEART

This *parashah* contains more mitzvos than any other *parashah*, and they are mitzvos that encompass many areas that sensitize our hearts and enable us to perceive that there is more to life than mere existence. It is not by coincidence that this *parashah* is read as we prepare for Rosh Hashanah and Yom Kippur.

The *parashah* opens with the stirring words, "When you will go out to war against your enemies, and Hashem, your God, will deliver them into your hand ...."[43]

These words are spoken, not only in regard to the battlefield, but more importantly, in connection with the personal struggle that each and every one of us must wage to conquer our most for-

---
43. Ibid. 21:10.

midable enemy, the *yetzer hara*. God promises us that if we make a decision to go forth and battle that enemy within ourselves, He will deliver it into our hands; that is, if we are truly determined to free ourselves of our negative traits and base habits, God will do the rest and we will gain control over our passions rather than be controlled by them.

The many and varied mitzvos in the *parashah* are here to sensitize our souls so that we might better fulfill our mission in our *Avodas Hashem* (service of God). For example, the laws pertaining to a rebellious son[44] make us realize the critical importance of parents speaking with the same voice and avoiding the tragedies that can result when there is a lack of *shalom bayis* and parents send conflicting messages.

The laws pertaining to helping unload a burdened animal[45] not only teach us that it is a positive commandment to relieve the animal of its burden, but that closing our eyes to its suffering is to transgress the prohibition of "*tzaar baalei chaim,*" which means that we may not be indifferent to the distress of an animal. This law should give us food for thought and compel us to re-think our relationships with our fellow man. If the Torah demands that we be so sensitive to the pain of an animal, how much more must we sensitize ourselves to the burdens and the pain in the hearts of our brethren.

Nowadays, there are so many problems that afflict people, so many who are lonely and hurting, so many who are ill, so many who have lost their jobs and have difficulty making ends meet, and so many who are suffering in Eretz Yisrael. We dare not turn our backs on them and pretend that we do not see or hear their cries. A kind word, a listening ear, a smile, a helping hand can all serve to ease their pain and lift their burdens.

---

44. Ibid. 21:18.
45. Ibid. 22:4.

Each of God's Creations Is Unique

The *parashah* also admonishes us not to harness an ox and a donkey together to plow.[46] Although this commandment is a *chok*, for which no reason is given, we can derive a moral lesson from it. The Torah has compassion on the animals, since they have different energy levels, and harnessing them together would pit one against the other, causing undue pain and stress. In addition, the ox chews its cud, while the donkey swallows grass or grain quickly, leading the donkey to believe that the ox, which takes longer to consume its food, was given a greater portion. Once again, there are lessons to be drawn in our human relations: Never pit people of different energy levels against one another. Never compare children, for each child is a star in his or her own right. Never should husbands and wives compare their spouses to others. All such comparisons can be painful and can leave deep scars. Each of us is God's creation, endowed with our own unique gifts and talents, and each of us has our own contribution to make.

Furthermore, if we jealously think that someone has more than we have, just remember the donkey that foolishly thinks that the ox has more than it does. God gives to each of us that which we need, so instead of focusing on that which the other has, let us concentrate on that with which God blessed us.

Returning That Which Is Lost

All the portions of the Torah that we read during the month of Elul have been designed to prepare us for the awesome days of Rosh Hashanah and Yom Kippur, when our destiny for the coming year is decided. In this *parashah* we learn about the mitzvah of *hashavas aveidah*, returning lost items.

---

46. Ibid. 22:10.

> "You shall not see the ox of your brother or his sheep cast off, and hide yourself from them; you shall surely return them to your brother. If your brother is not near you and you do not know him, then gather it inside your house and it shall remain with you until your brother inquires after it, and you shall return it to him."[47]

On a simple level, we understand this to mean that it is a mitzvah to return lost objects to their rightful owners, and this holds true even if we have to inconvenience ourselves to do so. On another level, this teaching takes on a powerful spiritual dimension. Allegorically, your brother Who lost something can be seen as a reference to the Almighty God, Who "lost" many of His children. But, you might ask, how does it happen that a Jew is lost? The answer can be found in our text: He becomes like an *ox* or a *sheep*; that is, he becomes stubborn as an ox or, sheeplike, he mindlessly follows the crowd.

We live in an age in which many stubbornly rationalize. No matter what befalls them, they refuse to see the hand of God and try to explain everything away as either happenstance or scientific phenomena. They deny the hand of God in their personal lives as well as in world events. On the other hand, others, like sheep, succumb to that which is in vogue. If their peers assimilate, they too will assimilate; if their peers give up the observance of mitzvos, they too will give up the observance of mitzvos, and so on. So we must all be on guard not to fall into the trap of the ox or the sheep. But regarding those who did fall, it is our responsibility to return them to Almighty God. The soul of every individual belongs to Him, for we are all God's children.

But what if we are not sufficiently erudite in Torah learning and feel inadequate to this task? We are nevertheless responsible, for the Torah teaches that if we find a lost item and do not know who the owner is, we must take it into our homes and safeguard it until the connection is made. How does that teaching apply to us? If we bring lost Jews into our home, a place where the holy

---

47. Ibid. 22:1-2.

lights of Shabbos burn bright, or if we bring them to a Torah class and thereby connect them to their roots, we will awaken the *pintele Yid* in their *neshamos* and thus return them to their true source, their Owner. And what if we ourselves are lost? The same formula applies to us. We must seek out a Torah teacher who will guide us on the path of return to our Heavenly Father.

It is only through Torah and mitzvos that we can reunite with Hashem, who is patiently and lovingly waiting for each and every one of us to come home.

The month of Elul is a time when God is holding "Open House" and is anxiously awaiting the return of all His children. In the month of Elul, anyone who knocks on God's door, so to speak, is welcomed and embraced. This truth is reinforced in the acronym formed by the Hebrew letters of the word ELUL — "*Ani l'dodi v'dodi li* — I am my Beloved's and my Beloved is mine."[48]

---

48. *Song of Songs* 6:3.

PARASHAS KI SAVO

How To Give

This *parashah* opens with the mitzvah of *bikkurim*, which requires that we bring the first fruits of our field to the Temple as an expression of gratitude to God. The Torah states that when we present those first fruits, we make the following declaration: "*V'atah hinei heiveisi* ... — And now, behold, I have brought the first fruits of the ground ...."[49]

The Midrash tells us that three words in this passage teach us the proper manner in which to give, for just as the nation is responsible to provide for the Kohanim, so too are we responsible for the needy.

1. "*V'atah* — And now," implies *immediacy* — alacrity. *Tzedakah* must be given with dispatch, for any delay might prolong the distress of the needy. Moreover, by giving immediately,

---

49. *Deuteronomy* 26:10.

without procrastination, we demonstrate our sensitivity to the pain of the recipient, and that, in and of itself, is therapeutic. The knowledge that someone truly cares and understands the urgency of their predicament lifts the spirits of those in need and gives them hope.

2. "*Hinei* — Behold." The word connotes joy, happiness. It is essential that when we give, we do so with a full heart, a smile, and a kindly word. By giving in such a manner, we shield the indigent from embarrassment and enable him to keep his dignity. Begging is a mortifying experience, and donors must exert every effort to protect the poor from humiliation.

3. "*Heiveisi* — I have brought." This word connotes that that which we give to the poor is not really *our* gift, but rather, a gift that we *bring* entrusted to us by God so that we might share it with others. But, if that be the case, what are we giving? If we give with a full heart, with those aforementioned qualities — identification with the plight of the indigent and a kindly spirit — then it is accounted to us that *we* gave, for that is truly the only thing that we can give. The money is not ours. These are important laws to bear in mind regarding *tzedukah*. Once we absorb them, our entire manner of giving will be different. It will leave us spiritually elevated rather than with the feeling of self-aggrandizement which, unfortunately, very often characterize the donor.

Happiness — A Command, Not an Option

And you shall rejoice with all the goodness that Hashem, your God, has given you and your household ...."[50]

We may have difficulty with this passage. This commandment pertains to those who had toiled over their crops and

---

50. Ibid. 26:11.

gathered their harvest. Surely, in the wake of such an accomplishment, they would not have to be told to be happy. They had every reason to rejoice and be satisfied. But herein we discover the perverseness of human nature, which never allows a man to be content with what he has. Even though he succeeds, he remains restless; *he desires more*, and then *some more again*. And worse, he measures his harvest, his attainments, against those of his neighbors, and if they should have more, his jealousy consumes him and his joy is marred. It is this jealousy that robs a person of his peace of mind, his happiness and contentment, and generates bitterness, greed, and hatred.

Gratitude: A Pillar of Judaism

To overcome these negative feelings, the Torah commands us to appreciate that whatever we have has been given to us by God. **He knows what we require for our well-being,** and we must condition ourselves to believe that, if He did not give it to us, then obviously, we can do without it. So, instead of bemoaning that which we do *not* have, let us rejoice in that which we *do* have. If we absorb this basic principle, if we bear in mind that it is God Who is in charge, that it is He Who provides us with all our needs, then we will be blessed with *simchas hachaim*. We will find fulfillment in our own lot, for we will realize that we do not need more. This spirit of *simchas hachaim* is the ticket to peace of mind, but if we lose sight of it, we underwrite our own undoing. This concept of *simchas hachaim* is at the root of *hakaras hatov*, the gratitude that is one of the basic pillars of the principles of our faith. Feelings of *hakaras hatov* are so crucial to the proper service of God that, toward the end of the *parashah*, we are told that our exile would come about because we did not serve God *with joy and goodness of heart*.[51]

---

51. See ibid. 28:47.

Jealousy Leads to Hatred

But, one might protest, does this not conflict with the dictum that our Temple was destroyed because of *sinas chinam* — baseless hatred — between Jew and Jew? Upon closer scrutiny, we will realize that there is no dichotomy between these two teachings, for as was explained, when one is *not* happy, when one is *not* content, at the root of his feelings is "I need more!" And such feelings easily lead to resentment and jealousy, culminating in hatred.

Those who indulge their covetous eyes will never be satisfied, and the consequences of their discontent will be their undoing. There will always be someone who is richer, whose house is bigger, who is smarter or prettier, etc., so the Torah commands us to work on ourselves and find happiness, contentment in all the good that God has bestowed upon us. In our competitive society, it is easy to fall into the trap of covetousness, to focus on *what we do not have* rather than on *what we do have*.

Let us count the many blessings that God has granted us and find our happiness in them. Let's start with a simple exercise: Upon opening our eyes every morning, let's not say, "*Modeh Ani,*" simply by rote, but let us declare those words with a sincere grateful heart, "I thank **You** for returning my soul." If we learn to commence our days with a genuine expression of gratitude, then, hopefully, those feelings will accompany us throughout the day, spill over into all our activities, and make us realize that we should not take any of the simple gifts of life for granted, for those gifts are not so simple after all. Alas, most of us appreciate God's blessings only after we lose them; only then do we realize how fortunate we once were. How sad!

You Need Not Be Blind To Have Faith, But You Have To Be Blind Not To Have Faith

In this *parashah*, we study the *tochachos*, the terrible curses and tragic calamities that will befall us throughout our history. There is no parallel in the annals of mankind to such prophecies in either theological or historical writings. This, in and of itself, is proof of the Torah's Divine authorship and the guiding hand of God in our history. Thousands of years ago, our forefathers were told of the painful, tragic events that would befall their descendants. As difficult as it may have been for them to accept such a fate, they did so, for they fully understood that ultimately, it would be for the good, for God was guiding it all. Throughout our long, dark centuries of exile, those who studied Torah understood and clung tenaciously to our faith, but those who lost sight of our Divine wisdom also lost their faith and coined the phrase, "You have to be blind to have faith." But we, who belong to this generation, even if our knowledge of Torah is minimal, have to be awed by the miraculous survival of that people. Despite the barbaric cruelties inflicted upon us by the nations, we are here, alive and vibrant. Today, we do not have to be blind to have faith, for we have seen prophecy unfold before our very eyes. Today, it is those who lack faith who are blind.

There are actually two places in the Torah where these curses are mentioned: in this *parashah* and in the Book of *Leviticus*, focusing on a different period in our history. In *Leviticus*, the destruction of the First Temple and the subsequent exile are foretold,[52] while in this *parashah*, Ki Savo,[53] the destruction of the Second Temple, with all the evil that followed and which continues to haunt us to this very day, is predicted.

After describing the many horrific events that would befall our

---

52. *Leviticus* 26.
53. *Deuteronomy* 28.

people in the Roman exile, the *parashah* states, "Hashem will return you to Egypt in ships,"[54] which at first glance is difficult to understand, for to travel from Israel to Egypt does not require a vessel. Historians of that period who recount the events of those days relate that our ancestors were taken to Rome in chains and sold as slaves. But there were so many Jewish slaves in Rome that the market became depressed and the price fell, so the Romans decided to ship our people to Egypt to be sold there. Thus, the tragic prophecy was fulfilled.

There are many terrible, painful curses enumerated in this *parashah*, with which anyone who experienced the Holocaust can easily identify, but since the curse of return to Egypt by ship is mentioned last, it appears that the Torah regards this to be the most devastating of all. And this, too, is puzzling, for it certainly cannot compare with the atrocities that were visited upon us during our long and painful exile.

Our rabbis explain that the greatest of all agonies that can befall someone is to discover that his entire life's work — all his efforts, his labors, and his hopes — were for naught; that all that he believed, all that he had accomplished were of no significance; and after it was all over, he was back where he started from. God brought us forth from Egypt thousands of years ago so that we might come to Sinai, receive His covenant, and become a Priestly Kingdom, a Holy Nation, and thus fortified, enter the Promised Land. But alas, we failed in our mission. We did not adhere to the commandments and after many centuries, *we were right back where we started from: once again, slaves in Egypt.*

There is a profound message in this tragedy that speaks to all of us. As we approach the High Holy Days, let us search our lives and ascertain whether our efforts, toil, and aspirations are rooted in our Torah and of lasting value, or whether they are superficial endeavors that evaporate. Let us make certain that the energy we expend has substance and merit so that our life's work will be something to which we can point with pride. At the conclusion of *Shacharis*, we beseech God, "*l'maan lo neega lareek,*" asking God to protect us

---

54. Ibid. 28:68.

from having labored in vain or produce for futility.

Despite all the curses that are prophesied, there is a blessing to be found therein, hinted at by the Hebrew word "*V'hayah* — And it will be," the phrase with which the curses are introduced[55] and which our Sages explain is an expression of joy. The very fact that God's guiding hand is directing us, that nothing happens randomly, that there is a beginning and an ultimate goal to our history, should fill us with happiness, for it assures us that God will never give up on us but will bring us to our final destination, our redemption, with the coming of *Mashiach*. May it be soon, in our own day.

---

55. Ibid. 28:15.

PARASHAS NITZAVIM

THE COVENANT OF MUTUAL RESPONSIBILITY

The study of the *parashah* is not only the study of our past, our present, our future, but most significantly, it is the Word of God. If you know how to study it and plumb its infinite depths, you will see that the *parashah* always gives illumination and enables you to better respond to the challenges of the moment. The reading of *Parashas Nitzavim* always coincides with the High Holy Days and gives us guidance as to how we might best prepare ourselves for the awesome days of Rosh Hashanah and Yom Kippur. The stirring opening words, "*Atem nitzavim hayom kulchem lifnei Hashem Elokeichem* — You are standing today, all of you, before

Hashem, your God,"[56] speak volumes. In *gematria* these words are the equivalent of *"La'amod l'selichos* — to stand before God and seek forgiveness." During the entire year we run from place to place, from activity to activity, and some of us *run* so fast that we forget why we are running, what our lives are all about.

But now, God's Day of Judgment is upon us and we are commanded to *stand still*, probe our souls, examine our hearts, and give an accounting of our lives. The passage goes on to enumerate the various strata of the population: the leaders, the elders, the officers, the men, the small children, the women, and the proselytes, down to the hewer of wood and the drawer of water. The question arises: Since the text already stated "all of you," why would the Torah find it necessary to mention each group separately? Surely they fall under the canopy of "all of you." So, since every word in the Torah is significant, why this redundancy?

The answer to this question can serve as our road map for life, and particularly for the season of High Holy Days. *We are all responsible one for the other. Our destiny is intertwined.* The Jewish people are like one body, and if just one joint is injured, the entire body hurts; if just one limb is amputated, the entire person is disabled. Similarly, if just one of us is missing, we are all diminished; if just one of us is guilty of a grievous wrong, all of us are implicated. To impress this teaching upon us, all our prayers are said in the plural, i.e., *r'fa'einu* — heal *us* — *shema koleinu* — hear *our* voices, and so on. This teaching is especially relevant to us today, for we are the generation that has been destined to experience the travails that accompany the birth pangs of *Mashiach*. Our Sages teach that one of the ways in which we may protect ourselves during that difficult period is to unify, to forgive and feel for one another. If we can do that, we can anticipate that God will forgive us as well.

To further reinforce this concept of mutual responsibility, the *parashah* teaches us: "The hidden [sins] are for Hashem, our God, but the revealed [sins] are for us and our children forever, to carry out all the words of this Torah."[57] From this we learn that we will

---

56. Ibid. 29:9.
57. Ibid. 29:28.

not be held accountable for sins of individuals who are unknown to us, but for those violations that are public, we are *all* liable, for our very silence signals our consent. In Judaism there is an adage: "*Shtikah k'hodaah* — silence is acceptance."[58] When we see a wrong, when we witness an injustice, when we see our Torah laws violated and abandoned, we have a responsibility to speak out and remind our brethren of their higher calling: to live as Jews by Torah Law.

This responsibility to remind one another of our God-given destiny, of our Jewish heritage, is, in and of itself, a covenant. In the holy tongue, it is referred to as "*areivus* — mutual responsibility. That is why, prior to his death, Moses addressed each and every segment of the population and charged them all with this mission. Has this covenant of mutual responsibility remained the hallmark of our lives? Has it been borne out throughout the centuries? Yes and no.

On one hand, we, the Jewish people, can be separated by oceans and continents, language and culture; nevertheless, we have remained one. If our brethren in Russian, Ethiopia, or wherever they may be are oppressed, we hear their cry, and if our people in Israel are under attack, we are there. Yes, we are one. The covenant of mutual responsibility that Moses engraved upon our Jewish hearts has survived the centuries. But, on the other hand, we are also witness to alienation, complacency, and indifference. Those of us who are sensitive to this covenant of mutual responsibility must try to make all our brethren aware if it.

What If It's Beyond You?

It is not only for those who are oppressed or in crisis that we must feel responsibility, but for those who are Torah-deprived and Jewishly impoverished as well. If our brethren are unaware of the meaning of our faith, it is incumbent upon each and every one of us to do everything in our power to make them aware of our mutual heritage.

---

58. Tractate *Yevamos* 87b.

Some situations, however, are beyond our capability, in which assimilation has been so all encompassing that individuals no longer identify as Jews and there is no way for us to reach them. Such cases fall under the umbrella of *hidden*. It is God Himself Who will bring them home. When Moses charged the nation with this covenant of mutual responsibility, he spoke to all of us, for all eternity. "Not with you alone do I seal this covenant … but … with whoever is not here with us today."[59]

From this we learn that every *Yiddishe neshamah* born in future generations was present and heard Moses' voice. Moses left nothing to chance, and in his message, he reminded us that God made His covenant with us for a special purpose: "[T]o establish you today as a people to Him, and that He be a God to you, as He spoke to you and as He swore to your forefathers, to Abraham, to Isaac, and to Jacob."[60] This, then, is our mission, our raison d'être as individuals and as a nation. If we would only take a few moments to contemplate these words, we would be filled with a sense of exhilaration. We have been granted the awesome privilege of being God's people. Can there be a greater calling than that? Tragically, however, so many of our people are unaware and do not know their true essence.

THE ETERNITY OF THE JEWISH PEOPLE

There is yet another interpretation to "*Atem nitzavim* — you are standing today, all of you, before Hashem, your God." In the previous *parashah*, the people were told of all the terrible and painful calamities that would befall them, and they became terrified. So much so, the Midrash teaches us, that they turned colors. Moses reassured them with the powerful opening words of our *parashah*: "*Atem nitzavim hayom kulchem lifnei Hashem*

---

59. *Deuteronomy* 29:13-14.
60. Ibid. 29:12.

Elokeichem .... You are standing today, all of you, before Hashem, your God." In those words are to be found the secret of our miraculous survival.

No matter where destiny may lead us, no matter in which century, in which culture, in which country we may reside, *we must always see ourselves standing before God*; that is the secret of our miraculous survival. So it is that we have outlived the tyrants of history. We have seen the empires, the great powers of the world, soar to their zenith, only to disappear. From Pharaoh to Hitler to contemporary demagogues, we have experienced them all and triumphed, because, at all times, we stand before Hashem, our God. And even if we should forget our calling, the words, "*Atem nitzavim hayom*," come to redeem us. In *gematria*, that is the equivalent of "standing up for *Selichos*, asking forgiveness, and returning to God. The Almighty granted us a magnificent gift — *Selichos*, giving us the ability to rejuvenate ourselves by asking for His forgiveness. At first glance, this may appear to be an overwhelming task, but in this *parashah* we are also assured that "... this commandment that I command you today — it is not hidden from you and it is not distant .... Rather, the matter is very near to you — in your mouth and in your heart — to perform it."[61] This covenant is embedded in our souls and is so deeply engraved on our hearts that we need only call out unto God and the covenant will emerge and transform us into the people that stood at Sinai.

Throughout the centuries, we have seen the amazing renewal of our people. Even those who appear to be hopelessly lost, can come back in an instant.

STEPS LEADING TO ASSIMILATION

How does it happen that a Jew loses his way? How does the assimilation process commence? The answer can be found in our *parashah*. "*Pen yesh bachem* ... — Perhaps

---

61. Ibid. 30:11, 14.

there is among you a man or woman, or a family or tribe, whose heart turns away today from being with Hashem, our God."[62] It all starts with that little insidious word, *"pen* — perhaps." When you render the Torah a "perhaps" and cast doubt upon God's Word … when you begin to think, *Maybe it's true, maybe it's not*, the assimilation process has commenced. Our covenant with God can never be a "perhaps," a *"possibility"* that may or may not have occurred. As Jews, we not only believe that God spoke to us at Sinai, but we know beyond any doubt that the revelation took place, that we all stood at Sinai and heard God proclaim His commandments. There is no room for *"pen"* in our faith. When, however, that little insidious word does enter the mind of a person, it plants toxic seeds. This little insidious word *"pen"* is so deadly, so infectious that, while it may begin with one man or one woman, it can eventually infect the entire family, the entire tribe, and result in *"shoresh poreh rosh v'laanah* — a root flourishing with gall and wormwood."[63] These words, "a root flourishing with gall and wormwood," require explanation. On one hand, they confine the doubter to a life detached from God and His people; but, on the other hand, a Jew is never lost, and within these very words the Torah provides a prescription for survival. In the holy tongue, the first letters of the words *Shoresh Poreh Rosh V'la'anoh* spell *shofar*. The call of the *shofar* has such an awesome power that it can revive even the most toxic, alienated *neshamah*, resuscitate it, and restore it to its original sanctity. And that is the miracle that we have witnessed time and again in our own generation through the spectacular *baal teshuvah* movement.

---

62. Ibid. 29:17.
63. Ibid.

PARASHAS VAYEILECH

The Torah Is Engraved on Every Jewish Soul

The *parashah* begins, "*Vayeilech Moshe* — And Moses went ...."[64] Where did Moses go? The Torah doesn't specify, but our Sages explain that he went into every Jewish heart so that the Torah might be engraved on the souls of our people for all eternity. But how did Moses accomplish that feat?

The answer to that question reveals the awesome greatness and sanctity of Moses. In the previous *parashah*, Nitzavim, Moses addressed the entire nation and renewed the covenant with them. In doing so, he also charged the people with a new covenant of *areivus*, which commanded each and every Jew to assume respon-

---

64. Ibid. 31:1.

sibility for his fellows. Henceforth, not only would individuals be held culpable for their own sins, but also for the sins of the nation: one nation, with one destiny, inexorably intertwined.

After Moses sealed this covenant, the people returned to their tents. Moses then did what only the greatest of men would be capable of doing. He went from tent to tent to bid them farewell, for he knew that on that day, he would return his soul to God and die. But if that be the case, we might well ask, why didn't Moses say his farewells and bless the nation when they were all gathered as one and stood before him? Visiting millions of people would be a superhuman undertaking for even a young man, and would take, not a day, but weeks or months. But Moses' love for his people was such that no undertaking was too much for him. And more, he wanted, on this last day of his life, to engrave not just faith, but also love for Torah on the heart of each and every individual. And for that, loving, personal contact was required.

Our Sages teach that Moses, our teacher, placed the Torah within the heart of every Jew for all eternity; because of that, wherever a Jew might find himself, at whatever time in history, whenever he sincerely desires to study Torah, Moses would be at his side and teach him.

When God's Face Is Hidden

> And Hashem spoke to Moses: "Behold, you will lie with your forefathers, but this people will rise up and stray after the gods of the foreigners of the Land ... it will forsake Me and annul My covenant that I have sealed with it. My anger will flare against it on that day and I will forsake them; and I will conceal My Face from them ... and many evils and distresses will encounter it. It will say on that day, 'Is it not because my God is not in my midst that these evils have come upon me?' But I will surely have concealed My face on that day because of all the evil that it did, for it had turned to the god of others."[65]

---

65. Ibid. 31:16-18.

Thus, God informs Moses that after his death, the nation will abandon the covenant; subsequently, God's wrath will be kindled against them and terrible suffering will befall them. And the people will realize, "God is not in our midst. It is because of this that these evils have come upon us."

One would have imagined that such an admission would be regarded as a positive step toward repentance. But strangely enough, the verse states that God would continue to hide His face from them. How do we understand this? Why doesn't Hashem accept their declaration as a true expression of repentance? The answer is simple. God never abandons us. He is our loving Father; when there is a breakdown in our relationship, it is not because He is not in *our* midst, but rather, because *we* have abandoned Him. Until such time as we realize our responsibility to return to Him with a full heart, there can be no real reconciliation.

But even under those painful circumstances, God's message is filled with hope. He does not say, "I will forsake them," but rather, "I will conceal My face from them." When someone hides, it means that he is still there; we need only find him.

Similarly, God, Who is our loving Father, never forsakes us. He is always there, watching over us, guarding us, even in our darkest moments. We are never alone ... God is in hiding, waiting for us to find Him.

There is a well-known story about a Chassidic rebbe who found a little boy crying. "Why are you crying, my son?" he asked.

"Because I am hiding, and no one is looking for me," the boy answered.

"Woe unto us!" the rebbe said. "God is hiding and we are not looking for Him. We don't even make an attempt to find Him!"

SONG OF THE JEWISH PEOPLE

So now, write this song for yourselves, and teach it to the Children of Israel. Place it in their mouth ...."[66]

This is the last mitzvah that *Moshe Rabbeinu* imparted

---

66. Ibid. 31:19.

to us, and it is a command for every Jew to write a Torah Scroll. This, of course, does not mean that every Jew must write his own *Sefer Torah*; what it does mean, however, is that by writing a single letter to complete a Torah Scroll, we can fulfill this mitzvah.

Throughout the centuries, no matter how dense the darkness of our exile, how bitter our persecution, and how abject our poverty, our people fulfilled this mitzvah of writing Torah scrolls with enormous zeal, sacrifice, and love. The celebration accompanying the dedication of a new Torah is akin to that of a wedding, and the joy that it generates envelopes the entire community.

Some years ago, our Hineni organization dedicated a new Torah Scroll and we celebrated the occasion by dancing with the Torah along Park Avenue, which was closed to traffic. The Torah was carried under the *chuppah,* and as we made our way down the avenue, multitudes of people joined us, dancing and singing with joy. Children waved flags, the music played, and men and women from every walk of life came to participate, their eyes brimming with tears of joy — tears that spanned the centuries, going back thousands of years to the moment when Moses proclaimed, "Write this song for yourself and teach it to the Children of Israel. Place it in their mouth …."

In thousands of years, we have never forgotten Moses' commandment, and when a new Torah is dedicated, even the most secular Jew comes forth to celebrate with a full heart.

But the question that still must be asked is why the writing of a Torah Scroll is compared to writing a song.

A song is something that you can never forget. Even if you forget the lyrics, the melody remains in your heart. Yes, the Torah is the song of our people. Even for those among us who may have forgotten the holy words, the melody nevertheless remains in their hearts, and in an instant, they can relearn the lyrics.

God Is Always With Us

"*Chizku* — Strengthen youselves ... do not be afraid ... for Hashem, your God — it is He Who goes before you. He will not release you nor will He forsake you."[67]

With these words, Moses assures the nation that they are not to fear, for God will always lead them. But what is curious in this passage is that it starts out in the plural verb, calling upon the nation, "*Chizku* — strengthen yourselves." But the passage closes with the singular pronoun, "*Lo yarpecha* — He [God] will not forsake you," the individual. Why the discrepancy? Why does the Torah commence with the charge to the nation and conclude with an assurance to the individual?

Many people may be under the erroneous impression that, while God may safeguard the nation, individuals are at risk. But God is our Heavenly Father, and even as the nation, the glorious family of Jacob, is precious and dear to Him, so is every person, every individual. He sees every sigh, hears every cry ... we need only call upon Him in truth. We are never alone. God has sworn never to abandon us.

---

67. Ibid. 31:6.

PARASHAS HAAZINU

Eternal Witnesses

"*Haazinu Hashamayim* — Give ear, O Heavens, and I will speak, and may the earth hear the words of my mouth." [68]

Moses reminds us that even when he is no longer here physically, the heavens and the earth will stand as eternal witnesses and testify that we sealed an irrevocable covenant with God. Moses calls upon heaven and earth to serve as witnesses, for even as they are constant and unchanging, so must our loyalty to Torah be constant and unchanging. Homiletically, the heavens represent our spiritual essence and the earth our physical being. Both must act in consonance to fulfill God's Will. Heaven and earth are chosen

---

68. Ibid. 32:1.

by Moses to testify that even as the covenant is eternally binding and can never be broken, similarly, heaven and earth are eternal and capable of taking punitive measures: The heavens can withhold rain and the earth can withhold its fruit, making this planet an inhospitable, dark place. And if anyone should know this, it is surely we, the Jewish people.

The Power of Listening

Our Sages ask why Moses proclaimed, "*haazinu* — listen," before "*adabeirah* — I shall speak." The answer should give us all pause. It is only if we are *desirous* of *listening* that God's Words will find a place in our hearts. If we are bent upon closing our ears and shutting our minds, then in vain is the message given. God sends us wake-up calls, but whether we hear them or not will depend strictly on us. And so, Moses called upon the nation, "*Haazinu* — listen!" — open your minds and hearts; only then does he say, "*adabeirah* — I will speak."

Formula for Jewish Living

Moses, the beloved teacher of Israel, gives us the formula that has accompanied us throughout our long journey and has guaranteed our survival even through the darkest moments of our exile.

Torah and Rain

Moses prays that his "teaching drop like the rain."[69] Why should Moses make such a wish? What is there about rain that is so special that he should compare it to the study of Torah?

---

69. Ibid. 32:2.

Rain in its season results in luscious fruit and vegetables. Rain makes flowers and trees bloom; rain can convert arid land into a beautiful garden, but if rain is to bring about this most wonderful growth and transformation, the earth must first be cultivated, plowed, and fertilized, and seeds have to be carefully planted. Similarly, if Torah is to take root in our hearts, if it is to transform us into a magnificent, fruitful garden in which luscious fruit, nourishing vegetables, and beautiful flowers grow, then we have to cultivate our hearts and minds and plant therein seeds of faith and love.

Rain that falls on barren land results in mud, and rain that falls on concrete forms a puddle. In the same way, if Torah is to transform and elevate us, then we must open our hearts and minds and make them ready receptacles for God's holy words. Thus, Moses prayed that we perceive the teachings of Torah as drops of rain, and properly prepare ourselves for its study and observance.

"*Ki Shem Hashem ekra* ... — When I call out the Name of Hashem, ascribe greatness to our God."[70]

This verse charges us with our responsibility to proclaim the praise of God in every situation. As Jews, the people who stood at Sinai, we recognize His many kindnesses as well as His corrective Hand when He disciplines us. We understand that blessings as well as that which is painful come from God, that He is just. Everything that He does is for our benefit, even if we do not perceive it as such. So it is that we, the Jewish people, whose calling is to be His witnesses here on Earth, have never abandoned our faith in Him. Even in our darkest moments, in the throes of persecution and oppression, we have proclaimed His praises and have never ceased to call out His Holy Name.

Based upon the verse, "*Ki Shem Hashem ekra*," our Sages have instructed us to recite a blessing before Torah study, and, when three or more men eat together, we call upon our fellow Jews to say Grace and proclaim His praises.

In the days of the Holy Temple, when the Holy Name of God was pronounced, the people would respond with "*Baruch Shem* ... — Blessed is the Name of His glorious kingdom forever and ever-

---

70. Ibid. 32:3.

more." Today, in the absence of our Temple, we recite this verse *"Ki Shem Hashem ekra ..."* before we commence the *Amidah* service.

WHO IS TO BLAME?

Shicheis lo Lo! Banav muman — Corruption is not His — the blemish is His children's ...."[71]

From the genesis of history, from the moment that God challenged Adam with the life-defining question *"Ayekah? —* Where are you?"[72] "What did you do?" And Adam responded with the audacious words, "The woman whom You gave to be with me — she gave me of the tree and I ate."[73] Man learned to scapegoat and to blame others for his failings. We, the Jewish people, have a responsibility to reverse Adam's response and accept accountability for our deeds, for only through accountability can we fulfill our mission with honor.

So it is that on Yom Kippur, when we confess our sins and declare our faith, we refrain from making excuses for our transgressions but accept full responsibility, without ifs, ands, or buts. With contrite hearts, we approach God and stand before Him. Only thus do we have the right to ask His forgiveness.

Scapegoating, however, has become so much a part of the human condition that many people have all but forgotten the meaning of personal accountability. They blame family members, friends, circumstances — anything and anyone but themselves — for their failings. But worse, when we violate the Law of God and then we suffer the consequences of our betrayal, we wonder how God could have allowed such evil to prevail. The words of Moses, the words of our Torah cry out to us, *"Shicheis lo Lo! Banav muman—* Corruption is *not* His — the blemish is His children's." But we have yet to absorb this lesson. It's always more convenient to blame God for the ills of our world, ills that we ourselves have choreographed.

---

71. Ibid. 32:5.
72. *Genesis* 3:9.
73. Ibid. 3:12.

Study Your Past To Understand Your Present

Parashas Haazinu is rich in teachings that keep us focused and enable us to understand the ups and downs of life, the good as well as the seemingly evil that we constantly encounter in our world. "*Zechor ...,*" Moses admonishes us, "Remember the days of yore, understand the years of generation after generation ...."[74] This means that if we are perplexed, if we have difficulty comprehending that which befalls us and that which transpires in the world, we need only search our history. Study the lives of past generations, the legacy of our Patriarchs and Matriarchs, and all will become clear.

And if we are still perplexed, if we still have questions, Moses advises us, "*Sh'al avicha ...* — Ask your father and he will relate it to you, your elders and they will tell you."[75] It's so simple, yet so profound. Seek the counsel of your father, your elders — your Torah Sages. Sadly, those who are questioning, those who have lost their way, search for guidance almost everywhere and consult almost everyone, but they fail to turn to their own Torah Sages, who could guide them and show them the way.

Red Flags To Watch For

Moses gave us red flags to beware of "*Vayishman Yeshurun va'yivat ...* —And *Jeshurun* became fat and kicked ...."[76]

The name *Jeshurun* is yet another august title for our people. It is a designation of honor, righteousness, and justice. Moses warns us to be on guard and watch for the red flags that could blemish even Jeshurun, a righteous nation. These red flags that Moses warned

---

74. *Deuteronomy* 32:7.
75. Ibid. 32:7.
76. Ibid. 32:15.

us against are prosperity, wealth, and an abundance of luxury and material possessions. While we all desire God's blessings, we have to be aware of our vulnerability, for when things go well and we prosper, it is easy to lose our way and become self-satisfied and arrogant. It is easy to delude ourselves into believing that it is our own hard work and our cunning that are responsible for our success. It is easy to become complacent and forget our responsibilities to our fellow Jews and to God. Moses, our beloved teacher, warns us to be especially vigilant when God blesses us with good fortune. We have to learn to master wealth and not allow wealth to master us.

Moses' Last Will and Testament

At the end of the *parashah,* Moses reviews his last will and testament for the Jewish people:

Vayomer aleihem … — And he [Moses] said to them, "Apply your hearts to all the words that I testify against you today, with which you are to instruct your children, to be careful to perform all the words of this Torah, for it [the Torah] is not an empty thing for you, for it is your life, and through this matter you shall prolong your days …."[77]

Moses' message is a threefold teaching that should guide us throughout life.

- If Torah is to be our life, it cannot be just a cerebral learning experience, but must saturate our entire being and guide all our thoughts and deeds.
- The Torah education of our children must be our top priority.
- We must bear in mind that the Torah is not *empty.* Every word, every letter, is laden with wisdom and hidden treasures that will prolong our days and give meaning to our lives.

---

77. Ibid. 32:46-47.

PARASHAS VEZOS HABERACHAH

THE BLESSINGS CONTINUE

In this, the closing *parashah* of the Five Books of the Torah, Moses continues the tradition of the Patriarch Jacob and blesses each tribe. Even as the Patriarch commenced his blessing with the word "*Zos* — this," so, too, does Moses imparts his blessing with the word "*Zos*." Even as the Patriarch Jacob's blessing spoke to each tribe individually and charged each with his unique mission, so, too, did Moses speak to each tribe to define its special role and the contribution it was to make to the greater mosaic of the Jewish people.

It is a blessing to have someone help you define your purpose in life and delineate the contributions that you can make to the greater good of your people; prior to their deaths, Moses and Jacob were both able to do that for their children and disciples. In their blessings, Jacob and Moses foretold the future. Their blessings were so powerful that they transcended the centuries and are with us to this very day. Today, when we rise to bless our children, we invoke the words of the Patriarch Jacob and the Priestly Blessing that God imparted to Aaron. Thus, our children become a continuous link in the endless chain that takes us back to the genesis of our history.

THE UNIQUENESS OF THE JEWISH PEOPLE

Prior to offering his blessing, Moses speaks of the greatness of the Jewish nation and recounts the merits that rendered them worthy of being God's chosen people. Thus, we learn from Moses the importance of referring to the good deeds of a person prior to imparting blessing so that God Himself may place His seal of approval on the *berachah*.

Moses recalls that God offered the Torah to all the nations, only to have them reject it after they learned what the Torah required of them. Although all the nations were consulted, Moses mentions only Esau and Ishmael. "Hashem came from Sinai — having shone forth to them from Seir, having appeared from Mount Paran ...."[78] (Seir and Paran were the habitations of Esau and Ishmael.) Why does the Torah focus only on these two nations and ignore all the others that also rejected God's offer?

Esau and Ishmael should have known better, for they were nurtured in Torah homes. Esau was the son of Isaac and Rebecca and he also had the privilege of knowing his *zeide*, Abraham. Moreover, he was the identical twin of Jacob, the paradigm of Torah, and could have learned from him. So yes, he should have known better. He should have said *yes* to the call of God.

Ishmael was also guilty, for he was raised in the loving home of Abraham and Sarah, yet he chose the bow and arrow and thievery

---

78. Ibid. 33:2.

over the teachings of his father. Both Esau and Ishmael rebelled and spurned their spiritual heritage, and it was this rebellion and contempt for Torah that they passed on to future generations.

So it was that when God approached their descendants and invited them to accept the Torah, they asked what those laws entailed, and when they found that there were prohibitions and disciplines that would curb their animalistic natures, they rejected God's Torah out of hand. From this we can learn that the way of life a man chooses has far-reaching consequences that transcend generations and can taint his descendants.

In contrast, when God approached the Jewish people, they never asked questions. They did not make their acceptance contingent upon anything. Their automatic response was *"Na'aseh v'nishma."* The Jewish nation understood that it would be the height of chutzpah to ask God to first reveal the contents of His gift, the Torah. How dare anyone question it? If it comes from God, it must be perfect. The people understood that it would be a privilege to be given commandments that come from God. It is this awareness that flows in the veins of our people and has enabled us to remain loyal to our Torah throughout the centuries and to humbly thank Hashem for the privilege of serving Him.

Torah Tzivah Lanu Moshe, Morashah Kehilas Yaakov

"The Torah that Moses commanded us is the heritage of the Congregation of Jacob."[79] Our Sages teach that this is the very first passage that a father is enjoined to teach when his child learns to talk. One might wonder why this passage has been singled out above all the others for the commencement of a child's life journey.

In the holy tongue, there are two ways in which we can say "inheritance": *nachalah* and *morashah*. Since we know that there are

---

79. Ibid. 33:4.

no exact synonyms in Hebrew, we must discover the difference between these two words. *Nachalah* is an inheritance that belongs solely to the heir, to use as he sees fit. *Morashah*, the term used in our passage, means a heritage that has been given in trust and cannot be tampered with. It is a heritage that must be preserved intact and passed from generation to generation. As we understand this, it becomes obvious why, of all the teachings, our Sages chose this to be the first to be engraved upon a Jewish child's heart. Even as a parent has a responsibility to pass on this heritage to his children, so the children should know that one day, they, too, will be charged with the same responsibility: to pass on this same heritage in the same manner in which they received it.

There is yet an additional meaning to the word *morashah*. It can also be read *morasah*, which means "married," for our relationship with the Torah is that of a bride and groom who are one in their love. The passage concludes with the words, "[It] is the heritage of the Congregation of Jacob." Indeed, every Jew, impoverished or wealthy, prominent or humble, young or old, is part of the "Congregation of Jacob," and has the right to this heritage.

MOSES DIED AND YET HE LIVES

Vayamas sham Moshe, eved Hashem ... — So Moses, servant of Hashem, died there, in the land of Moab, by the mouth of Hashem."[80] Our sages ask, "What is the meaning of 'died there'?" And they answer, "He only died *there*, but he lives on in our hearts. His teachings are forever with us."

Our Sages further ask, "If Moses died, who wrote the last passages of the Torah?"

There are two views. One is that up to this point, Moses wrote, and Joshua completed these final passages. The other teaching is that God dictated the words to Moses and he wrote them with his tears.

---

80. Ibid. 34:5.

Throughout his life, Moses was known as *"Ish Ha Elokeim* — Man of God." But as death confronts him, his title is changed to *"Eved Hashem* — servant of God." There can be no greater testimony to a man than to be called *"Eved Hashem."* A servant has no identity of his own; he belongs totally to his master. Similarly, Moses' entire life was dedicated to his Master, his God.

Moreover, in contrast to other members of a royal house, the servant has access to the inner chambers of the king at all times. Similarly, Moses was able to communicate with God at all times, speak to Him face to face, and now, in his death, as he sheds the barrier of his physical self, he is given this new title, "Servant of God," and is invited to enter the inner chambers of Hashem, the King.

Moses died "by the mouth of God," meaning that God drew forth his soul with a Divine kiss. God Himself buried him, and to this day, no one knows the exact location of his burial place.

The Last Letter

The concluding word of the Torah is *"Yisrael* — Israel," teaching us that the Torah was given for the sake of Israel — the Jewish people. The last letter of the Torah, *lamed*, is also instructive, teaching that if we combine that letter with the first letter of the Torah, *"beis"* from *Bereshis*, we will come up with the word *"lev* — heart." The entire Torah, from beginning to end, was given in order to refine our hearts and make us the compassionate, merciful children of God.

GLOSSARY

adamah — the earth.
adon — 1. socket; 2. master.
a.h. — acronym for "*alav* (or *aleha*) *hashalom*," literally, peace be on him/her.
ahavah — love.
Akeidah — Binding of Isaac.
al pi Hashem — at the bidding of God.
ameilus — toiling in Torah
Amidah — lit., standing; the *Shemoneh Esrei*, a prayer recited while standing.
areivus — mutual responsibility.
aval — 1. indeed; 2. but.
Avinu — our father (used to describe the Patriarchs).
Avodah — service (of God); the sacrificial offerings in the Temple.
Avodas Hashem — service of God
Ayekah — Where are you?
baal chesed — one who practices *chesed*.
baal teshuvah — one who repents and returns to Orthodoxy.
b'ahavah — with love.

Baruch Hashem — "Blessed is Hashem!"; thank God.
Bas Kol — divine Voice.
basherte — Divinely destined life-partner.
Bayis Ne'eman — a home that is a true bastion of faith.
Beis HaMikdash — the Holy Temple.
berachah (pl. *berachos*) — a blessing.
bikkurim — first fruits of the field.
bikores — investigation.
bikur — visit.
bikur cholim — visiting the sick; also, organizations established for visiting and helping people who are ill or hospitalized.
binah — understanding.
Birkas HaKohanim – the Priestly Blessing.
bo — come.
bobbe (pl. *bubbies*) — (Yiddish) grandmother.
boker — morning.
bris — circumcision.
Chazal — acronym for *Chachameinu zichronam livrachah*; our Sages, blessed be their memory.
chesed — loving-kindness.
chok — statute.
chuppah — marriage canopy.
Daas Torah — faith in our Torah Sages.
daven — to pray.
derech eretz — respect and proper conduct
eichah — how.
eid — witness.
eishes chayil — woman of valor.
Elul — acronym for *"Ani l'dodi v'dodi li"*; in the Jewish calendar the last month, preceding Rosh Hashanah.
emes — truth.
emunah — faith.
Eretz Yisrael — the Land of Israel.
Gadol — a great man.
gematria — numerology.
gemilus chassadim — acts of loving-kindness.
geulah — redemption.

gilgul — reincarnation.
gomlei chasadim — men and women who impart loving-kindness to others.
goral — 1. drawing of lots; 2. destiny..
hachnasas kallah — helping poor brides; also, organizations established to help brides pay for their wedding and/or furnish their homes.
hachnasas orchim — hospitality; lit., welcoming guests.
hakaras hatov — gratitude; acknowledgment of the good.
halachah — the body of Jewish law.
hashavas aveidah — returning lost items.
Hashem — God.
Ikvesa D'Meshicha — lit., the Footsteps of Messiah; the period preceding the Messianic period.
Imeinu — our mother (used to refer to the Matriarchs).
ir miklat (pl. *arei miklat*) — city of refuge.
ish — man
Kaddish — prayer said in memory of the dead.
karov — to come near.
kashering — purifying.
kashruth — Jewish dietery laws.
kelev —dog.
Kiddush — the prayer recited over wine before a Sabbath or holiday meal.
Kohen (pl. Kohanim) — a priest descended from Aaron HaKohen.
Kohen Gadol (pl. Kohanim Gedolim)— High Priest.
kol — 1. voice; 2. prayer.
korban (pl. *korbanos*) — a sacrificial offering.
lashon haKodesh — lit., the holy tongue; the language in which the Torah is written.
lashon hara — derogatory speech; slander.
lech — go.
Maamad Har Sinai — the Revelation at Sinai.
Maariv — the evening prayer service.
Ma'aseh Avos siman l'banim — What happened to our Forefathers is a portent for their children.
maggid — lit., a storyteller; a (usually itinerant) preacher who used

Glossary / 333

parables to make his points.
makom — a place.
makom kavua — designating a set place, i.e., for prayer.
Malchus HaShamayim — the Kingdom of G-d here on earth.
Mamleches Kohanim — a Priestly Kingdom,
mamon — 1. money; 2. charity.
Mashiach — Messiah.
Menachem Av — lit., a comforting father; the Jewish month preceding Elul.
Menorah — the 7-branched candelabrum standing in the Holy Temple.
mentsch — (Yiddish) lit., man; connotes a person who exemplifies integrity, respect, and kindness.
mesiras nefesh — self-sacrifice.
middah (pl. *middos*) — character trait(s).
middah k'neged middah — measure for measure.
Midrash — classic anthology of Sages' homiletical teachings on the Torah or a particular passage therefrom; the body of the Sages' teaching.
mikveh — ritual bath.
Minchah — the afternoon prayer service.
Mishkan — the Holy Tabernacle.
mitzvah, (pl. mitzvos) — 1. commandment; 2. good deed.
Mizbei'ach — Altar.
Moshe Rabbeinu — lit., Moses, our teacher.
Na'aseh v'nishma — lit., "We will do and we will hear," also, "We will do it and we will study it," the Jews' expression of obedience to God.
nachas — satisfaction; pleasure, esp. spiritual or emotional pleasure.
neshamah (pl. *neshamos*) — a soul.
nisayon — a test.
Nusach Sefard — the manner of carrying out prayer liturgy in certain communities.
o.b.m — (acronym) of blessed memory.
parah adumah — Red Heifer.
parashah (pl. *parshiyos*) — the weekly Torah portion.

pasuk (pl. *pesukim*) — Biblical verse.
Pesach Sheni — a day on which those who were ritually impure at the time the Pesach offering was brought were permitted to bring the offering.
pintele Yid — spark of Jewishness.
rachamim, rachmanus — compassion.
rachmanim, bnei rachmanim — compassionate ones, sons of compassionate ones.
rechem — womb.
remez — hint.
Ro'eh Ne'eman — the loyal shepherd.
Ruach Hakodesh — the gift of prophecy.
sefer (pl. *seforim*) — a book, specifically a book on holy subjects.
Sefer Torah — Torah scroll.
selichos — prayers for forgiveness.
Shabbos — the Sabbath.
Shacharis — the morning prayer service.
shadchan — matchmaker.
shalom — peace.
shalom bayis – peace and harmony in the home.
Shechinah — the Presence of G-d.
Shema — short for "*Shema Yisrael, HaShem Elokeinu, HaShem Echod!*" — Hear O Israel, Hashem is our G-d, Hashem is the One and Only"; this prayer, recited twice daily, expresses the essence of Jewish faith.
shemittah — the Sabbatical year
shidduch (pl. *shidduchim*) — a marriage match.
shofar — ram's horn.
shteiging — growing.
shtetl — a village, esp. in pre-war Europe.
simchas hachaim — a positive attitude toward life.
sinas chinam — baseless hatred.
sulam — ladder.
ta'am — a taste; a reason.
ta'amei haMitzvos — underlying meanings we may derive from the mitzvos.
tachlis — a God-given purpose.

teshuvah — repentance.
tichyeh — may she live.
tikun — rectification.
tikun olam — perfecting the world.
tochachos — curses and calamities that will befall us throughout our history.
tzaar baalei chaim — cruelty to animals.
tzaraas — spiritual leprosy.
tzedakah — charity.
tzohar — 1. a window 2. a brilliant jewel that sheds light.
tzom — fasting/repentance.
vayiven — to build.
Vidui — confessions.
yahrzeit — anniversary of a death.
Yasher Koach — Thank you.
yetzer hara — the evil inclination.
Yetzias Mitzraim — Exodus from Egypt.
Yiddishe — Jewish.
Yiddishkeit — Judaism.
yiras Shamayim — reverence for G-d.
zechus avos — the merit of our ancestors.
Zeicher l'Churban — in memory of the destruction of the Holy Temple in Jerusalem.
zeide (pl. *zeides*) — (Yiddish) grandfather.
zemiros — songs of praise and thanksgiving, esp. those sung at the Shabbos table.
z"tl — acronym for *zecher tzaddik l'berachah,* may the righteous person be remembered as a blessing.